America's Best Day Hiking Series

Hiking ARIZONA

CHRISTINE MAXA

Human Kinetics

Library of Congress Cataloging-in-Publication Data

Maxa, Christine.
  Hiking Arizona / Christine Maxa.
    p. cm. — (America's best day hiking series)
  Includes bibliographical references.
  ISBN 0-7360-4157-5 (Soft cover)
  1. Hiking—Arizona—Guidebooks. 2. Trails—Arizona—Guidebooks. 3.
Arizona—Guidebooks. I. Title. II. Series.
  GV199.42.A7 M387 2003
  917.9104'54—dc21

                          2002153242

ISBN: 0-7360-4157-5

Acquisitions Editor: Todd Jensen; **Production Editor:** Melinda Graham; **Assistant Editor:** John Wentworth; **Copyeditor:** Jacqueline Eaton Blakley; **Proofreader:** Sue Fetters; **Permission Manager:** Toni Harte; **Graphic Designer:** Robert Reuther; **Photo Manager:** Dan Wendt; **Cover Designer:** Jack W. Davis; **Photographer (cover and interior):** Christine Maxa; **Art Manager:** Dan Wendt; **Illustrator:** Tim Shedelbower; **Printer:** Versa Press

Maps on pages 4 and 10 reprinted, by permission, from Michael R. Kelsey, 1999, *Canyon Hiking Guide to the Colorado Plateau* (Provo, Utah: Kelsey Publishing). Maps on pages 84 and 142 reprinted by permission of the Arizona State Parks.

Human Kinetics books are available at special discounts for bulk purchase. Special editions or book excerpts can also be created to specification. For details, contact the Special Sales Manager at Human Kinetics.

Printed in the United States of America
10 9 8 7 6 5 4 3 2 1

Human Kinetics
Web site: www.HumanKinetics.com

United States: Human Kinetics
P.O. Box 5076
Champaign, IL 61825-5076
800-747-4457
e-mail: humank@hkusa.com

Canada: Human Kinetics
475 Devonshire Road Unit 100
Windsor, ON N8Y 2L5
800-465-7301 (in Canada only)
e-mail: orders@hkcanada.com

Europe: Human Kinetics
107 Bradford Road
Stanningley
Leeds LS28 6AT, United Kingdom
+44 (0) 113 255 5665
e-mail: hk@hkeurope.com

Australia: Human Kinetics
57A Price Avenue
Lower Mitcham, South Australia 5062
08 8277 1555
e-mail: liahka@senet.com.au

New Zealand: Human Kinetics
P.O. Box 105-231, Auckland Central
09-523-3462
e-mail: hkp@ihug.co.nz

To Jan H. and Jeffrey H.

Acknowledgments

To my contacts at the managing agencies who double-checked my work and went the extra mile in obtaining answers to my questions: Thank you!

To Gregory F. Hansen, National Leave No Trace Program coordinator—USDA Forest Service, for providing the section on Leave No Trace ethics: Thank you!

To Rory Aikens, public information officer, Arizona Game & Fish Department's Phoenix office, for providing the section on snakes: Thank you!

To Barbara Bain at the Department of Mines & Mineral Resources for providing mine information: Thank you!

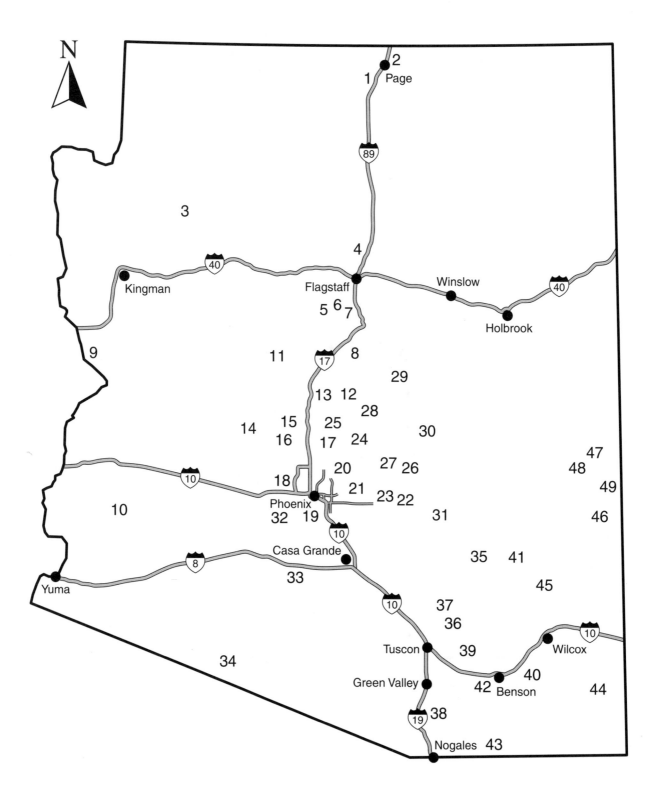

N

2
1 Page

89

3

40
Kingman
Flagstaff
5 6 7
Winslow
40
Holbrook

9

11
17
8
29
13 12
28
14 15
25
30
16 17
24
47
48
10
18
20
27 26
49
Phoenix
21
23 22
46
32 19
31
10
Casa Grande
35 41
33
45
8
10
37
Yuma
36
34
Tuscon
39
Wilcox
10
40
Green Valley
42 Benson
44
19 38
Nogales 43

Contents

Leave No Trace

The Leave No Trace idea began with the U.S. Forest Service, as the popularity of hiking and backpacking in the 1970s led millions of people out to enjoy their national forests and other public lands. With this increased use came an overwhelming increase in human impact, and something had to be done to save these special places from being "loved to death." The Leave No Trace program grew out of a need to teach the American people about minimum-impact camping and to encourage them to tread lightly on the land. But Leave No Trace is much more than just minimum-impact camping. It is an awareness, an understanding of one's responsibility and connection to our natural environment.

The following seven principles have been developed to help you enjoy your outdoor experience in a way that will leave our public lands unimpaired for future generations. If you are visiting a desert, mountain, seashore, or wetland environment, each will require different Leave No Trace methods. Make the effort to contact the local managing agency before your trip to get information about the proper land ethics for that specific area. We can all help to protect the natural integrity and value of our precious natural resources by working hard to Leave No Trace.

Plan Ahead and Prepare

Proper trip planning and preparation helps hikers accomplish trip goals safely and enjoyably while minimizing damage to natural and cultural resources. Proper planning ensures low-risk adventures because hikers can obtain information concerning geography and weather to prepare properly.

Travel and Camp on Durable Surfaces

Damage to land occurs when visitors trample beyond recovery vegetation or communities of organisms. The resulting barren areas develop into undesirable trails, campsites, and soil erosion. When hiking, stay on the trail. If you must hike off the trail, hike on the most durable surface, and spread out when in a group.

Dispose of Waste Properly (Pack It In, Pack It Out)

Whatever you take into the backcountry should be packed out. Double-check rest and lunch spots for anything left behind. To help prevent disease and contamination of water sources, dispose of human waste at least 200 feet from water, trails, and campsites in a cathole dug 6 to 8 inches deep.

Leave What You Find

Allow other hikers a sense of discovery—preserve the past. Leave rocks, plants, animals, archaeological artifacts, and other objects as you find them. Examine but do not touch cultural or historical structures.

Minimize Campfire Impacts

If you must build a fire, consider the potential for resource damage. Make a small fire, and use dead or downed wood. Whenever possible, use an existing campfire ring in a well-placed campsite. Don't build a fire in areas where wood is scarce, such as in higher elevations, in heavily used areas with limited wood supply, or in desert settings.

Respect Wildlife

Quick movements and loud noises are stressful to animals. Try to observe animals from afar to avoid disturbing them. You are too close to an animal if your presence alters its normal activity. Give animals a wide berth, especially during breeding, nesting, and birthing seasons.

Be Considerate of Other Visitors

- Travel in small groups.
- Keep your noise level down. Let nature's sounds prevail.
- Wear clothing with colors that blend with the environment.
- Respect private property; leave gates the way you found them (opened or closed).

Gregory F. Hansen
National Leave No Trace Program Coordinator
USDA Forest Service

Hiking in Arizona

As soon as you feel thirsty, you've already stepped onto the weary path of dehydration—fatigue, loss of energy, foggy thinking, dry mouth, irritability. Because the dry desert air evaporates perspiration (your body's method of cooling down) so quickly, hikers often experience some level of dehydration during a hike no matter what the season or terrain.

Hiking an Arizona trail requires thoroughly hydrating before you start, methodically hydrating during the hike, and drinking extra liquids afterward to replace any deficiency. And water is not enough.

In the Grand Canyon, where summer temperatures can reach 120 degrees at the Colorado River, backcountry rescues (about 75 per month) often involve hikers who have consumed so much water, they get "drunk." This condition is technically called *hyponatremia* (water intoxication caused by low sodium levels in the body). The symptoms—which include nausea, disorientation, slurred speech, and confusion—appear when you drink more water than

your system can handle. When you sweat, you lose body salts. If you drink liquids without electrolyte replacements or do not eat salty foods, the sodium levels in your body get diluted, and you become water intoxicated.

So along with drinking plenty of water, you must eat salty foods. Even if you make your liquids an electrolyte replacement drink, don't leave out the food. "Plenty," as in the amount of water, can have several definitions. "Plenty" depends on your level of acclimation to hiking in Arizona, the temperatures, and the strenuousness of a trail. A general rule of thumb is to drink a quart of liquids every hour on hot stretches of trail and every two hours under more favorable conditions, such as mild temperatures and shade.

If you plan to acquire water along the trail from streams or springs, you must purify all water from all sources. This requires boiling water to produce half-inch bubbles, adding iodine tablets to the water, or using a water filter with at least an absolute pour size.

If you use iodine, make sure you allow at least an hour for the iodine to kill the germs in the water before drinking, especially if the water is cold. Iodine may kill giardia protozoa, but not cryptosporidium.

More Sunshine Than You Need

The Arizona Sun Awareness Project says Arizonans have the highest rate of skin cancer in the United States and the second highest in the world. Arizona's geographic location, altitude, and high number of sunny days precipitate sun damage. In the summer, as little as 12 minutes of exposure at noon can burn unprotected skin.

Sun damage has a cumulative effect, with the most damage occurring during the first 18 years of your life. The Arizona Sun Awareness Project offers the following guidelines if you spend time outdoors:

- Spend as little time as possible in the sun between 10 A.M. and 3 P.M.
- Wear a wide-brimmed hat, long-sleeved shirt, and long pants.
- Wear a sunscreen with a sun protection factor (SPF) of at least 15.

Cool Clothes Versus the Right Clothes

Wearing the right clothes can mean life or death in the desert. If you're hiking in the heat without much shade, you need all the cooling power you can get. Wear cotton. But if you venture into canyons, forests, or cool highcountry, stick with synthetics that wick moisture from your body.

When wet, cotton cools your body. Dipping your cotton T-shirt in a cold stream can cool you down tremendously on a hot, sunny day in a canyon. But let's say it starts to rain; you have no warmth from the sun, and the temperatures have dropped to 60 degrees. Your cotton T-shirt is still cooling you down. Dangerously. You start to get chilled. Then your body shakes uncontrollably. Now the same cotton T-shirt that saved your life from heat exhaustion is on its way to killing you with hypothermia. The same can happen with a sudden storm on a mountaintop when snow is possible—even in July on Arizona's subalpine peaks.

If you need to conserve as much body heat as possible, follow these guidelines:

- Wear synthetics, all the way to your underwear.
- Wear a hat.
- Never venture into the highcountry without a polar fleece jacket and rain gear.

When overheating is a factor, follow these guidelines.

- Feel free to wear cotton and wet down your clothes to help a natural refrigeration process.
- Wear a lightweight hat for sun protection.
- Wear lightweight hiking boots.
- Unless you have weak ankles, trail running shoes or sports sandals with Vibram soles make excellent alternatives.

No matter what the weather (hot or cold), wear sunscreen and a hat.

Monsoon Season

During the summer, usually from July 4 to mid-September, Arizona experiences its monsoon season. Thunderstorms occur when warm, moist air from the Gulf of Mexico rises into the state. In the highcountry, these storms occur almost daily. A hike started in the morning sunshine will see clouds gathering by midmorning, a thunderstorm around noon, and calm skies by sunset.

During these storms, temperatures can drop 20 to 30 degrees, hail may form, and flash floods may thunder down creeks and drainage areas. Lightning strikes, hypothermia, and drowning become potential dangers. The best chance to avoid the rain is to start your hike at first light and plan to end the hike by noon.

How to Avoid Lightning Strikes

An average of four people per year die of lightning strikes during the short monsoon season in Arizona. The Mogollon Rim has the second highest incidence of lightning in the U.S. You can decrease your chances of becoming a prime target for a lightning strike if you

- don't stand under the tallest trees;
- head for the lowest spot, crouch down, and make yourself into a ball; and
- don't lie on the ground, because lightning travels into the ground and you want as little contact as possible with its 50,000-degree bolts.

How to Avoid Hypothermia

Hypothermia, when the core body temperature falls below safe levels, becomes a threat during highcountry storms. The combination of wet clothes and dramatic drops in temperatures makes you a prime target for hypothermia. Hypothermia takes place most often in temperatures between 30 and 50 degrees; it is the number one outdoor recreation killer.

- Stay dry. Always bring rain gear on every hike, and wear it. Wet clothes lose 90 percent of their insulation value.
- Bring a synthetic jacket (or wool sweater) to keep warm when the temperature drops.
- Bring waterproof matches or a lighter in case you must light a fire for warmth.
- Eat carbohydrate snacks to help fuel your body.

Flash Floods

Water levels in highcountry creeks can rise quickly during a thunderstorm. An easy rockhop across a creek at the start of your hike can turn into a major production when crossing it during or after a rainstorm. Footing becomes slippery when rain wets down stepping-stones. Water levels can rise, turn murky, and swallow stepping-stones. Currents can become too strong to wade—three feet of water traveling three seconds per foot can knock a man down. If any of these happen, follow these guidelines.

- Use a walking stick to help you keep your balance when crossing high, fast-moving creeks.
- Make sure your footing is secure before taking your next step.
- Try to cross near objects you can hold on to, such as tree branches or boulders.

- Do not cross water three feet or deeper that is traveling three feet per second.

Wildlife Dangers

Wildlife usually poses a danger only when you get in its way. On more remote trails, keep attentive to the possible presence of animals to preclude surprise encounters. If you see wildlife, keep a safe, respectful distance to avoid self-defensive maneuvers from the animal.

Bears

Highcountry trails bring you to black bear country. Most wild bears will detect and avoid humans, and sighting one can make an exciting experience during a hike. But when a bear has become accustomed to humans and their food, it may not run away. The exciting moment can turn into a conflict.

Most conflicts between humans and black bears happen because of human-supplied foods. When you're in the highcountry, make sure all of your food and toiletries are inaccessible to bears. Wild bears with a taste for human food often will not run away from humans. Here's what to do if a conflict arises.

- Do not run. Slowly back away while facing the bear.
- Keep children and pets close to your side.

- Make noise. Clap your hands, yell, whistle, break sticks.
- Stand upright—do not crouch or kneel—and wave your arms.
- Don't go between a mother and her cubs.
- Don't approach the bear.
- Fight back if a bear attacks you.

Snakes

Around 53 species of snakes make their home in Arizona. Only a dozen of them are poisonous—coral snakes and 11 species of rattlesnakes. If you are bitten by a poisonous snake, and you have a couple of friends with you, keep quiet and have someone stay with you while another goes for help. If you're alone, the best action to take is the same required for any emergency situation. Practice the *three Cs:* staying as *cool, calm,* and *collected* as you can so you can assess the variables.

Is the Bite Poisonous?
Nonpoisonous snakes have teeth, and the poisonous pit vipers (which include rattlesnakes) have fangs. Fang marks always indicate a poisonous bite. Coral snakes will leave a semicircle mark from their teeth. About 25 percent of rattlesnake bites and 50 percent of coral snake bites receive no venom.

If So, What Are Your Chances of Survival?
If only one bite was inflicted, the bite was quick or shallow, the snake was a smaller one, and the victim was not a child or elderly person, chances of survival are excellent. Of the 7,000 people in the U.S. who get

poisonous snake bites each year, only 15 people die. If you don't feel any symptoms, the bite probably didn't contain any venom. You can tell how much venom was injected, if any, by how quickly and severely the symptoms occur.

- Within five minutes, the immediate area around the bite will swell and burn.
- In 8 to 36 hours the whole limb will swell.
- A purple discoloration will appear around the bite in two to three hours with possible blistering and numbing.
- The numbness will start to include the mouth and tongue.
- Nausea, vomiting, fever, chills, muscle spasms, and convulsions may occur.

If you think the bite contained venom, you may use a snake bite kit that suctions out the poison or apply clay or charcoal poultices; but you must get to a hospital as quickly and calmly as you can.

Preventing a Bite
The best-case scenario is the snake bite you prevent. Rory Aikens, public information officer with the Arizona Game and Fish Department, gives the following tips:

- Stay on established trails. Snakes are less likely to hang around barren human trails, and you can clearly see the ground in front of you.
- Use a walking stick. The stick gives you better balance, makes additional noise that helps warn the snake of your approach, and extends out in front of your body.
- Keep your children and dogs behind you, or at least close by. Kids and dogs tend to move quicker, often without looking.
- Put your hands and feet only in places where you can see.
- Don't try to move or pick up any snakes you encounter. Also, don't try to get the snake to move by throwing objects at it. Instead, go around the snake. A good rule of thumb is to keep about six feet away and walk slowly around the snake.

Insects

Arizona has two poisonous spiders, the black widow and brown recluse; and one poisonous species of scorpion, the small, yellowish, translucent bark scorpion. If you are bitten by these poisonous critters, get to a hospital right away.

How to Use This Book

Hiking is an antidote to modern life. It gives our bodies some much needed (and enjoyable) exercise, and it gives our minds both rest and stimulation. It even lifts the spirit as we connect again with the earth that we're a part of, but seldom have time to think about. With the America's Best Trails series, we hope to provide you with an incentive to start or continue hiking, for the pleasure and the challenge of it.

Each book in the series offers around 100 of the most interesting and scenic trails of each state, as well as information on recreational, historical, and sightseeing destinations located near each trail. The assortment of trails ranges from short, easy hikes for occasional hikers and families with young children to longer, more rugged ones for the experienced trail-blazer. None of the trails individually takes more than a day to hike, although some may be linked together to create a hike of several days.

The trails are divided into six main areas—North, West, Central, South, Southeast, and East. Divider pages signal the beginning of each new area, and those pages include information on the local topography, major rivers and lakes, flora and fauna, weather, and best features of the area.

The innovative format is designed to make exploring trails easy. Information on each area always appears on a right-hand page. It begins with the area's name and a small state map that shows the general location. Bulleted highlights then point out the trail's most interesting features. A description of the area's terrain comes next with practical information on how to get to the park, park hours, available facilities, permits and rules, and a contact address and phone number follow. The section entitled "Other Areas of Interest" briefly mentions other parks and recreational opportunities nearby, with phone numbers to call for more information.

The next pages are generally descriptions of the two best hikes in that park, along with a trail map at the bottom of each page and a difficulty rating at the top shown by boot icons, with 1 being easiest and 5 being most difficult. Each hike begins with information on the length and difficulty of the trail, estimated time to walk it, and cautions to help you avoid possible annoyances or problems.

easiest 1 2 3 4 5 most difficult

This book supplies a general overview of trail locations in each area. For more detailed information, refer to the maps suggested in the information section listed for each hike. Each trail has a United States Geological Survey (USGS) topographical map listed, which provides intricate details of the terrain the trail traverses; most trails also have a map produced by the land manager (such as a national forest or Bureau of Land Management—BLM) that often shows updated information but no topography.

The description of the trail isn't just directions but a guided tour of what you will see as you hike along. The scenery, wildlife, and history of the trail are all brought to life. Points of interest along the trail are numbered in the text, and those numbers are shown on the trail map to guide you. The approximate distance from the trailhead to each point of interest is given.

The park descriptions, maps, and trails are all kept as a unit within an even number of pages so you can easily copy that unit for your own personal use and carry it with you when you travel. Parks for which only one trail is highlighted take up no more than two pages. You might want to use a plastic sleeve to protect the copied pages from the elements, and you can make notes on those pages to remind you of your favorite parts of the park or trail.

If you want to find a park or trail quickly, use the trail finder that appears on the next pages. It gives essential information about each highlighted trail in the book, including the trail's length, difficulty, special features, and facilities.

We hope the books in the America's Best Trails series inspire you to get out and enjoy outdoor experiences. For each state, we've tried to find interesting trails in all parts of that state. Some are unexpected treasures — places you'd never dream would be in that state. Some may be favorites that you've already hiked and recommended to friends. But whether you live in a city or in the country, are vacationing or live there, some of these trails will be near you. Find one you like, lace up your hiking boots, and go!

Trail Finder

KEY

Icon	Icon	Icon	Icon
RV camping	tent camping	swimming	canoeing
fishing	boating	picnicking	biking

Trail Sites and Trails	Facilities	Miles	Trail Difficulty Rating	Mountains	Meadows	Forests	Canyons	Lakes	Vistas	River/Stream	Page #
1 Vermilion Cliffs National Monument											
Soap Creek Canyon		4	5 boots				✓			✓	4
2 Glen Canyon National Recreation Area/Page	All facilities										
Cathedral Canyon		1.25	5 boots				✓			✓	7
Rimview Trail		10	3 boots					✓	✓		8
3 Hualapai Indian Reservation	tent camping, picnicking										
Diamond Creek		2.5+	3 boots				✓			✓	10
4 San Francisco Volcanic Field	tent camping, picnicking, biking										
Red Mountain Trail		1.5	2 boots	✓							13
Strawbery Crater		0.5	3 boots	✓					✓		14
Little Bear Loop		9	3 boots	✓	✓	✓			✓		15
Inner Basin Trail		3	3 boots	✓	✓	✓			✓	✓	16
Weatherford Trail		5-8.7	3 boots	✓	✓	✓			✓		17
Sandys Canyon Trail		1	3 boots		✓	✓	✓		✓		18
5 Sycamore Canyon Wilderness											
Sycamore Rim Trail		11	3 boots		✓	✓	✓		✓		21
Dogie Trail		5.4	3 boots				✓		✓		22
6 Red Rock/Secret Mountain Wilderness	tent camping, picnicking, fishing, swimming										
Bear Sign Trail		3.5	3 boots			✓	✓		✓	✓	25
Wilson Canyon Trail		1	2 boots			✓	✓		✓	✓	26

Continued ☞

	Trail Sites and Trails	Facilities	Miles	Trail Difficulty Rating	Mountains	Meadows	Forests	Canyons	Lakes	Vistas	River/Stream	Page #
6	**Red Rock (contd.)**	(icons)										
	Secret Canyon Trail		5.5	3 boots			✓	✓			✓	27
	West Fork Trail		3	3 boots			✓	✓			✓	28
7	**Sedona Area (Coconino National Forest)**	(icons)										
	Pumphouse Wash		3.5	5 boots				✓			✓	31
	Huckaby Trail		2.5	2 boots				✓		✓	✓	32
8	**Wet Beaver Creek Wilderness**	(icon)										
	Bell Trail		3-6	3 boots				✓		✓	✓	35
	Weir Trail		.75	2 boots				✓			✓	36
9	**Lake Havasu State Park**	All facilities										
	Balance Rock Cove		3	4 boots	✓			✓	✓	✓		40
10	**Kofa National Wildlife Refuge**	(icons)										
	Kofa Queen Canyon		3.75	3 boots				✓		✓		43
	Burro Canyon		4.7	3 boots				✓				44
11	**Bradshaw Mountains**	(icons)										
	Granite Mountain Loop		9.1-13.7	3 boots	✓		✓			✓		49
	Grapevine Trail		2	2 boots			✓	✓			✓	50
12	**Pine Mountain Wilderness**	(icons)										
	Pine Mountain Loop		9.6	3 boots	✓		✓			✓	✓	52
13	**Agua Fria National Monument**											
	Agua Fria River		2	4 boots				✓			✓	54
14	**Hassayampa River Area**	(icons)										
	Vulture Peak Trail		2	4 boots	✓					✓		57
	Treasure Canyon		1.5	4 boots				✓			✓	58
15	**Hell's Canyon Wilderness**											
	Burro Flats Trail		3	3 boots	✓	✓		✓		✓	✓	61
	Spring Valley Trail		2	3 boots	✓			✓		✓	✓	62

Terrain/Landscape

Continued ☞

#	Trail Sites and Trails	Facilities	Miles	Trail Difficulty Rating	Mountains	Meadows	Forests	Canyons	Lakes	Vistas	River/Stream	Page #
16	**Lake Pleasant Regional Park**	All facilities										
	Pipeline Canyon Trail		1.8	🥾🥾🥾				✓	✓	✓		64
17	**Cave Creek Recreation Area**	[RV] [camp] [picnic] [bike]										
	Go John Trail		4.8	🥾🥾🥾	✓			✓		✓		66
18	**White Tank Mountain Regional Park**	[RV] [picnic] [bike]										
	Waterfall Trail		1	🥾🥾🥾				✓				68
19	**South Mountain Park**	[picnic] [bike]										
	Bajada Loop		8	🥾🥾🥾	✓			✓		✓		71
	Alta Trail		4.5	🥾🥾🥾	✓					✓		72
20	**McDowell Moutain Preserve**	[RV] [camp] [picnic] [bike]										
	Scenic Trail Loop		3.4	🥾🥾🥾	✓					✓		74
21	**Usery Mountain Recreation Area**	[RV] [camp] [picnic] [bike]										
	Wind Cave Trail		1.6	🥾🥾🥾	✓					✓		76
22	**Superstition Mountains**											
	JF-Rogers Canyon Trails to Angel Basin		5	🥾🥾🥾	✓	✓		✓		✓	✓	79
	Whitford Canyon		1.5	🥾🥾				✓		✓	✓	80
	Boulder Canyon Trail		7.3	🥾🥾🥾🥾	✓			✓		✓	✓	81
	Bluff Springs Loop		9.5	🥾🥾🥾	✓			✓		✓	✓	82
23	**Lost Dutchman State Park**	[camp] [RV] [picnic] [bike]										
	Siphon Draw Trail		0.7-1.6	🥾🥾🥾	✓			✓		✓		84
24	**Bartlett Reservoir**	All facilities										
	Palo Verde Trail		3.8-4.7	🥾🥾🥾	✓				✓	✓		86
25	**Cave Creek Area**	[camp] [bike]										
	Cave Creek Loop		10	🥾🥾🥾	✓			✓		✓	✓	89
	Hogan Trail		6.5-7.5	🥾🥾🥾	✓					✓	✓	90

Continued ☞

Continued ☞

Terrain/Landscape

Continued ☞

	Trail Sites and Trails	Facilities	Miles	Trail Difficulty Rating	Mountains	Meadows	Forests	Canyons	Lakes	Vistas	River/Stream	Page #
												Terrain/Landscape
43	**Huachuca Mountains**	🌲⛺ 🚶⛱										
	Scheelite Canyon Trail		4	👢👢👢👢	✓		✓	✓		✓	✓	161
	Huachuca Mountains Loop		10.4	👢👢👢	✓	✓	✓	✓		✓	✓	162
44	**Chiricahua Wilderness**	🌲⛺ 🚶⛱										
	South Fork Trail		5.8	👢👢👢	✓		✓	✓		✓	✓	165
	Rucker Canyon Trail		4.6	👢👢👢	✓		✓	✓		✓	✓	166
45	**Pinaleño Mountains**	🌲⛺ 🚶⛱ 🚲	5.1-									
	Arcadia Trail		6.1	👢👢👢	✓		✓	✓		✓	✓	168
46	**Lower Coronado Trail**	🌲⛺ 🚶⛱	1.8-									
	Sardine Canyon Trail		3.6	👢👢👢👢	✓		✓	✓			✓	173
	Spur Cross Trail		5.9	👢👢👢👢	✓			✓		✓	✓	174
47	**White Mountains**	🚐 ⛺ 🚶⛱ 🚲 🐟 🛶										
	Thompson Trail		2.5	👢👢👢		✓	✓	✓			✓	177
	Ackre Lake Trail		7	👢👢👢		✓	✓	✓			✓	178
	Lower Fish Creek		5.5	👢👢👢		✓	✓	✓			✓	179
	KP Trail		2.9	👢👢👢		✓	✓	✓			✓	180
48	**Bear Wallow Wilderness**	🐟										
	Bear Wallow Trail		7.6	👢👢👢		✓	✓	✓			✓	183
	Rose Spring Trail		5.4	👢👢👢			✓			✓		184
49	**Blue Range Primitive Area**	🐟										
	Lanphier Trail		5.6	👢👢👢	✓	✓	✓	✓		✓	✓	187
	Grant Creek Loop		11.4	👢👢👢👢		✓	✓	✓		✓	✓	188

North

The northern section of Arizona covered in this book spans the Colorado Plateau. Heading north from the plateau's 2,000-foot-high escarpment called the Mogollon Rim, the plateau extends into southern Utah and Colorado and into eastern New Mexico.

Topography

Erosion-carved, painted, and utterly breathtaking, the plateau land that makes up northern Arizona presents several charismatic scenes. Early on, Anglo adventurers were drawn to the enchanting geology of the Colorado Plateau with its sandstone cliffs, red rock canyons, and Painted Desert. More than a century later, the land's remoteness and beauty still carry a mystique that draws people looking for a challenge.

Canyons are big in quantity and in size, but they narrow to a slot in some areas. The Grand Canyon, near the top of the state, is the grandest of the canyons in the plateau. A geologic object lesson, the canyon contains some of the oldest rocks on the planet in the Inner Gorge.

Moving eastward from the Grand Canyon, mesas and cliffs create dramatic panoramas. Colors paint the landscape in shades of red, purple, ochre, and white. Narrow canyons drip with seeps and springs, attracting ferns and colorful flowers that deck the red rock walls.

The San Francisco Volcanic Field erupts just below the Painted Desert. Cinder cones, volcanic mountains, and lava tubes show the aesthetic conclusion of the tumult of centuries-old volcanism.

The region abruptly ends at the edge of the Mogollon Rim. The 2,000-foot high escarpment, called the backbone of Arizona, runs with the plateau into New Mexico. Canyons carved by perennial creeks gushing from the rim's side stream down the rim toward the central mountains.

Major Rivers and Lakes

The Colorado River makes the biggest statement in the northern region as it slices across the northwest corner of the state to form the Grand Canyon. This major western United States drainage gets pooled several times as it makes its way across this region.

The first dam, at Page, forms Lake Powell. After a raucous run through the Grand Canyon, the river bloats from dams at Lake Mead.

The Little Colorado River travels a northward course to the Colorado River from its headwaters in the eastern region of the state. The river starts as a sliver of a stream and ends as an enchanting turquoise flow at its confluence with the Colorado River in Marble Canyon.

Common Plant Life

The vegetation of the north section varies as much as its terrain. This inspired Clinton Hart Merriam, the first chief of the USDA's Division of Economic Ornithology and Mammalogy (an agency that preceded the National Wildlife Research Center), to make a study about the area's vegetation. He came up with the *life zone* concept.

Merriam made a base camp just north of the San Francisco Peaks around 1889 when he researched the feasibility of his famous life zones theory. Merriam believed that climate gradients produced by elevation and latitude influenced the type of vegetation in an area.

Merriam conducted his research from the desert floor of the Grand Canyon to the tundra mountaintops on the San Francisco Peaks, coming up with six ecological communities where vegetation types reflected climate changes produced by elevation gains: *Lower Sonoran, Upper Sonoran, Transition, Canadian, Hudsonian,* and *Arctic Alpine*. Merriam identified each zone with a major vegetation feature.

Vegetation in the north section of Arizona spans from cactus and desert shrubs of the Lower Sonoran zone at the bottom of the Grand Canyon to the spruce-alpine fir community of the San Francisco Peaks. The Upper Sonoran life zone of evergreen oaks, piñon pines, and junipers sprawl across the section. The Transition zone, composed of ponderosa pines, appears on lower mountaintops. The Canadian life zone features firs in groves of aspen on the taller peaks. The Hudsonian zone has spruce, alpine fir, and bristlecone pine trees. The Alpine zone mirrors tundra life above the treeline.

Common Birds and Mammals

Like the vegetation, the birds and mammals vary in the north section with the terrain and life zones. In the lower elevation of the bottom of the Grand Canyon, watch for rattlesnakes, scorpions, and lizards. Ground squirrels and ringtailed cats may purloin food if you don't watch your pack.

In the Upper Sonoran and Transition life zones, you may spot coyotes, mountain lions, deer, and bears. Elk appear in the higher elevations of the mountains and are especially comfortable in the cooler Hudsonian zone.

Canyons have their own unique ecosystems. In the middle of a parched sandstone landscape, a spring-fed stream may create an Edenic environment that draws birds, reptiles, and animals.

Listen for canyon wrens in steep-walled canyons. Watch condors glide along the Arizona Strip and Grand Canyon areas. Enjoy the sweet sound of hermit thrushes in high-altitude canyons. Expect the squawk of Stellar's jays in Transition zones. Always watch for ravens.

Climate

You'll find every weather scenario that occurs in the state of Arizona occurring in the north section. Temperatures in the bottom of the Grand Canyon mirror those of the desert: hot in the summer and mild in the winter. On its rim, you find the cooler influence you'll also find in the higher mountains, where moderate summer temperatures make life comfortable but winters see snow and freezing cold. Most of the section, however, has extreme weather patterns: hot and dry in the summer with mild nights; warm and dry in the spring and fall with cool nights; and cold winter days with frosty nights.

Like the rest of the state, the north section experiences monsoon season from early July through mid-September, when thunderstorms often occur by (or after) noon, especially in the higher elevations. Always watch for lightning. In the higher mountains be prepared for hail, and even snow, during these storms.

If snows falls on the plateaus, it will probably melt when the sun comes out. The mountaintops won't see spring until April or May. The highest elevations in the San Francisco Peaks will keep winter snow, which often accumulates several feet, until May or June.

Best Natural Features

- The Grand Canyon and other canyons with perennial streams, where natural elements have carved through layers of rock
- Lake Powell, surrounded by colorful sandstone cliffs, along the Colorado River
- Mesas, extraordinary rock formations, and colors in the Painted Desert
- Volcanism in the San Francisco Volcanic Field
- The red rock country of Sedona, where the Supai Formation has eroded into stunning cliffs and formations

1. Vermilion Cliffs National Monument

- Explore side canyons of the Grand Canyon National Park.
- Watch California condors soar in the sky.

Area Information

Wild, weather-wracked, and remote, the Vermilion Cliffs National Monument presents a true backcountry experience to anyone wanting to explore its dramatic features. Users will need good route-finding skills to follow the unmaintained routes the area offers. But anyone who likes to explore with a healthy dose of adventure will have fun here.

The area has always drawn explorers. Through the last few centuries, the Vermilion Cliffs have hosted several historic expeditions.

The cliffs got their name during an expedition led by John Wesley Powell. When the exploration party wintered in the area in 1872, geologist Clarence Dutton recognized a geologic stairway composed of different-colored cliffs that successively rise 5,500 feet up to Bryce Canyon in Utah. He named them the Grand Staircase. The Grand Staircase became part the Grand Staircase-Escalante National Monument in 1996. The Vermilion Cliffs, showing red tones as intense as the name implies, make up the bottom "stair" of the Grand Staircase.

Different cultures have left their marks on the monument. Ancestral Pueblo ruins and rock art, Mormon settlements, mining paraphernalia, and ranching signs all appear around the Vermilion Cliffs.

The medicinal pungency from sage bushes wafts among the area's high desert vegetation mix of cacti and grasses. Piñon and juniper trees cast stingy pools of shade in the harsh environment.

The area has a variety of reptiles, raptors, pronghorn antelope, bighorn sheep, and mountain lions. An exciting addition to the wildlife lineup is the California condor, reintroduced in 1996. Wildlife viewers can usually get a glimpse of the four-foot-high scavenger birds if they travel to the release site on House Rock Valley Road. Even if the birds aren't around, a biologist from the Peregrine Fund usually is there during the day to discuss the birds and their behavior.

Directions: Located near Marble Canyon along U.S. 89A on the Arizona Strip.

Hours Open: No restrictions.

Facilities: No facilities.

Permits and Rules: The Archaeological Resource Protection Act and state antiquity laws protect ancient and historic ruins. Anyone found excavating, collecting, defacing, or removing an artifact can be fined $500 to $250,000 and imprisoned up to five years. If you see a relic from a historic or ancient culture, you may inspect it, but you may not take it.

Further Information: Bureau of Land Management, Arizona Strip Field Office, 345 E. Riverside Dr., St. George UT 84790; 435-688-3200.

Other Areas of Interest

Take a drive on House Rock Valley Road north of U.S. 89 to get to know more about the California condors living in the area. A biologist from the Peregrine Fund is usually stationed along the road observing the big scavenger birds.

Soap Creek Canyon

Distance Round-Trip: 8 miles

Estimated Hiking Time: 8 hours

Elevation: 4,220 to 3,050 feet

Map: USGS Navajo Bridge

Cautions: Only experienced hikers should attempt this hike. Overnight use requires a permit from Grand Canyon National Park.

Directions: Drive west on U.S. 89A about 9 miles just past mile marker 548, then turn south (left); go through a gate, then drive 0.5 mile to the trailhead. Soap Creek presents a daring route that will push less experienced hikers past their envelope of comfort, but provides a fun challenge for seasoned hikers.

The route starts **[1]** along a gravelly section on the canyon's floor past ledged Kaibab limestone cliffs the color of dirty dishwater. The rocks show occasional crusts of calcite crystals. Fossils of coral and brachiopods tell how the area once had an saltwater cover.

At mile 0.75, the ledge-forming Toroweap Formation comes on the scene. The route climbs down a 10-foot pouroff, then does a simple scramble down several ledges that eventually drop you about 100 feet.

By mile 1, a platform of rock overlooking the canyon shows a jumble of huge limestone boulders on the canyon floor **[2]**. You will notice rock cairns demarcating two different routes. One leads into the boulder field in the canyon; another leads to a suggestion of a path that climbs nearly to the top of the talus slope on the north wall, then skids down at the other end of the boulder field. This makes a good turnaround point.

Hiking through the boulder field requires hopping, twisting, and squeezing among square house-sized boulders and giant dimpled rock slabs. The route that climbs the canyon wall requires steady footing on a perpendicular talus slope.

At about mile 1.3, you come to another pouroff. A path on the right climbs up to a sliver of a trail, often less than a foot wide, that teeters midslope around a 100-foot pouroff. An alternate route requires a traverse along a narrow 50-foot ledge on the left.

At about mile 2, cairns lead the way to a 10-foot downclimb **[3]**. A handhold on the middle of three large boulders makes the climb fairly simple. Once on the canyon floor again, maneuver through boulders until about mile 2.5, at the North Fork of Soap Creek **[4]**, which enters on your left. From here, the route eases up, weaving around rocks and boulders to the canyon's mouth at the Colorado River.

At the river **[5]**, you can have lunch, fish for trout if you have an Arizona fishing license and trout stamp, or watch for a rafting trip to negotiate Soap Creek Rapids. When you have finished enjoying the river, return the way you came.

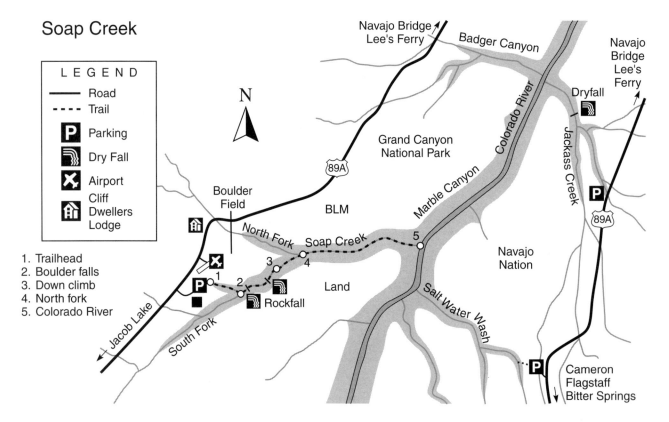

Soap Creek

LEGEND
— Road
---- Trail
P Parking
Dry Fall
X Airport
Cliff Dwellers Lodge

1. Trailhead
2. Boulder falls
3. Down climb
4. North fork
5. Colorado River

2. Glen Canyon National Recreation Area/ Page

- Swim, fish, and boat in one of the most beautiful lakes in the United States.
- Hike along Lake Powell and the Navajo Nation.
- Have lunch on the banks of the Colorado River in the Grand Canyon.

Area Information

The area around Lake Powell has gone through radical changes over the years. On a geological timeline, the land once saw ancient seas and freshwater lakes, and experienced the creation of mountains and plateau uplifting. All this millenniumish activity that took thousands of years produced a gorgeous landscape of sandstone cliffs cut by the Colorado and Escalante rivers.

The cliffs, predominantly Navajo sandstone, were formed by sand dunes hardened by minerals in the groundwater. Fossils of small sea creatures reveal its oceanic ties. Petrified wood and fossilized dinosaur bones tell about the era when marshes oozed and volcanoes steamed.

In the middle of the 20th century, only the most adventurous explored the area, which was beautiful but not user friendly. The area's sanguine sandstone cliffs, buttes, mesas, and canyons created a captivating landscape. A hike in a lonely canyon saw intricate features of limestone cracks, fluted walls, clefts, and boxed canyons. But things changed in the 1960s. The esoteric high desert hideaway became a world-class water world.

Much to California's relief, and environmentalists' chagrin, the Glen Canyon Dam came on the scene. Built to meet western U.S. energy demands, the dam made dramatic changes to the area. Construction on the dam started in 1956.

The Colorado River, with its volatile flow that wavered from a muddy sludge to a raging flood, pooled to form Lake Powell. By 1980 the lake reached full pool. The waters now run crystal clear and hundreds of feet deep. The prehistoric-looking chub and sucker natives that lurked in the river's pre-dam muddy flow have taken a back seat to the trophy bass in Lake Powell and the rainbow trout below the dam. Swimming and boating have become activities of choice.

A hike in the area can take you into intriguing canyons that require a bit of adventure, or it can stay along the lakeshore for a mild-mannered stroll. When you're done with the hike you can take a swim, or just enjoy the stunning oddity of such a big pool of blue water contained in red rock cliffs in the middle of the desert.

Directions: The recreation area is located at the northern edge of Arizona. Take U.S. 89A to Page.

Hours Open: No restrictions.

Facilities: Developed campgrounds, restrooms, picnic areas, boat launch sites, a restaurant, and a motel at Glen Canyon National Recreation Area. The National Park Service charges an entrance fee of $10 per car.

Permits and Rules:

- Pets must be leashed at all times.
- Fireworks are illegal.
- Removing, disturbing, or destroying plants, animals, rocks, fossils, or natural features is illegal.
- The Archaeological Resource Protection Act and state antiquity laws protect ancient and historic ruins. Anyone found excavating, collecting, defacing, or removing an artifact can be fined $500 to $250,000 and imprisoned up to five years.

Further Information: Glen Canyon National Recreation Area, P.O. Box 1507, Page, AZ 86040-1507; 928-608-6404. Also the City of Page, P.O. Box 1180, Page, AZ 86040; 928-645-8861.

Other Areas of Interest

If you want to learn about the dam that formed Lake Powell, go on a free tour that takes you inside Glen Canyon Dam. The tour starts at the Carl Hayden Visitor Center in Page. If you want to tour Glen Canyon, take a smoothwater river trip on the Colorado River's peaceful passage through Glen Canyon on a Wilderness River Adventures tour. Call 800-992-8022 for more information.

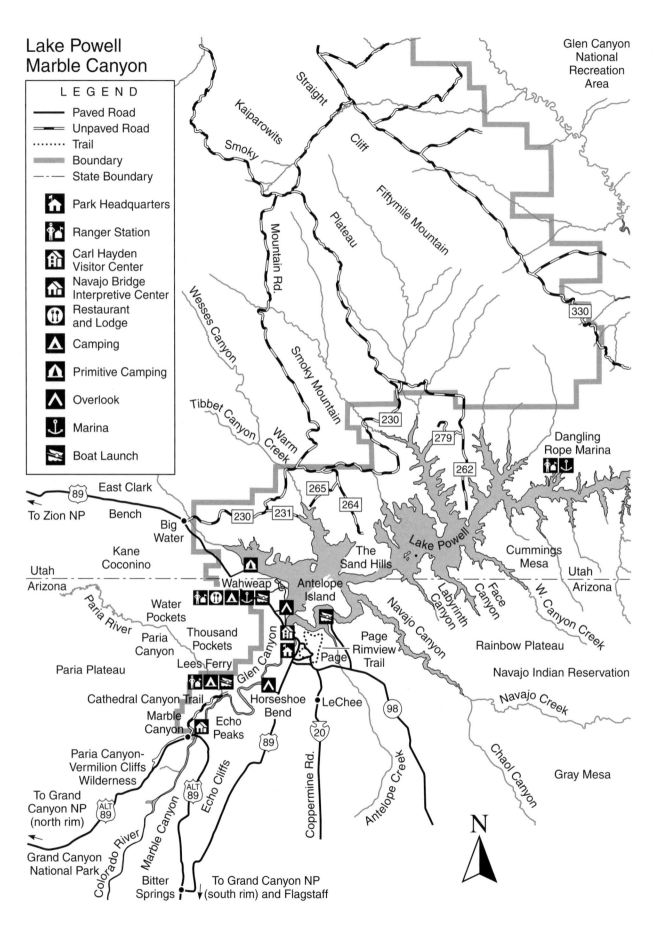

Lake Powell
Marble Canyon

L E G E N D

——	Paved Road
▬▬	Unpaved Road
......	Trail
▬▬	Boundary
—·—	State Boundary
🏠	Park Headquarters
🧍	Ranger Station
🏛	Carl Hayden Visitor Center
🏠	Navajo Bridge Interpretive Center
🍽	Restaurant and Lodge
⛺	Camping
⛺	Primitive Camping
⛰	Overlook
⚓	Marina
🛥	Boat Launch

Glen Canyon National Recreation Area

Straight

Kaiparowits

Smoky

Cliff

Plateau

Fiftymile Mountain

Mountain Rd.

Smoky Mountain

Wesses Canyon

Tibbet Canyon

Warm Creek

330

Dangling Rope Marina

279

262

230

265

264

231

230

US 89 East Clark

To Zion NP   Bench

Big Water

Kane Coconino

Utah
Arizona

Lake Powell

The Sand Hills

Cummings Mesa

Utah
Arizona

W. Canyon Creek

Wahweap

Antelope Island

Labyrinth Canyon

Face Canyon

Water Pockets

Paria River

Thousand Pockets

Navajo Canyon

Rainbow Plateau

Paria Canyon

Page Rimview Trail

Paria Plateau

Lees Ferry

Glen Canyon

Page

Navajo Indian Reservation

Cathedral Canyon Trail

Horseshoe Bend

LeChee

98

Navajo Creek

Marble Canyon

Echo Peaks

20

Paria Canyon-Vermilion Cliffs Wilderness

Echo Cliffs

US 89

Coppermine Rd.

Chaol Canyon

Gray Mesa

To Grand Canyon NP (north rim)

ALT 89

ALT 89

Marble Canyon

Colorado River

Grand Canyon National Park

Bitter Springs

To Grand Canyon NP (south rim) and Flagstaff

Antelope Creek

N

Cathedral Canyon

🥾 🥾 🥾 🥾 🥾

Distance Round-Trip: 2.5 miles

Estimated Hiking Time: 2.5 hours

Elevation: 3,400 to 3,600 feet

Map: USGS Lees Ferry

Cautions: Do not hike if rain threatens. Hikers with vertigo should not attempt the route.

Directions: From U.S. 89A, turn north onto Lees Ferry Road; drive 1.5 miles to the turnout at Cathedral Rock. Drop into Cathedral Wash on the east (right) side of the road and head into the canyon to the Colorado River.

Neither hair-raising nor a cakewalk, the route down Cathedral Wash to the Colorado River near Lees Ferry makes a fun change of pace from a designated trail. The route connects cairns while traipsing on ledges and climbing up and down the canyon's walls.

Generally sharp and raspy, the Kaibab limestone walls at the route's beginning [1] stand smooth, well worn by flooding that has created a series of chute-like pouroffs. A metal sign near the first pouroff designates the boundary of the Grand Canyon National Park, informing hikers that permits are required for overnight use.

From there, the walls grow as the route drops deeper into the canyon. Along the way, arches appear [2], one near a set of utility wires strung across the rim of the canyon and one near the river; and strangely sculpted rocks peer into the canyon from its rim.

Starting at about mile 0.25, the route has you hoisting yourself up and down ledges, ducking under low-hanging alcoves, and plodding across the sandy wash floor. Cairns will always show you the easier way to negotiate around pouroffs and where to access ledges.

By mile 1, you can hear the roar of Cathedral Rapids at the Colorado River. The weaker Toroweap sandstone walls have caved in under the force of erosion in spots, creating an obstacle course of boulders [3] for you to wend around on your way to the river's edge. The canyon ends at Cathedral Rapids [4] on the Colorado River.

The Colorado River makes a perfect destination. After all, it's not often a hiker can hike into the Grand Canyon and have lunch at the Colorado River in a day.

1. Trailhead
2. Arch
3. Toroweap formation
4. Cathedral Rapids

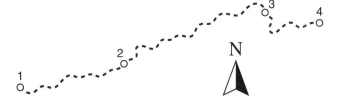

Rimview Trail 👢 👢 👢

Distance Round-Trip: 10-mile loop

Estimated Hiking Time: 5 hours

Elevation: 3,250 to 3,850 feet

Map: USGS Page

Cautions: To avoid hiking in the town of Page, plan your hike to stay on the western half of the trail. This trail is managed by the city of Page.

Directions: From U.S. 89 in Page, turn right at the second turnoff for Lake Powell Boulevard near the Courtyard by Marriott; drive about 1.5 miles to North Navajo Road and turn north (left); drive one mile to the trailhead.

Circling the city of Page on Manson Mesa, the Rimview Trail gives you an idea of the tenuous hold civilization has in the midst of the powerful wilderness that surrounds this area. The trail travels the stunning shoreline of Lake Powell, passes through the town of Page, then travels near the Navajo Nation, giving you a variety of experiences on this high desert hike.

Starting on Page's Nature Trail **[1]**, veer left at a pink post with the number 5 on it. The trail will eventually meet the single-track Rimview Trail that traces the edge of the mesa.

Lake Powell's surreal landscape will occupy your attention for the next couple of miles until the dramatic geology of Marble Canyon takes over. About when the velvety greens of Page's golf course come into view **[2]**, you can pick out the Vermilion Cliffs, Glen Canyon Dam, and the Kaiparowits Plateau.

The trail crosses Lake Powell Boulevard, then resumes at the end of the guardrail, about 70 yards east. After a brief pass through the golf course, the trail continues along a wooden fence as it rounds its way to the southern side of the mesa. Follow the trail signs as the trail heads east, making two more street crossings and a jog around Page's water treatment plant **[3]**. At the Lake Powell Yacht Club, the path scrambles back down to the single-track trail hugging the edge of the mesa.

Heading north **[4]**, the loneliness of the Navajo Nation, its red rock land stretching to the horizons, encroaches on the trail, taking you into a remote atmosphere. But the warm shades of orange that paint slickrock haystacks rising from the landscape add a cozy feeling. The dome-shaped mountain in the distant east is Sacred Navajo Mountain. As the trail heads west back to the Nature Trail, Lake Powell once again becomes the main attraction. At a pink post with the number 23 on it, veer left onto the Nature Trail and follow the pink posts back to the parking area.

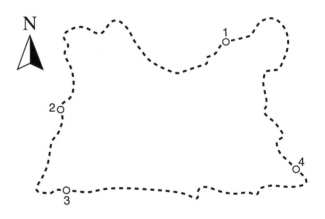

1. Trailhead
2. Golf course
3. Street crossings
4. Navajo Nation

3. Hualapai Indian Reservation

- Drive the only road that travels into the Grand Canyon to the banks of the Colorado River.

- Hike into a remote side canyon of the Grand Canyon.

Area Information

The name *Hualapai* derives from *Hwal'bay*, which means "people of the tall pine." Most of the million acres of land on which the Hualapai live, located on plateau uplands in northwestern Arizona bordering the Colorado River in the western end of the Grand Canyon, have a piñon pine and juniper tree cover. The reservation's forested land attracts hunters; its 108 miles of the Colorado River and the Grand Canyon bring outdoor enthusiasts.

The Hualapai call their 108 miles of river *Hakataya*, "the backbone of the river," because it's placed in the middle river corridor. The Colorado River has a significant place in Hualapai tradition. All of the Yuman language family tribes, of which they are a part, were located close to the Colorado River. These tribes have similar myths that creation occurred at a place near Bullhead City called *Wikahme*, which means "Spirit Mountain."

The Hualapai have always delved into the Grand Canyon to obtain edibles for food and medicinal purposes. Historically, they have hunted, gathered, and farmed in the canyon. Today, Hualapai River Running, the only tribal river outfitter in the Grand Canyon, offers tours on the Colorado River.

The Hualapai reservation presents remote hiking in side canyons of the Colorado River. Most of these hikes require that hikers have canyoneering experience. Diamond Creek gives hikers of all experience levels a chance at hiking all or part of the route.

Directions: Peach Springs, the main town in the Hualapai Reservation, is located about 50 miles east of Kingman and 110 miles west of Flagstaff along U.S. 66. At Peach Springs, turn north onto Diamond Creek Road (across the street from the Hualapai Lodge). This road takes you to the banks of the Colorado River in the Grand Canyon.

Hours Open: No restrictions.

Facilities: Camping and picnic areas.

Permits and Rules: Visitors must obtain a permit to enter the Hualapai Reservation from the Department of Wildlife and Recreation or the Hualapai Lodge in Peach Springs ($5 for each day and an additional $3 for each night).

Further Information: Department of Wildlife and Recreation, P.O. Box 300, Peach Springs, AZ 86434; 928-769-2227.

Other Areas of Interest

You can visit the town of Supai, nestled next to a blue-green stream under the Grand Canyon's soaring red rock cliffs on the floor of the Grand Canyon. Travel there by foot or horseback via the 8-mile Supai Trail; the trailhead is located about 66 miles northeast of Peach Springs on the Havasupai Indian Reservation, or arrive via helicopter. For more information (permits required), call the Havasupai Tribal Council at 928-448-2731.

Diamond Creek 🥾 🥾 🥾

Distance Round-Trip: 5-plus miles

Estimated Hiking Time: +3.5 hours

Elevation: 1,335 to 6,560 feet

Map: USGS Peach Springs NE

Cautions: This route follows no maintained trail. Purify all water.

Directions: From Peach Springs, drive 19.2 miles on Diamond Creek Road to the trailhead parking area on the west side of the road.

During his 1857 passage through Diamond Canyon, a tributary of the Grand Canyon on the Hualapai Indian Reservation, Joseph Ives described the gorge as having an "unearthly character." Claiming he heard screams from its shadowy 2,000-foot heights, he likened the canyon to "the portals of the infernal regions."

The lower canyon's remote atmosphere and towering sable-colored walls could easily fuel the fire of Ives' lively imagination. An ancient meld of sandstone, shale, limestone, and lava crushed, folded, and melted by heat and pressure has produced breathtaking formations and passageways with an eerie but aesthetic appeal.

With no maintained trail or even a beaten path, the route [1] picks its way along the rocky canyon bottom and wades the shallow creek into Diamond Canyon. In the canyon, the creek wends between dark-colored schists of the Vishnu Group—some of the oldest rocks on the planet.

By mile 2.5 [2], the canyon walls become cavernous and swallow all but traces of sunlight as they grow to 2,000 feet high and narrow to a mere 20 feet in some spots. The short stretch of narrows ends just beyond a moderate climb up a 10-foot pouroff. The pouroff makes a good turnaround point for a short day hike.

Those looking for a more adventurous hike can continue past the cascade toward Diamond Spring. Craggy peaks form peculiar and dramatic formations in the rockwalls, which have shortened and widened enough to absorb a constant drenching of the sun [3]. The canyon floor climbs perceptibly, creating cascades that take more attention and time to negotiate.

A backpack will take you to Diamond Spring [4], once a meeting place for the Hualapai, where small pools congregate as the canyon narrows to a small ravine and fills with galleries of mesquite and mature hackberry trees. Beyond the spring, water may be intermittent, and the relatively mild-mannered route becomes an aggressive challenge suitable for experienced hikers only as it climbs out of the canyon on a faint trail and scrambles 3,000 feet to a trailhead on Wilder Springs Road (about 10 miles from Indian Route 18).

Hikers not accustomed to remote areas may feel overwhelmed by the distant atmosphere they encounter between the narrows and Diamond Spring. However, if they take a moment to observe and absorb their surroundings, they may feel as comfortable as the Hualapai Indians did when they once made this canyon their home.

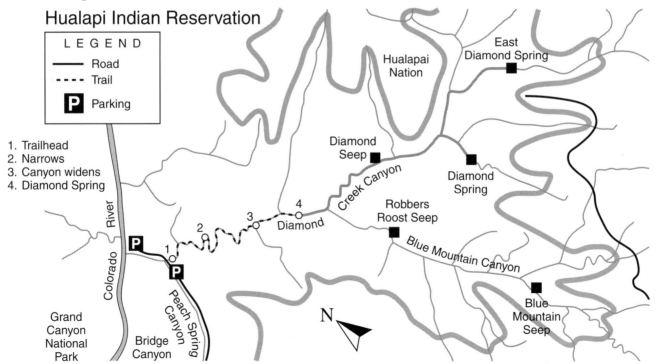

Hualapi Indian Reservation

LEGEND
— Road
- - - Trail
P Parking

1. Trailhead
2. Narrows
3. Canyon widens
4. Diamond Spring

4. San Francisco Volcanic Field

- Hike up volcanic cinder cones.
- Picnic in alpine meadows full of dozens of different wildflowers.
- Enjoy panoramas reaching to the Grand Canyon and the Painted Desert.
- Stand on Arizona's tallest peak.

Area Information

In the San Francisco Volcanic Field near Flagstaff, you get a look at several different examples of volcanism. A rich array of volcanoes, and the weird landscape formed in their tumultuous aftermath, cluster in the area.

"Someday there will be another eruption in the Flagstaff area," volcano expert Wendell Duffield says. "During the past five to six millions years there have been hundreds. From a geological perspective, another eruption seems inevitable."

Volcanoes help cool the earth by creating an escape hatch for releasing thermal energy through eruptions. When pressure builds to the point that magma must escape, the magma erupts onto the earth's surface in the form of a new volcano. The next eruption's harbingers, Duffield says, will be hundreds—if not thousands—of earthquakes, perceptible at first only by seismograph. Magma will rise through cracks in the earth's surface, and the earthquakes will get more shallow as the molten river rises.

"If things start shaking up," Duffield says about the Flagstaff area, "the place would teem with geologists from around the world who would have an immediate interest in the area. Chances are, however, it will not be in my lifetime."

For now, Flagstaff's volcanic assemblage remains peaceful, and its beautiful volcanic landscape prevails. The San Francisco Volcanic Field, with the San Francisco Peaks in its heart, harbors over 600 volcanoes, most of them cones that rise in flat grasslands. The San Francisco Volcanic Field's biggest volcano, Mount Humphreys, is the area's only stratovolcano. Duffield calls the mountain northern Arizona's version of Mount Fuji.

Mount St. Helens is a recent example of a stratovolcano that blew its top quarter away. Duffield surmises Mount Humphreys' pre-eruption summit once stood about 16,000 feet—the same height as that of Mount St. Helens—and left a caldera of Humphreys, Agassiz, Fremont, Aubineau, Reese, Doyle, and Sugarloaf peaks. Hikers who head for the Inner Basin Trail in Lockett Meadow can stand in the palm of the caldera.

The best time to hike the San Francisco Volcanic Field is between May and October. Its highcountry elevations make summer the perfect time. Wildflowers put on a springtime show in May, then another wave appears from mid-July to mid-August during summer monsoons. Autumn color appears any time from late September to early October.

Directions: This area is located near Flagstaff. Trails can be reached by driving north on U.S. 180 or U.S. 89 from Flagstaff.

Hours Open: No restrictions.

Facilities: Restrooms at some trailheads; camping at Lockett Meadow; developed campgrounds, picnic area, restrooms, and visitors center at Sunset Crater Volcano National Monument.

Permits and Rules:

- Some trails are located in the Kachina Peaks Wilderness, where no mechanized vehicles or mountain bikes are allowed.
- In developed recreation sites, pets must be restrained on a leash no longer than 6 feet.
- Fireworks are prohibited.
- Fires must be attended at all times.
- Maximum stay is 14 days.
- Maximum group size is 10 people.

Further Information: Coconino National Forest, Peaks District Ranger District, 5075 N. Highway 89, Flagstaff, AZ 86004; 928-526-0866.

Other Areas of Interest

You can learn more about the vegetation along the trails in this area at The Arboretum at Flagstaff, located on Woody Mountain Road at the northern end of Flagstaff. Call 928-774-1442 for more information. You can find out all about the volcanic and archaeological history in the area at the Sunset Crater Volcano National Monument, located about 11 miles north of Flagstaff on U.S. 89. Call 800-842-7293.

San Francisco Volcanic Field

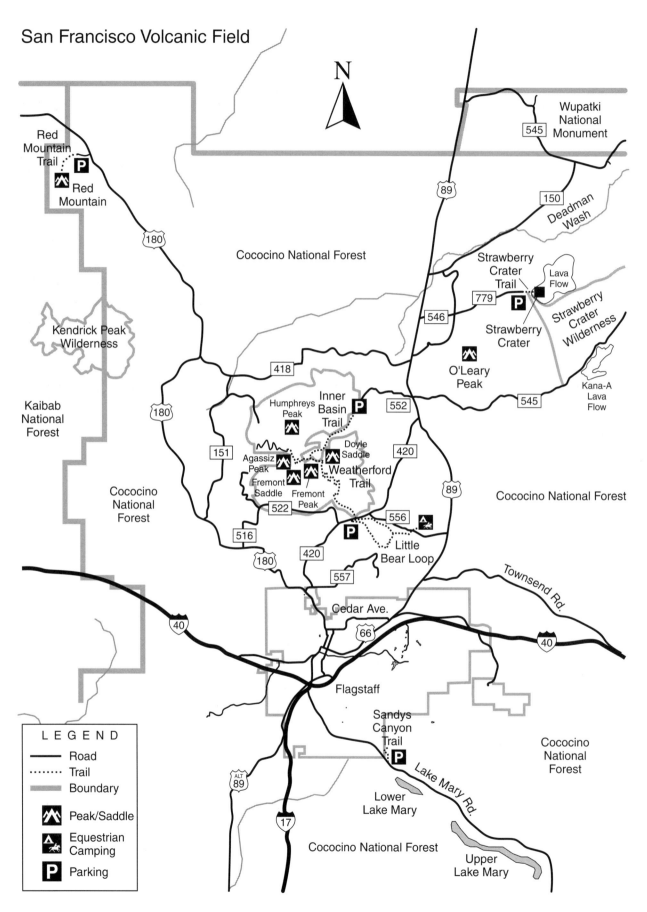

Red Mountain Trail 🥾 🥾

Distance Round-Trip: 3 miles

Estimated Hiking Time: 1.5 hours

Elevation: 6,800 to 7,000 feet

Map: USGS Chapel Mountain

Caution: If you explore inside the volcano, wear footgear with good tread because the cindered landscape can be treacherous.

Directions: Drive north on U.S. 180 about 33.2 miles to milepost 247 and turn west (left) onto FR 9023V; drive 0.3 mile to the trailhead.

The Red Mountain Trail takes you to a ruddy volcano on the San Francisco Volcanic Field. The surreal amphitheater of orange-tinged volcanic rock at the end of the trail is actually the blown-out side of the volcano, and not the vent. The area has eroded into fantasy forms of peaks and spires reminiscent of Bryce Canyon National Park.

By mile 0.1, the trail enters a piñon-juniper forest **[1]**, also called a *pygmy forest*. Desolate-looking juniper snags and trunks writhing on the warm ruddy-colored ground produces an odd coziness. The aroma of sap oozing from the piñon trees smells like incense.

By mile 1, the trail steps into, and follows, a wash lined with cliffrose and current bushes **[2]**. Ponderosa pines show up about mile 1.3.

The wash twines around a handful of ponderosa pines, then enters a corridor where black cinder slopes rise on either side of the trail. The slopes, sparse of vegetation, have a dramatic look akin to a moonscape.

The corridor **[3]** leads to a manmade spillway where a seven-rung ladder lifts you up the wall and onto the volcano. From here, you can explore the eroded formations in the volcano. When you have finished exploring the volcano, return the way you came.

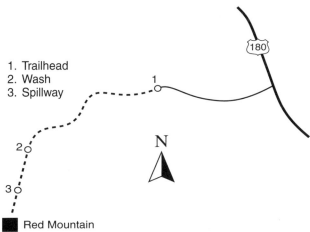

1. Trailhead
2. Wash
3. Spillway

Coconino National Forest

Strawberry Crater

Distance Round-Trip: 1 mile

Estimated Hiking Time: 1 hour

Elevation: 6,000 to 6,500 feet

Map: USGS Strawberry Crater

Caution: Enclosed footgear will help to keep out pebble-sized cinders along the path.

Directions: Drive about 15 miles north on U.S. Route 89 to FR 546 (just past mile marker 434), then turn east (right); drive 3.5 miles and continue straight on FR 779; drive about 2 miles to the parking area.

Grayed juniper limbs strewn across the black cinder landscape set a moody scene for this half-mile hike [1]. The Forest Service has lined the route between the parking area and the cinder cone with juniper limbs to lead you in the right direction. Raspy cobbles of ruddy basalt stacked into craggy cairns further mark the route. You need them both. Aside from clusters of Apache plume, skunkbush, and current bushes, the landscape has no grasses to delineate a footpath.

Once the trail gets to the cinder cone, said to look like an upside-down strawberry, get ready for a climb. Even with its handful of switchbacks, the trail zips vertically up the cone. And it's two steps forward, one step back as you plow up the cindered route as if hiking in sand. At the crater's top [2], the path makes a quick jog through a jagged wall of lava onto the crater.

The lava flow, a frozen flash of volcanism, spreads across the crater. The flow looks like a chocolate coral reef. If you study the raspy wall, you can see scrape marks in the rock where it oozed through cracks in the cooler surface. You may also notice how the volcano's boiling rock cooled into petrified bubbles.

Panoramas from the top of the crater give a sweeping view of the San Francisco Volcanic Field. The landscape to the northeast shows cinder hillsides sloping casually like swells of the sea until the ruddy colors of the Painted Desert streak across the horizon. To the west, you can see the San Francisco Peaks, the heart of the San Francisco Volcanic Field. After you have enjoyed the panorama of the landscape below, return the way you came.

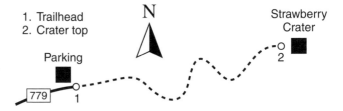

1. Trailhead
2. Crater top

N

Parking

Strawberry Crater

779

Little Bear Loop

Distance Round-Trip: 9 miles

Estimated Hiking Time: 4.5 hours

Elevation: 7,600 to 9,275 feet

Map: USGS Coconino National Forest

Caution: This is a multiuse trail. Proper trail etiquette requires that mountain bikers yield to runners and hikers, runners yield to hikers, and all yield to horses.

Directions: From Flagstaff, drive north on Arizona 89 about 5 miles to Elden Springs Road (just north of mile marker 423), then turn left; drive about 2.4 miles to the trailhead.

Located in the Dry Lake Hills just north of Flagstaff, this loop takes you through a variety of landscapes. The trail starts in a highcountry meadow, takes a look at Mount Humphreys in the San Francisco Peaks, and ducks under subalpine forests.

Starting **[1]** on the Little Elden Trail, the route makes an imperceptible ascent across a sunny meadow scattered with ponderosa pines. During the summer, wildflowers dot the grasses. The trail waits until about mile 1.5 **[2]** before it starts to climb into a fir and aspen forest. Flashes of Mount Humphreys appear in small clearings. When the trail arrives at Schultz Tank, about mile 3, you get a good look at Arizona's tallest peak rising just behind the pond **[3]**.

At a signed trail junction, about mile 3.2, turn left onto the Sunset Trail **[4]**. The route proceeds on a pleasant grade through a pine forest. You might catch a deer peering at you from the other side of a grassy meadow, or hear an Abert's squirrel's chatter. Elk, black bears, and porcupines also roam the area this trail treads. If you do see wildlife, try to keep maximum distance with minimum noise.

At another signed junction **[5]**, about mile 4.9, continue on the Sunset Trail, taking a hard left toward the Elden Lookout. At about mile 5.2, turn left onto the Little Bear Trail.

The trail starts a 1,200-foot descent back to the Little Elden Trail **[6]** in a forest of fir, pine, and aspen. As the trail zigzags down the mountain, several excellent views of Sunset Crater, located less than 10 miles north; and the Painted Desert, spreading in the distant north, show up in openings in the forest. An unusual stretch of terraced outcroppings right along the trail have cascades of plants spilling over, and claret cactus nestle in niches on their ledges.

The trail takes you back to the Little Elden Trail **[7]**, where you turn right and return to the trailhead.

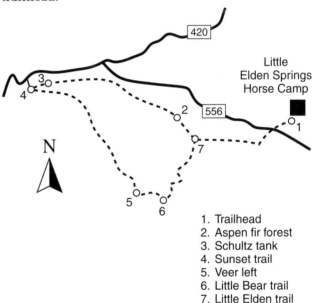

1. Trailhead
2. Aspen fir forest
3. Schultz tank
4. Sunset trail
5. Veer left
6. Little Bear trail
7. Little Elden trail

Inner Basin Trail 👢 👢 👢

Distance Round-Trip: 6 miles

Estimated Hiking Time: 3 hours

Elevation: 8,600 to 10,000 feet

Maps: Coconino National Forest, USGS Humphreys Peak

Caution: Camping and horses are not allowed in the Inner Basin.

Directions: Drive north on Highway 89 for 12 miles and turn left (east) onto FR 552 (across from the Sunset Crater turnoff); drive 1.5 miles and turn right at a sign for Lockett Meadow; drive 3 more miles to the trailhead.

The Inner Basin Trail takes you into a meadow that was the heart of an extinct volcano. The mountain, once 15,000 feet high, shattered when it erupted millions of years ago, just as Mount St. Helens did in 1980. The San Francisco Peaks' highest mountaintops—Doyle, Fremont, Agassiz, and Humphreys—make up the caldera of the volcano. These peaks ring the meadow, showing off a striking subalpine scene.

The trail keeps a shady profile as it purposefully climbs on a primitive road up to the Inner Basin [1] through a forest of aspen trees and mixed conifers. At mile 1, almost to the Inner Basin [2], the sun breaks through when a handful of buildings push the trees back and the trail turns a bend in the road.

A variety of bushes congregate in this area. Two attractive ones, especially in the summer, are the red-stemmed red-osier dogwood and red elder-berry, which hangs with clusters of red berries in August. Twinberry may have two dark berries nestled in the remains of its twin red flowers.

As the trail edges up to the Inner Basin, it enters into full sun. A drainage on the east side of the meadow draws wild raspberry bushes and a number of botanicals in the summer.

Mountain panoramas of the San Francisco Peaks appear when the trail reaches the old spring house located on the edge of the basin.

Once in the Inner Basin meadow, you can see avalanches of rocks jumble down the surrounding mountain slopes. In the fall, the slopes gleam gold from thick stands of aspen trees [3]. You can continue on the trail as it climbs up the side of the caldera through a corridor of spruce toward the Weatherford Trail. If you look behind you during the climb up, you can see the rosy tinge of the Painted Desert along the eastern horizon. Return the way you came.

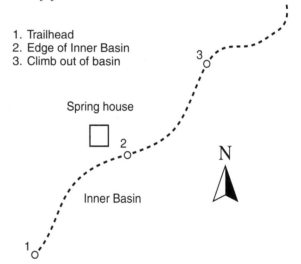

1. Trailhead
2. Edge of Inner Basin
3. Climb out of basin

Weatherford Trail 👢 👢 👢

Distance Round-Trip: 10 to 17.4 miles

Estimated Hiking Time: 5 to 9 hours

Elevation: 8,800 to 12,000 feet

Maps: Coconino National Forest, USGS Humphreys Peak

Caution: Horses are not allowed beyond the Doyle Saddle, which enters the Inner Basin Watershed.

Directions: Drive north on U.S. 180 about 2 miles to FR 420 (Schultz Pass Road) and turn right (east). At the intersection with FR 557, turn left (north) and continue on FR 420 for 6 miles to the trailhead at Schultz Tank.

This trail gets it name from John Weatherford, who in the 1920s built a road up the north side of the Peaks. Weatherford charged motoring tourists a toll to use his namesake road until the Great Depression put the kibosh on his moneymaking scheme.

The trail gets a mild-mannered start **[1]** as it crosses a meadow on the old road. Soon the path starts an almost continuous climb that eventually takes you past Fremont, Doyle, and Agassiz peaks to Agassiz Saddle just shy of Humphreys Peak.

By mile 1, the trail enters a mixed conifer forest woven with aspen trees that squeeze the trail down to a single track as it marches up a steady grade **[2]**. The path eases its way up in elevation on long switchbacks with reasonable grades, vacillating between stands of aspen trees, shadowy mixed conifer forests, and sun-drenched meadows **[3]**.

At Doyle Saddle, about mile 5, the trail approaches an extraordinary mountain scene where the sparse vegetation produces a stark but beautiful landscape that exposes reddish rock formations **[4]**. Doyle Saddle makes a good turnaround point for a shorter dayhike.

For a longer day hike, continue heading east on the trail, which contours the north face of Fremont Peak, picking through an avalanche that pours volcanic rock down the peak's slope while eyeing neighboring mountainsides. Keeping generally level, the trail passes through a dainty forest of Engelmann spruce and bristlecone pines, past the intersection with the Inner Basin Trail at mile 6.5, and starts a slow climb to rise above the treeline **[5]**. You can see the rouge of the Painted Desert beyond.

As the air and the trees thin out, you may feel the effects of the high altitude—headache, weakness, and nausea. If you do, take your time, drink electrolyte fluids, and eat some snacks. You might alleviate altitude troubles if you acclimate yourself by spending the night before the hike near the trailhead.

When the trail starts to climb across the barren, rocky slope of Agassiz Peak **[6]**, a sign informs you that off-trail hiking is prohibited to protect the endangered and federally protected San Francisco Peaks groundsel found exclusively on the Peaks. The inches-high plant, one of only a few on the barren landscape, has a yellow daisy flower about the size of a quarter.

The trail reaches its end as it crests Agassiz Saddle **[7]**. You may return the way you came, or continue on the Mount Humphreys Trail another three-quarters of a mile and 633 feet to its end, which will bring you to the top of Arizona.

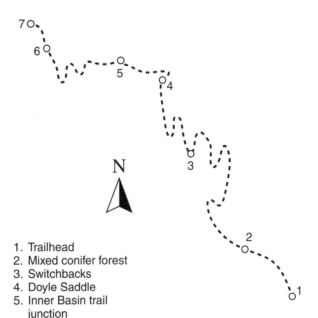

1. Trailhead
2. Mixed conifer forest
3. Switchbacks
4. Doyle Saddle
5. Inner Basin trail junction
6. Agassiz Peak
7. Agassiz Saddle

Sandys Canyon Trail 🥾 🥾 🥾

Distance Round-Trip: 2 miles

Estimated Hiking Time: 1 hour

Elevation: 7,400 to 7,800 feet

Maps: USGS Flagstaff east

Caution: Certain sections of the trail may flood after wet weather, especially during snowmelt.

Directions: From Flagstaff, go southeast on Lake Mary Road (exit 339 off I-17) and drive 5 miles; turn left just after a cattle guard into a day-use area; drive to the end of the parking area to the trailhead.

Sandys Canyon, once a wildlife path, gives you an interesting geologic perspective of the Colorado Plateau with moments mirroring shades of the Grand Canyon. The trail was named for Sandy Hartman, owner of the local Hitchin' Post Stables. Hartman used to like to ride the wildlife path privately, and never took a guided tour into the canyon.

As you hike the trail, you can see why Hartman kept it to herself. The trail skirts the rim of Sandys Canyon, past an anomalous lava flow, then digs into the canyon's limestone walls down to red-hued sandstone walls near Walnut Canyon. Spreads of wildflowers color meadows in the summertime. Aspen glow gold in the fall.

The trail starts **[1]** in a meadow and heads to the rim of Sandys Canyon. At the rim, a right turn will take you to a popular rockclimbing area. If you walk to the edge of the canyon, you might see rockclimbers on the north wall of the canyon. To stay on the Sandys Canyon Trail, turn left.

The trail leaves the meadow and ventures into an open forest of ponderosa pines, staying near the rim of the canyon. At a small clearing, about mile 0.3, take a moment to hike to the edge of the canyon rim **[2]** to look at the dramatic avalanches of volcanic rock that have tumbled into the canyon.

The white bark on aspen trees picking through the rubble makes a stunning contrast against the porous midnight rock.

At a large meadow, mile 0.5, veer right to enter Sandys Canyon **[3]**. As the trail drops into the canyon, watch for poison ivy, which sometimes encroaches into the trail.

The environment takes on a cozy feel as the trail slowly descends Sandys Canyon's narrow gorge. Rockmat drapes over outcroppings that push toward the trail, canyon grape clings to trees and bushes, and colonies of Arizona rose line up along the path. Red-osier dogwood bushes pack into a gulch along the trail.

Once you're on the canyon bottom, clumps of Rocky Mountain iris appear along the trail, indicating that this section has boggy moments, especially during snowmelt or wet weather. The irises usually bloom during May.

The trail makes a quick climb out of the lowland area and comes to a fork. Veer left and follow the trail through an open ponderosa forest. As the canyon widens, ruddy sandstone walls poke through the pines. The trail ends at its intersection with the Arizona Trail **[4]**. You may continue on the Arizona Trail or return the way you came.

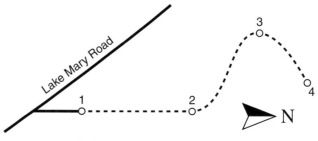

1. Trailhead
2. Rock avalanche
3. Drop into Sandys Canyon
4. Junction with Arizona Trail

5. Sycamore Canyon Wilderness

- Find oasis-like natural tanks floating with water lilies.
- View stunning panoramas in a wild and remote wilderness area.
- Hike along a perennial creek.

Area Information

Neighbor to the more traveled Red Rock–Secret Mountain Wilderness, the 55,936-acre Sycamore Canyon Wilderness presents an untamed, more remote area for more experienced hikers to explore. The wilderness' namesake, Sycamore Canyon, is the largest, and definitely the wildest, canyon in the red rock country. Red and cream sandstone and midnight lava stratify the canyon walls.

The landscape never seems to sit still in the Sycamore Canyon Wilderness. Shadows drift around outcroppings, peaks, and spires like ghosts playing hide-and-seek. Sanguine colors burst on the sandstone walls, then fade with the light of the sun. The sandstone starts to burn like embers at twilight and a penetrating quiet swallows up every sound.

Besides having a wild and remote reputation, the wilderness has accumulated some interesting lore. This is where transdimensional beings lurk. Where UFOs abscond with unsuspecting hikers. Where Bigfoot prowls. You're more apt, however, to see bears, deer, and javelina.

Forest Service officials remain unfazed by this hearsay of otherworldly activity. More concerned about hikers getting hurt or overextending themselves on the wilderness' rugged trails that head to the middle of nowhere and miles away from help, the Forest Service dismisses the reports as rumors.

The wilderness topography ranges from 3,000 to just under 7,000 feet, with most trails exposed to the sun. This makes hiking more pleasant in spring and fall. Many of the wilderness trails follow old cattle routes that meander along piñon and juniper trees or brush through catclaw or manzanita bushes.

Sycamore Creek sees only a seasonal flow of water north of Parsons Spring. Pools, ruddy with red clay, linger near outcroppings. Cottonwood, sycamore, walnut, velvet ash, and alder trees congregate along well-watered creek banks.

A hike in this wilderness might take more experience and effort, but the solitude and beauty you experience make a big payback.

Directions: Located about 20 miles south of Williams and just north of Cottonwood, just east of the Red Rock–Secret Mountain Wilderness. Take U.S. 89A to access the south end of the wilderness; then take the Garland Prairie Road exit (167) off Interstate 40 to access the northern end of the wilderness.

Hours Open: No restrictions.

Facilities: None.

Permits and Rules:
- No mechanized vehicles or mountain bikes are allowed.
- In developed recreation sites, pets must be restrained on a leash no longer than 6 feet.
- Fireworks are prohibited.
- Fires must be attended at all times.
- Maximum stay is 14 days.
- Maximum group size is 10 people.

Further Information: Red Rock Ranger District, P.O. Box 300, Sedona, AZ 86336; 928-282-4119. You may also contact the Williams Ranger District, 742 South Clover Road, Williams, AZ 86046; 928-635-5600.

Other Areas of Interest

If you want to know more about the Indians who lived in Sycamore Canyon and the surrounding area, visit the Tuzigoot National Monument, right next to the south end of the wilderness. The monument has cliff dwellings and information about the culture. Call 928-534-5564 for more information. Farther down the road on Arizona 89A, Dead Horse State Park has trails that follow along the Verde River, as well as fishing, camping, and swimming. Call 928-634-5283 for more information.

Sycamore Canyon Wilderness

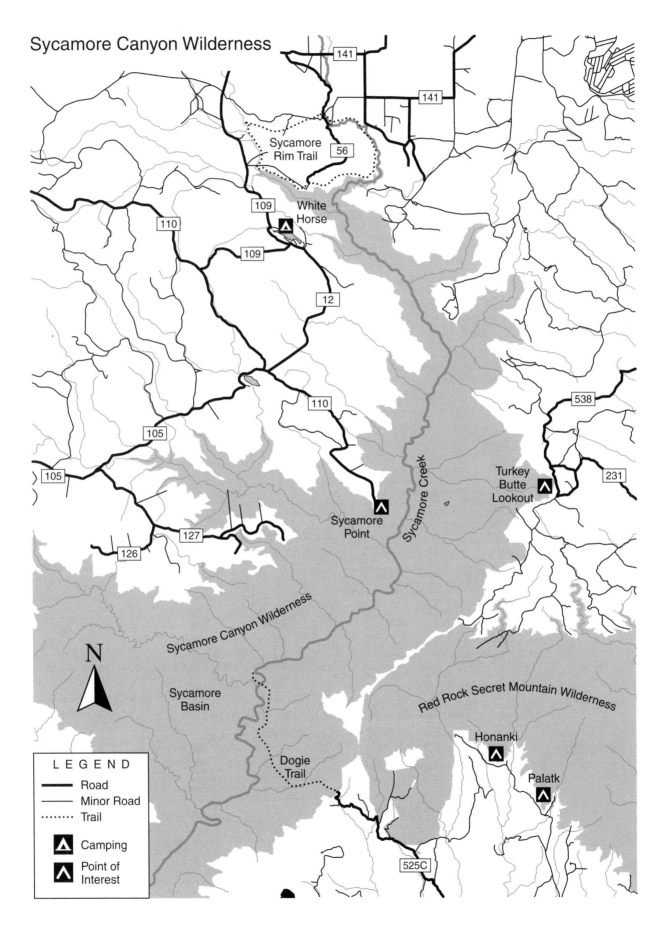

LEGEND

▬▬▬ Road

──── Minor Road

········ Trail

⛺ Camping

⛺ Point of Interest

Sycamore Rim Trail

Distance Round-Trip: 11-mile loop

Estimated Hiking Time: 5.5 hours

Elevation: 6,500 to 7,280 feet

Maps: Coconino National Forest, USGS Bill William Mountain and Sycamore Point

Caution: This loop trail has five trailheads.

Directions: Drive south on Garland Prairie Road (FR 141), veer right at a fork and continue on FR 141; drive 8.6 miles and turn right onto FR 56; drive 1.7 miles to the trailhead.

The start [1] of this hike at the KA Hill Trailhead trail passes through a meadow populated by Rocky Mountain iris. The iris favors boggy ground, a frequent occurrence along the trail as it alternates between stands of ponderosa pines and sunny meadows. The best time to catch the Rocky Mountain iris in bloom is mid-May.

At mile 0.5, the trail passes a series of attractions as it drops into a shallow chasm: a sawmill site that operated between 1910 to 1920; Dow Springs, a water stop along the 85-mile Overland Road; and a collection of ponds. If you're hiking this trail during the summer, yellow pond lily will beam from the water surface.

The trail climbs back on the rim long enough to look at the ruins of a small log cabin, the only remains of the Dow Springs settlement [2], then down into the chasm again. The path has you stepping on stones for about 0.1 mile in this particularly boggy section, then climbs back onto the rim, staying high and dry for several miles and paralleling the edge of Sycamore Canyon.

At mile 4.5, the Sycamore Vista Point [3] shows a scenic view of the canyon, which has dug deep enough to expose blushing sandstone walls. At mile 5.5, the trail looks down at Sycamore Falls, an exceptionally scenic gorge where a spectacular waterfall pours during snowmelt. The smooth perpendicular wall attracts technical rockclimbers.

The trail parts company with the canyon, and after a mile-long walk in a pine forest comes to a particularly scenic area call Pomeroy Tanks [4], an oasis-like gathering of natural reservoirs nestled between jagged stone walls.

After traveling through a mix of meadows and ponderosa pines, the trail starts its gradual climb up KA Hill [5] in the shade of ponderosa pines. By mile 10, the trail tops out at 7,280 feet, where you'll get views of Garland Prairie and the San Francisco Peaks. From there, it's another mile back to the trailhead.

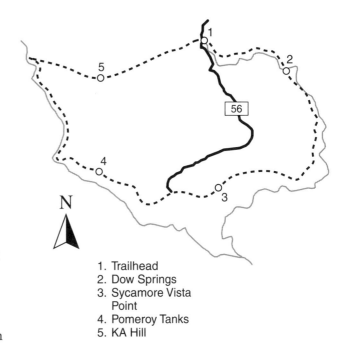

1. Trailhead
2. Dow Springs
3. Sycamore Vista Point
4. Pomeroy Tanks
5. KA Hill

Dogie Trail 👢 👢 👢

Distance Round-Trip: 10.8 miles

Estimated Hiking Time: 5 hours

Elevation: 4,900 to 4,200 feet

Maps: Coconino National Forest, USGS Loy Butte

Cautions: The trail has no shade. Sycamore Creek often has no water, so bring plenty of drinking water.

Directions: From Cottonwood, drive 9 miles east on U.S. 89A, then turn north (left) onto Red Canyon Road (FR 525); drive 3 miles and turn northwest (veer left) onto FR 525C and drive 9 miles to the trailhead. A high-clearance vehicle may be necessary for a couple spots in this road, and certainly for the last half-mile.

The panorama from this hike's trailhead **[1]** gives you an overall view of the sanguine ruggedness of Sycamore Canyon. The cliffs, colored red, orange, and buff, are marbled with green from piñon, juniper, and Arizona cypress trees. Red spires run just below the canyon rim.

The trail starts its drop into the canyon right away, heading in a westerly direction on an old rock-ribbed jeep trail. Crevices cut deep into the canyon wall and red rock buttes loom like unfinished statues. The trail forms a corridor through a thick cover of manzanita bushes. The small fruit, having the same size of and a kindred taste to rosehips, is a favorite food of black bears.

At about mile 1, the old road slims into a footpath at Dogie Tank **[2]**. Once a cattle route between the Verde Valley and Flagstaff, the Sycamore Canyon Wilderness contains remnants from these cattle days, such as cattle tanks. The Dogie Trail, named for the slang name cowboys called motherless calves, has several tanks along its route.

The trail winds deeper into the canyon, keeping on a strong downhill tack until it comes to Sycamore Pass, where it nearly levels out. The trail's atmosphere takes on a cozy loneliness here, and the red rock cliffs present interesting visuals. Formations seem to take on different appearances as the trail meanders around and under them.

After passing Sycamore Pass Tank, about mile 2, the trail heads northwest **[3]**. Contouring the base of the eastern wall, the trail dips in and out of crevices while gradually dropping to Sycamore Creek.

As you walk the high desert landscape, a covey of quail may flutter away at the sound of your presence. You may follow heart-shaped deer tracks on your way to Sycamore Basin Tank **[4]** in the folds of the canyon at about mile 3.4. As the trail gets closer to the creek, bear prints may appear on the ruddy earth.

At mile 5, let cairns guide you across the rock-covered bed of Sycamore Creek **[5]**, then wend with the trail through the bankside growth of Arizona cypress trees. The path teeters along the east canyon wall for a short stretch, then climbs up on Sycamore Basin to meet the Sycamore Basin Trail and this trail's end at mile 5.4.

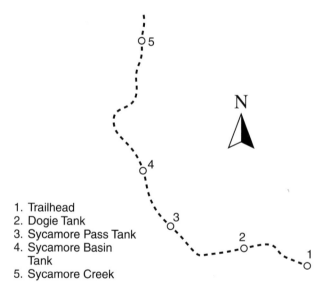

1. Trailhead
2. Dogie Tank
3. Sycamore Pass Tank
4. Sycamore Basin Tank
5. Sycamore Creek

6. Red Rock–Secret Mountain Wilderness

- Hike enchanting red rock canyons.
- Experience rich shows of autumn color.
- Identify dozens of species of wildflowers in the spring and summer in a research natural area.

Area Information

Sprawling under the Colorado Plateau north and west of Sedona, the Red Rock–Secret Mountain Wilderness shows off some of the most scenic country in the state. Wind- and water-carved pinnacles, arches, and canyons give the wilderness its distinctive appeal known throughout the world.

The basalt-capped mesas of Secret Mountain and Wilson Mountain rise above tree-shaded canyons dug as much as 1,500 feet into layers of sandstone. This striking geology presents a fascinating history of the earth, going back 300 million years according to geologists' estimates.

On a scientific timetable, the Secret Mountain Wilderness took millions of years to form. Eight different layers of sandstone, siltstone, and limestone stack on a base of Redwall limestone formed by an ancient tropical sea. The red sandstone Schnebly Hill Formation, topped by a cream-colored layer of Coconino sandstone, makes up some of the most spectacular formations of the cliffs in the wilderness.

If you look close enough, you might see Sinagua Indian cliff dwellings nestled in alcoves in these cliffs, or petroglyphs carved on the walls. The Sinagua lived in the area between 650 A.D. and 1400 A.D., then they abruptly disappeared.

The wilderness presents a high desert vegetation of Arizona cypress trees, manzanita bushes, juniper and piñon trees, and a variety of cacti. The canyons, however, create a lush environment full of bigtooth maple, cottonwood, sycamore, and velvet ash trees, plus dozens of species of wildflowers. This vegetative span supports a variety of wildlife, including elk, mule deer, white-tailed deer, javelina, coyotes, rabbits, mountain lions, and black bears.

You can hike the wilderness year-round. But leave the exposed hikes for October through April, when daytime temperatures stay in the comfort range of 50 to 80 degrees; and stick to the canyons in the hotter summertime, when temperatures can dwell in the 90s.

Directions: From Sedona exit 298, drive north on Arizona 179 about 15 miles to U.S. 89A in Sedona.

Hours Open: No restrictions.

Facilities: Campgrounds, picnic areas, and restrooms.

Permits and Rules:

- A Red Rock Pass (obtained from the Forest Service and roadside machines for $5) is required to park on Forest Service land, including parking areas.
- No mechanized vehicles or mountain bikes are allowed.
- In developed recreation sites, pets must be restrained on a leash no longer than 6 feet.
- Fireworks are prohibited.
- Fires must be attended at all times.
- Maximum stay is 14 days.
- Maximum group size is 10 people.
- The Archaeological Resource Protection Act and state antiquity laws protect ancient and historic ruins. Anyone found excavating, collecting, defacing, or removing an artifact can be fined $500 to $250,000 and imprisoned up to five years. If you see a relic from a historic or ancient culture, you may inspect it, but you may not take it.

Further Information: Red Rock Ranger District, P.O. Box 300, Sedona, AZ 86336; 928-282-4119.

Other Areas of Interest

Red Rock State Park, on the southwest side of Sedona off AZ 89, gives you more opportunities to hike among the red rocks along Oak Creek. For more information, call 928-282-6907.

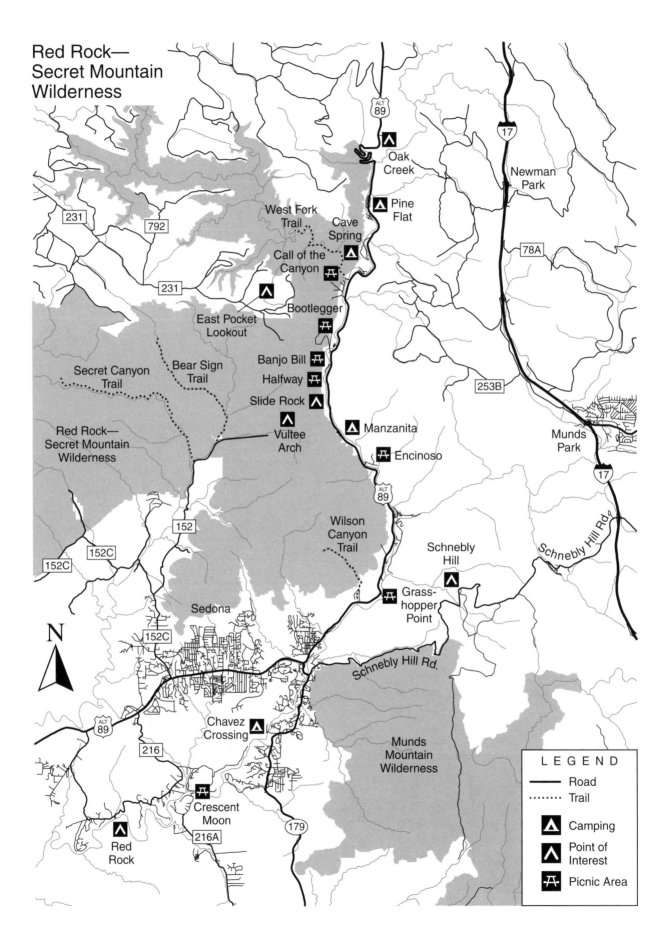

Red Rock—
Secret Mountain
Wilderness

231
792
231
West Fork Trail
Cave Spring
Call of the Canyon
East Pocket Lookout
Bootlegger
Bear Sign Trail
Secret Canyon Trail
Banjo Bill
Halfway
Slide Rock
Red Rock—Secret Mountain Wilderness
Vultee Arch
Manzanita
Encinoso
152
152C
152C
Wilson Canyon Trail
Schnebly Hill
Grass-hopper Point
Sedona
152C
Chavez Crossing
Munds Mountain Wilderness
Crescent Moon
216
216A
179
Red Rock

ALT 89
Oak Creek
Pine Flat
17
Newman Park
78A
253B
Munds Park
17
Schnebly Hill Rd.
ALT 89
Schnebly Hill Rd.

N

LEGEND
——— Road
········· Trail
▲ Camping
⋀ Point of Interest
🔆 Picnic Area

Bear Sign Trail 🥾 🥾 🥾

Distance Round-Trip: 7 miles

Estimated Hiking Time: 3.5 hours

Elevation: 4,800 to 5,400 feet

Maps: Coconino National Forest, USGS Wilson Mountain

Caution: Watch for poison ivy, especially at streambed crossings.

Directions: Drive west on U.S. 89A; drive about 3 miles to Dry Creek Road and turn right (north); drive 1.9 miles to FR 152 and turn right (east); drive about 4.4 miles to the Dry Creek Trailhead on the left. High-clearance vehicles are best for this road.

This hike starts out on the Dry Creek Trail in a high desert vegetative zone **[1]**. The trail follows along Dry Creek, normally dry except in wet weather, through a stand of Arizona cypress, an evergreen with mottled shaggy bark. At mile 0.5, the trail crosses a stream **[2]**, then enters an exceptionally beautiful area when it drops into the streambed at the confluence with Bear Sign Canyon. Red sandstone walls brace the rock-ribbed creekbed. The trail picks through the streambed to an island of red rock that creates a fork. Veer left for the Bear Sign Trail.

The trail climbs above the streambed onto a bench for a short distance, then drops back into the canyon and settles there for a while. The path crisscrosses the streambed several times while maintaining a moderate climb up the canyon.

By mile 1.7, the canyon opens up and fills with Arizona cypress. The surrounding cliffs rise powerfully several hundred feet above the canyon floor. A feeling of remoteness starts to impose on the

trail. Because of this solitude, you have a good chance of finding black bear signs—or even spotting one of the bruins—along the path, giving credence to the trail's name.

The canyon walls narrow once again at about mile 2, creating a comfortable environment for hardwoods such as Gambel oak, bigtooth maple, and Arizona walnut trees. When the trail comes to a junction with the David Miller Trail at about mile 2.5, continue on the Bear Sign Trail, which follows the drainage as it bends right **[3]**.

The atmosphere takes on a wild demeanor as the trail climbs up the canyon. The grade steepens, the forest darkens with fir trees, and the stream crossings become more rugged from fallen logs and boulders. When the trail suddenly fades **[4]** at about mile 3.5, return the way you came.

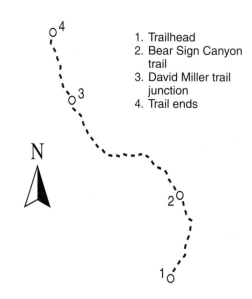

1. Trailhead
2. Bear Sign Canyon trail
3. David Miller trail junction
4. Trail ends

Wilson Canyon Trail 👢 👢

Distance Round-Trip: 2 miles

Estimated Hiking Time: 1 hour

Elevation: 4,500 to 5,000 feet

Maps: Coconino National Forest, USGS Wilson Mountain

Caution: Watch for poison ivy along the trail.

Directions: From the intersection of AZ 179 and U.S. 89A in Sedona, turn north onto U.S. 89A and drive about 1.6 miles to the Midgley Bridge parking lot.

The trail starts on an old sun-drenched road **[1]** along the canyon's rim lined with sugar sumac and manzanita bushes. Follow the signs directing you to the Wilson Canyon Trail. The path runs along the shallow north slope of the canyon for a bit before it drops to the canyon floor. When it does, look down the canyon a short distance for the ruins of an old red rock bridge. The bridge was once part of the original dirt road that traveled into Oak Creek Canyon. The road, dusty in dry weather and slick as axle grease in wet weather, has been replaced by the present U.S. 89.

The trail keeps its course following along the streambed of the canyon. A pouroff, often pooled with water, may cause you to tread on soggy ground as the trail steps alongside it.

At the junction with the Jim Thompson Trail, about mile 0.4, the trail crosses into the Red Rock–Secret Mountain Wilderness **[2]**. From here, continue straight on the Wilson Canyon Trail as it parallels the creek, climbing up and down gentle rises and crossing from one side of the stream to the other. By about mile 0.6, you can see Wilson Mountain rise in the near distance.

A bit farther, the path crosses the drainage past a dryfall that may have threads of water streaming from it in wet weather. Shortly after the trail situates itself on the canyon slope again, Arizona cypress trees squeeze in on the trail **[3]** at about mile 0.75. The path starts flirting with the canyon floor, taking turns crossing it and spending time walking down its sanguine stretches of bedrock. The trail finally stays put on the floor, then starts scrambling up a bouldered route.

The path ends at a bouldered logjam in the drainage. All around, red and white sandstone mountains show off an extraordinary scene. Return the way you came.

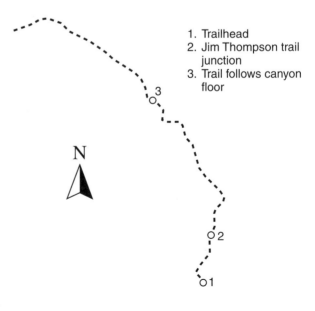

1. Trailhead
2. Jim Thompson trail junction
3. Trail follows canyon floor

N

Secret Canyon Trail 🥾🥾🥾

Distance Round-Trip: 11 miles

Estimated Hiking Time: 5.5 hours

Elevation: 4,640 to 5,300 feet

Maps: Coconino National Forest, USGS Wilson Mountain

Caution: Watch for poison ivy along the trail.

Directions: Drive east about 3 miles on U.S. 89A to Dry Creek Road and turn right (north); drive 1.9 miles to FR 152 and turn right (east); drive about 3.2 miles to the trailhead on the left. High-clearance vehicles are best for this road.

The trail gets its start by crossing the Dry Creek [1] streambed that normally lives up to its name. However, in wet weather, you'll have to rockhop. After climbing out of the drainage, the trail immediately enters the Red Rock–Secret Mountain Wilderness. A panorama of sandstone cliffs embrace the high desert cover of manzanita, piñon trees, and juniper trees that surround the trail, creating a beautiful red rock backdrop for the sea of green vegetation.

At about mile 1, the trail begins to climb gradually, pulling away from the streambed. The trail comes to a junction with the David Miller Trail [2] at about mile 1.7. Continue on the Secret Canyon Trail. The trail will drop in and out of the drainage, then duck under a pine forest into the depths of Secret Canyon.

As the trail continues up Secret Canyon, the path passes distinctive rock formations, brushes next to sandstone walls, and clatters along the rocky stream bottom. At about mile 3, the trail climbs out of the drainage onto a bench filled with a grove of Gambel oak trees. Bigtooth maple trees line the stream below. Lush during the summer, this mix of hardwoods creates a burst of color in the fall. By mile 3.2, the path heads back to the canyon floor for its place alongside the stream, and from this point vacillates between bench walking and creek crossings.

Around mile 4.5, the attention switches from the trail's lush hardwood forest to the surrounding Supai and Coconino sandstone cliffs that rise over 1,000 feet above the canyon floor [3]. The cliffs create an inspiring mood in the canyon. When you reach the trail's end at several pools, return the way you came [4].

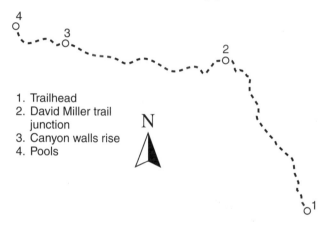

1. Trailhead
2. David Miller trail junction
3. Canyon walls rise
4. Pools

N

West Fork Trail 🥾🥾🥾

Distance Round-Trip: 6 miles

Estimated Hiking Time: 3 hours

Elevation: 5,400 to 5,500 feet

Maps: Coconino National Forest, USGS Dutton Hill

Cautions: The Forest Service requests that hikers keep their group to 12 or less and stay on the maintained trail to preserve the plants and the soil stabilization and watershed protection of this delicate area. Watch for poison ivy along the trail.

Directions: From the intersection of Arizona 179 and U.S. 89A in Sedona, drive 9.9 miles north on U.S. 89A to the Call of the Canyon parking area on the west side of the highway.

The West Fork of Oak Creek lies in a research natural area that has many of the general area's best representatives of natural plant communities. As soon as you pass the sign identifying the West Fork Trail **[1]**, you pass from the dry high desert to the lusciousness of a canyon riparian environment.

The blackberry brambles and horehound colonies you see near a bridge just beyond the sign were introduced to the area by European homesteaders. Both are considered invasive plants, and the Forest Service plans to decrease the number of these plants to allow natural plant species to return.

About mile 0.2, watch for the ruins of the Mayhew Lodge **[2]**. The lodge, which saw the likes of Warren Harding, Clark Gable, and Carole Lombard, no longer stands. But you can see its cellar and storage building on the north side of the trail in the red rock walls.

As you pass the trail registry, about mile 0.3, the trail comes to the first of several creek crossings to give you a look at the red-tinged cliffs rising alongside the clear creek water. The Coconino sandstone canyon walls rise from a base of Schnebly Hill Formation. The red color comes from iron oxide, and the black stains stroking down the cliff faces (called *desert varnish*) come from manganese.

The path brushes next to bushes, bracken ferns, and dozens of different wildflowers that grow thick along the creek. Poison ivy and red-osier dogwood bushes like to congregate near the creek crossing. Both of these plants show white flowers in the spring, white berries in the summer, and bold-colored leaves in the fall. The poison ivy generally grows up to a yard, and its three-leaf clusters will cause an itchy, weepy rash. The dogwood, however, grows up to eight feet and will not give you a rash if you touch its leaves.

At about mile 1.7, the canyon walls close in on the trail **[3]**, giving the hike an intimate feeling. Mixed conifers climb the red rock walls and walk their ledges. Near the creek, plants grow from cracks and niches. The trail passes slabs of sandstone piled along the path from a landslide. You may get a glimpse into the erosion process if you hear rockfall during your hike along the West Fork Trail. Though unusual to witness, the natural process plays a part in the formation of canyons and their exquisite features.

The trail pulls closer to the creek at its seventh creek crossing, clatters over a stretch of bedrock, then winds through a distinctive S-curve in the canyon. A colony of horsetail, which looks like a green reed, spreads around the trail and follows the path as it crosses the creek again and ducks under a curl of sandstone in the canyon wall. Also called *scouring rush*, silica-rich horsetail was used by homesteaders to clean pots.

The trail drops into the drainage, then makes its last creek crossing. The path climbs high above the creek, then drops back into the drainage and its end, where the canyon walls squeeze into the creek, requiring you to wade.

If you don't mind getting your feet wet, you may wade through the water and continue. An unmaintained trail will take you deeper into the canyon, crossing knee- to thigh-deep water. At mile 5, a chest-deep pool makes a good turnaround point. Return the way you came **[4]**.

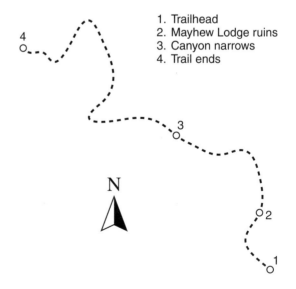

1. Trailhead
2. Mayhew Lodge ruins
3. Canyon narrows
4. Trail ends

N

7. Sedona Area (Coconino National Forest)

- View red rock panoramas and formations.
- Explore scenic stream courses.

Area Information

They were warned not to stay. Spirit guides sternly directed them not to indulge themselves in the idyllic atmosphere of Palatkwapi, the "place of the red rocks." But, the story goes, early Hopis ignored the spiritual guidance of their deities and pursued with abandon their life of leisure. Finally, a few virtuous Hopis entreated the deities to bring a flood.

Before the flood forced the early Hopis to higher ground, and their eventual settlement at First Mesa in northern Arizona, they built Palatkwapi into a thriving cultural and religious center. Palatkwapi, now the Sedona area, was once a meeting and healing place for Indians all over the Southwest over a thousand years ago.

Now the red-rocked town, located right in the Coconino National Forest, has the world passing through its doorways—over three million visitors a year. And it hasn't changed much from its legendary Palatkwapian nature. Dozens of art galleries and public art landmarks reflect its cultural side. Metaphysical shops line its streets. Even nature exudes the aesthetic and ethereal. The area's red rock cliffs, canyons, and mesas ooze with enchanting beauty and purported vortexes.

Most of the Sedona area's trails travel a comfortable distance of two to four miles one way to scenic destinations. The high desert landscape, usually offering little shade except in canyons, is best hiked in spring or fall. A wet winter will bring an exquisite display of wildflowers in April. Bigtooth maple, cottonwood, and velvet ash trees will flame red and yellow around mid-October in the canyons.

The wilderness gets about as many visitors each year as the Grand Canyon. Because of the high volume of visitation to the Sedona area, hikers should pay close attention to leave-no-trace principles. If you stay on the trail, pack out all your trash (including toilet paper), and honor your physical limitations, you should have an extraordinary hike in an extraordinary part of the country.

Because of the prior Indian habitation in the area, you may find relics from their culture. The Archaeological Resource Protection Act and state antiquity laws protect ancient and historic ruins. If you see a relic from a historic or ancient culture, you may inspect it, but you may not take it.

Directions: Sedona is located about 15 miles northwest of Interstate 17 on Arizona 179.

Hours Open: No restrictions.

Facilities: Campgrounds, washrooms, and picnic areas.

Permits and Rules:

- A Red Rock Pass (obtained from the Forest Service and automated machines at trailheads for $5) is required to park on Forest Service land, including parking areas.
- Vehicles must stay on established roadways.
- In developed recreation sites, pets must be restrained on a leash no longer than 6 feet.
- Fireworks are prohibited.
- Fires must be attended at all times. During May, June, and early July, the forests may have campfire and smoking restrictions.
- Maximum stay is 14 days.
- Maximum group size is 10 people.

Further Information: Red Rock Ranger District, P.O. Box 300, Sedona, AZ 86336; 928-282-4119.

Other Areas of Interest

A drive up Schnebly Hill Road, accessed off AZ 179 at the south end of town, will give you fabulous views of the town and the beautiful red rock formations surrounding it.

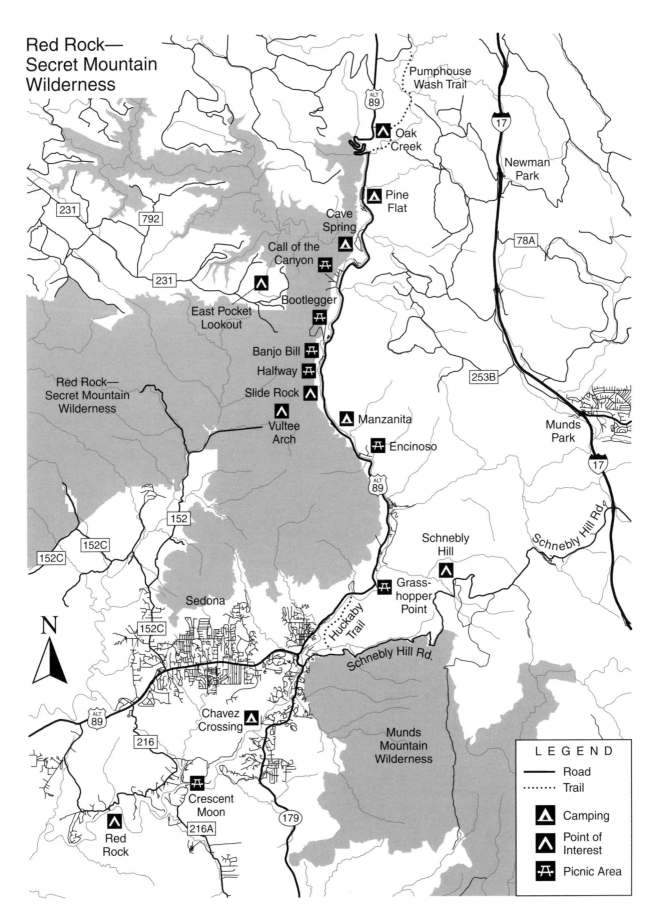

Red Rock—Secret Mountain Wilderness

Pumphouse Wash Trail

ALT 89

17

Oak Creek

Newman Park

Pine Flat

Cave Spring

Call of the Canyon

78A

Bootlegger

East Pocket Lookout

253B

Banjo Bill

Halfway

Slide Rock

Red Rock—Secret Mountain Wilderness

Vultee Arch

Manzanita

Munds Park

Encinoso

ALT 89

17

Schnebly Hill Rd.

152

Schnebly Hill

152C

152C

Grass-hopper Point

Sedona

152C

N

Huckaby Trail

Schnebly Hill Rd.

ALT 89

216

Chavez Crossing

Munds Mountain Wilderness

Crescent Moon

216A

179

Red Rock

LEGEND
——— Road

········· Trail

Camping

Point of Interest

Picnic Area

Pumphouse Wash 🥾 🥾 🥾 🥾 🥾

Distance Round-Trip: 7 miles

Estimated Hiking Time: 6 hours

Elevation: 6,400 to 5,690 feet

Maps: Coconino National Forest, USGS Mountainaire

Cautions: Only experienced hikers comfortable with canyoneering should attempt this hike. Do not hike in wet weather or during snowmelt.

Directions: Drive 12.6 miles north on U.S. 89A to just over a half-mile past mile marker 187. Park on the road just south of the Pumphouse Wash Bridge. You may arrange a shuttle by continuing past the bridge up to the rim and 1.5 miles past the Oak Creek Overlook to FR 237; turn right (east) and drive 1.5 miles to a parking area.

As soon as you drop into Pumphouse Wash **[1]** and see its canyon floor heaped with rocks and boulders (your route) you'll know whether you want to continue with the hike. The route through the canyon consists of hopping rocks and boulders in the first mile, climbing around pools during the second mile, and more rockhopping with intermittent stretches of beaten paths along the third mile.

The route starts out under the canyon's buff-colored Coconino sandstone walls, etched with crossbedding as deep as a furrowed brow, that rise several hundred feet above the canyon floor. Sandstone outcroppings jut into the wash like jagged gateposts chewed by erosion. Sometimes giant logjams bridge these narrow passages.

At mile 1, a ledge of sandstone requires a bit of help to negotiate **[2]**. You may have the advantage of previous hikers' ingenuity in the form of a stack of rocks or a heavy log to aid your climb up the ledge. As soon as you boost yourself up, you have to edge around a couple of deep cylinder-shaped holes carved by whirlpools of floodwater. The rest of the shelf shows ornate patterns of erosion where floodwater churned, chiseled, whirled, and smoothed the rock with slots, troughs, pools, and potholes.

At about mile 2, the canyon curls to the northwest **[3]** and makes a quick yawn that allows a dousing of sunshine. The canyon immediately tapers again, and you're back to rockhopping and edging past pools.

At mile 2.5, watch for a column arch at the bottom of the canyon where floodwaters have dissolved a portion of the canyon wall. A bit farther, the canyon widens dramatically. Look for a trail that hops onto the bench into a forest of pines. At mile 3.25, the trail crosses the wash **[4]**, then climbs a quarter-mile up to the rim. Return the way you came if you have not arranged a shuttle.

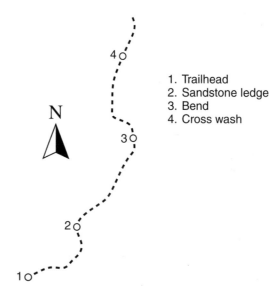

N

1. Trailhead
2. Sandstone ledge
3. Bend
4. Cross wash

Huckaby Trail 🥾 🥾

Distance Round-Trip: 5 miles

Estimated Hiking Time: 2.5 hours

Elevation: 4,400 to 4,550 feet

Maps: Coconino National Forest, USGS Sedona

Caution: Oak Creek may run too deep and swiftly to cross after heavy precipitation or snowmelt.

Directions: Drive south on Arizona 179; turn left (east) onto Schnebly Hill Road; drive 0.9 miles to the trailhead.

Built as a wagon road in 1887, the Huckaby Trail got its name from Jim Huckaby, who lived just opposite the Midgley Bridge along Oak Creek. The trail offers a different perspective of Sedona and its surrounding red rock hillsides as it peers, with an

innuendo of remoteness, at the activity of the town from the eastern rim of Oak Creek Canyon.

From the Schnebly Hill trailhead **[1]**, the trail quickly drops in and out of Bear Wallow Canyon, then climbs for a half-mile up to a ridge. From the ridgetop, you get outstanding views of several formations around town. The sprawling cliff to the north is Steamboat Rock, and the Fin juts just to the left of it. The dome-shaped gray rock on the west end of Sedona is Capital Butte. You may be able to find Coffeepot Rock in the congregation of formations just to the right of it. Snoopy Rock sits right above you.

The trail levels off and curves around Mitten Ridge **[2]**, then watches a line of trees bend with the flow of Oak Creek in the canyon below. The trail eventually drops into the canyon and parallels Oak Creek **[3]**, traveling over terra cotta-colored slick rock and sandy paths in the riparian cover of Arizona sycamore, cottonwood, and pine trees it viewed from above.

At mile 2, the trail makes its first creek crossing **[4]**, and then another a quarter-mile later. You will have to rockhop or wade each crossing. If the weather's nice, and the stream flow normal, take a moment to wade up- or downstream in the creek a bit to experience the lush habitat along its banks. The often emerald water flows right under red rock walls. The color contrasts create a stunning scene.

Once out of the creek, the trail starts a switchback up to the Midgley Bridge parking area. Along the way, you get a face-on view of massive Steamboat Rock, which overlooks the bridge. At the parking area, return the way you came if you have not set up a shuttle.

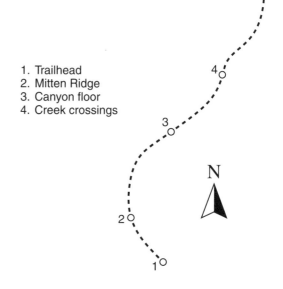

1. Trailhead
2. Mitten Ridge
3. Canyon floor
4. Creek crossings

N

8. Wet Beaver Creek Wilderness

- Swim in emerald pools between red rock cliffs.
- Hike a creekside trail.

Area Information

This 6,700-acre wilderness travels about 12 miles up the Wet Beaver Creek canyon system. Red rock cliffs bracing the clear mountain water of Wet Beaver Creek are the signature of this scenic area. The three major layers of rock—Supai Formation, Coconino sandstone, and volcanic deposits—create the extraordinary scenery.

The Sinagua Indians lived in the area hundreds of years ago, and some signs of their civilization remain, such as artifacts or petroglyph panels. (If you do come across any relics, be sure to leave them just as you found them, where you found them. If you see a relic from a historic or ancient culture, you may inspect it, but you may not take it.) Later, ranchers moved into the area. Charlie Bell used the Bell Trail to move his cattle between the top of the Mogollon Rim to the valley during the seasons.

Most of the wilderness trails travel between the canyon floor and the Mogollon Rim. Expect to see a diversity of plant life. The high desert vegetation in the western end and south-facing slopes of the canyon has prickly pear cactus, catclaw, scrub oak, juniper trees, and piñon pines. The higher sections in the east have douglas fir and ponderosa pine trees.

The wilderness has its popular areas, especially the Bell Trail. But if you travel beyond Bell's Crossing, whether on the Bell Trail or right in the canyon upstream, you enter more remote sections of the wilderness that give you an intimate experience with the canyon. Wildlife tend toward these more remote areas, but wander the entire wilderness. You may see bears, mountain lions, deer, elk, javelina, foxes, ringtailed cats, coyotes, and skunks.

Rattlesnakes, scorpions, and centipedes crawl around the wilderness, too. Be mindful of where you put your hands and feet. Mosquitoes and gnats hang around the creek.

Directions: From the intersection of I-17 and Arizona 179, turn right (east) on FR 618 for 2 miles; turn left (east) on FR 618A (follow signs to the trail); continue 0.25 mile to the trailhead.

Hours Open: No restrictions.

Facilities: None.

Permits and Rules:
- No mechanized vehicles or mountain bikes are allowed.
- In developed recreation sites, pets must be restrained on a leash no longer than 6 feet.
- Fireworks are prohibited.
- Fires must be attended at all times.
- Maximum stay is 14 days.
- Maximum group size is 10 people.
- The Archaeological Resource Protection Act and state antiquity laws protect ancient and historic ruins. Anyone found excavating, collecting, defacing, or removing an artifact can be fined $500 to $250,000 and imprisoned up to five years. If you see a relic from a historic or ancient culture, you may inspect it, but you may not take it.

Further Information: Red Rock Ranger District, P.O. Box 300, Sedona, AZ 86336; 928-282-4119.

Other Areas of Interest

If you don't find any Indian signs along the trails in the Wet Beaver Creek Wilderness, you can see one of the best-preserved cliff dwellings in the Southwest at Montezuma Castle National Monument near Camp Verde, where Sinagua Indians lived between 1100 and 1400 A.D. About 11 miles north of the ruins at Montezuma's Well, you can view a sinkhole, the Indians' main water source, which measures 368 feet across and 55 feet deep. For more information, call 928-567-3322.

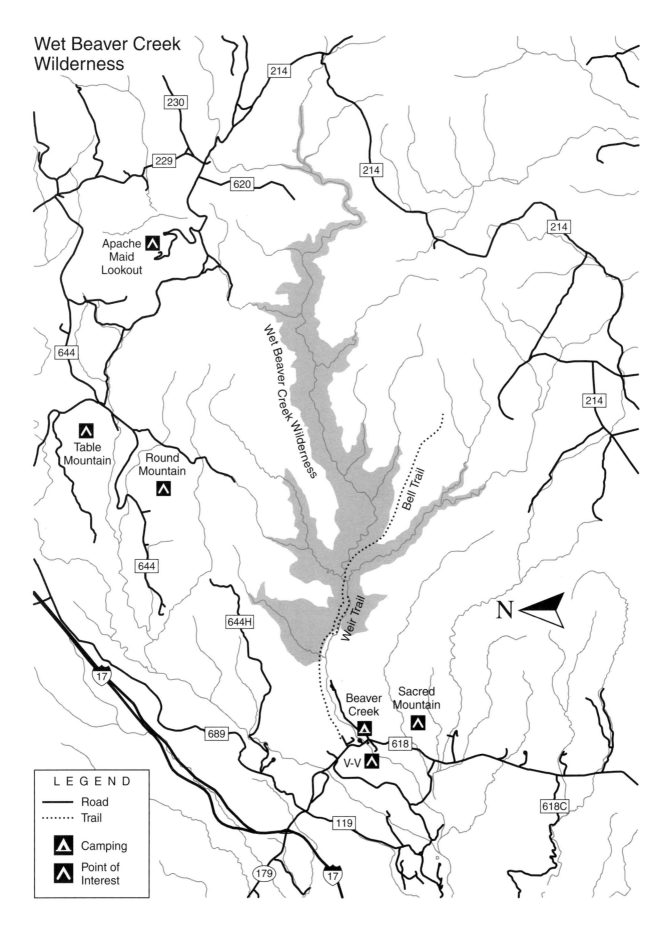

Wet Beaver Creek Wilderness

214
230
229
620
214
214
Apache Maid Lookout
644
214
Table Mountain
Round Mountain
Wet Beaver Creek Wilderness
Bell Trail
644
644H
Weir Trail
N
17
Beaver Creek
Sacred Mountain
689
618
V-V
618C
119
179
17

LEGEND
——— Road
.... Trail
Camping
Point of Interest

Bell Trail 🥾 🥾 🥾

Distance Round-Trip: 6-12 miles

Estimated Hiking Time: 3 to 6 hours

Elevation: 3,820 to 5,900 feet

Maps: Coconino National Forest, USGS Casner Butte

Caution: The last 4.8 miles of the Bell Trail (not included in this hike) travel a faint route over rocky ground atop the Mogollon Rim. Excellent route-finding skills are necessary.

Directions: As you start out on the Bell Trail [1], you follow an old Jeep road into the canyon now wide with cactus-covered slopes dotted with juniper trees. By mile 0.5, you can hear Wet Beaver Creek beyond a thick riparian barrier.

If you take one of the handful of beaten paths [2] leading into the forested cover, you get a glimpse of Wet Beaver Creek flowing past red rock outcroppings glowing in a mix of cottonwood, Arizona sycamore, and Arizona walnut trees. You can venture to the creekbanks and watch the clear, cool water cascade down large slabs of red sandstone. Moss-green pools of water briefly collect in deeper pockets of the sandstone before tumbling toward a jumble of smooth gray boulders littered across the spillway.

Back on the Bell Trail, the landscape turns high desert dry again. Twinges of red Supai sandstone, the same you saw creekside, streak the basalt-capped slopes.

At mile 1.5, the trail passes the White Mesa Trail on your left [3]. At mile 2, the trail passes the Apache Maid Trail, also on your left [4]. In another quarter-mile, the trail comes to a fork where the Weir Trail comes in. Veer left to continue on the Bell Trail.

The trail takes a colorful turn as red Supai formation cliffs jut into the canyon. The trail starts to climb up the north wall of the canyon [5], a scenic route that brushes right against bold red sandstone outcroppings in the wall. The path makes itself at home along a ledge in the wall several hundred feet above the creek, where it gives you an uninhibited view of the creek articulated by a band of cottonwood and Arizona sycamore trees.

Just past mile 3, the path dips into Bell's Crossing [6], where it crosses Wet Beaver Creek and continues its steep climb up the Mogollon Rim. The exceptionally pretty area has deep pools sunk between red rock walls.

From Bell's Crossing, you may continue on the Bell Trail or return the way you came. If you continue, you must rockhop across Wet Beaver Creek, then make your way up the southern wall of the canyon. Since most of the hikers on the Bell Trail make Bell's Crossing their turnaround point, this part of the trail takes on a more remote quality.

As you make your way about 1,000 feet up the canyon, the trail crosses the mouth of a side canyon, Long Canyon [7], jutting to the south. Orange Coconino sandstone walls make a stunning scene as the trail continues its slog up the canyon wall. Higher up, you get fabulous panoramic views of the Wet Beaver Creek drainage.

When the trail tops out on the Mogollon Rim [8], about mile 6, it continues for another 4.8 miles on a sketchy path on the rocky rim top to Forest Road 214. This last section of trail is hard to follow and is not recommended.

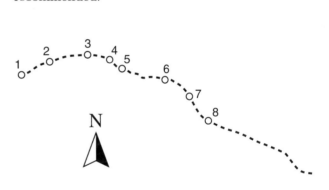

1. Trailhead
2. Side trails to creek
3. White Mesa trail junction
4. Apache Maid trail junction
5. Trail climbs cliffs
6. Bell's Crossing
7. Long Canyon
8. Mogollon Rim

Weir Trail 👢👢

Distance Round-Trip: 1.5 miles

Estimated Hiking Time: 1 hour

Elevation: 4,000 feet

Maps: Coconino National Forest, USGS Casner Butte

Cautions: The canyon is subject to flash floods, so use caution at stream crossings after wet weather, when the creek runs higher and faster. Also, do not hike in or near the creek if the possibility of wet weather exists.

Directions: To get to the Weir Trail, hike 2 miles on the Bell Trail (see page 35) to a registry and bike rack, where the Wet Beaver Wilderness begins **[1]**. At this point, motorized vehicles, bicycles, and hangliders are prohibited. The Weir Trail branches off to the right.

As it parts company with the Bell Trail, which climbs above the creek along red rock cliffs, the Weir Trail heads right for the creek, dropping quickly toward the drainage. At about mile 0.3, the trail reaches the creek, and the atmosphere turns intimate as the trail exits the high desert terrain of prickly pear cactus, juniper trees, and catclaw, and enters a riparian environment of Arizona sycamore, cottonwood, and willow trees.

As soon as the trail comes creekside, look for a gaging station and cable car over the creek **[2]**. Both are remnants from a watershed program created in 1960 designed to clear vegetation on the rim to possibly enhance water flow into the Verde and Salt drainages.

The program has since been abandoned, and so has the cable car, which was used to measure speed and volume of the water at the creek's center. The gaging station is still used to measure runoff levels.

The path keeps a cozy feeling as it continues, nuzzled next to the creek, passing several prime camping spots. The path swerves around cottonwood and sycamore trees, always keeping an eye on the crystal water. The trail comes to its end at a flood-wracked cove covered with cobbles **[3]**. Gnarled branches and caked mud stuffed into the lower branches of juniper and Arizona sycamore trees tell of past floods that ripped through the area.

The flood of 1993, considered a 100-year flood, thoroughly scoured the creekbanks and altered the topography of the canyon. In an unobtrusive section of the Weir Trail, you may find a panel of petroglyphs—sheep, spirals, and amorphic creatures. The flood of 1993 exposed another row of sheep. The whole panel is only visible at certain times of the year when the sunlight is at the right angle.

If you find these petroglyphs, or any others, while hiking in the wilderness, remember that the Archaeological Resource Protection Act and state antiquity laws protect these and other ancient and historic ruins and artifacts.

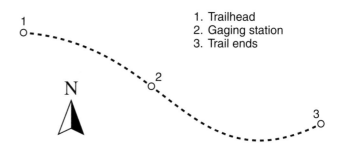

1. Trailhead
2. Gaging station
3. Trail ends

West

Mohave, LaPaz, and Yuma counties make up the western region of Arizona. The region runs along western Arizona to the Colorado Plateau in the north, the central highlands in the state's midsection, and the eastern end of Yuma County in the south.

Topography

The western region dips as close to sea level as the state can get. All of the high points mill around the northern part of the region, just below the Grand Canyon. Some rise up to 8,000 feet. As you travel down the western region of the state, the elevations decrease. The mountain ranges' citadels hover in the 3,000-foot levels. Nearer the southwestern end of the state, desert mountains rise only a couple thousand feet. The very southwestern tip measures 141 feet.

Many of the western region's mountains tend toward a volcanic tuff composition. This type of rock makes for fantastic formations, such as spires, arches, needles, and columns.

Major Rivers and Lakes

The Lower Colorado River forms the western boundary of Arizona and the western region. This major drainage gets its start in the Rocky Mountains. Flowing southward from Lake Mead after its tumultuous westward trip through the Grand Canyon, the river pools several times from dams as it makes its way to the Gulf of California.

Common Plant Life

The western region hosts plants not found in the rest of the state because of its rendezvous with a corner of the Mojave Desert—Joshua trees, for example. The low elevations invite herbaceous species that aren't found elsewhere. After a wet winter, sand verbena emits a sweet scent, birdcage primrose leaves a curious-looking skeleton that resembles a cage with a stem, and ghostflower has translucent yellow petals with red spots.

Creosote bushes, saguaro cactus, assorted cholla, and ocotillo are common sights across the desert landscape.

Common Birds and Mammals

At first blush, the dry areas in the western region seem to have little wildlife activity. But if you're looking, and lucky, you may spot a jackrabbit or

desert tortoise during the day. At night, you might catch a kit fox, coyote, owl, or rattlesnake on the roam for a dinner, such as a kangaroo rat. Desert bighorn sheep take to the rugged mountain ranges that rise along the western region. You often can discern sheep trails traversing the slopes of the ranges.

The Colorado River attracts a rich array of avian life. Hundreds of species of birds visit the river, its lakes, and the marshes around them, as well as parts of the Kofa National Wildlife Refuge. Like people who flock to the area in the winter, birds do too. Wintering fowl hang out around Yuma and surrounding wildlife refuges.

Climate

The generally low desert elevation of the western region makes for excellent winter weather. In January and February the western region becomes the domain of RVers who converge on the area.

By spring, temperatures rise to the mid-80s in western Arizona, and rarely dip below 100 in the summer. Lake Havasu City boasts record temperatures that commonly rise over 115 degrees.

The lower western region is prone to heavy doses of rain from Mexican weather systems that reach into the southwestern portion of the state, especially during autumn. This can bring exceptional spreads of wildflowers if enough precipitation continues during the winter.

Best Natural Features

- The blue-green water of Lake Havasu
- Volcanic tuff ranges in the Kofa National Wildlife Refuge
- Carpets of Mexican gold poppies and other wildflowers in the spring after a wet winter
- Rich array of aquatic avian life along the shores of the Colorado River

9. Lake Havasu State Park

- Scramble through a slot canyon.
- Have a picnic on the shores of Lake Havasu.
- Catch a trophy fish in a blue-green lake.

Area Information:

Lake Havasu, which runs 45 miles from its riverine flow between the Davis Dam and the Topock Gorge down to its swollen waters just south of the gorge to Parker Dam, spreads its blue-green waters like a lucid jewel between Arizona and California. *Havasu* is an Indian name meaning "blue-green." When the lake first formed, the water was muddy, but as it settled it took on a blue-green color. Hearsay has it the lake got its name from an old Indian couple.

Lake Havasu State Park's northern-edged Windsor Beach in Lake Havasu City draws day-use activity with its developed beach and picnic areas. The beach eyes the most expensive antique in the world, the $2.3 million London Bridge.

Year-round warm to hot temperatures make the lake a prime destination. Quiet times on the lake run from November through March, when the temperatures usually dip no lower than the 60s during the day. At Easter, when the temperatures rise to the 80s, the harbor near Windsor Beach fills with boats. By the summer, the air temperatures will hit 120 degrees, and the water will hover in the high 80s.

Record temperatures have become a novelty on the lower Colorado. During the last decade Lake Havasu City logged over 500 days as the hottest spot in the nation. When temperatures run amok, boaters simply find a cool pocket in the lake, grab a cold drink, don a life jacket, and bob in the refreshing currents.

The volcanic ragged-edged ridgelines that brace the lake dip and swell more turbulently than a storm-tossed sea. Their raw beauty makes a boat ride on the lake a scenic trip. Columned cliffs and balanced rocks rise in ruddy-rock coves along the shoreline. Hikers can find game trails to hike along the low mountains, and maybe spot bighorn sheep.

One of the park's unique features is its boat camping. About 150 campsites accessible only by boat line the shores between Cattail Cove and Windsor Beach.

Directions: Access this state park from Lake Havasu City, located on Arizona 95 about 60 miles south of Kingman in northwest Arizona.

Hours Open: No restrictions.

Facilities: Camping, fishing, boat ramp, boating, picnic area, ramada, hiking, restrooms, showers.

Permits and Rules:

- Arizona State Parks charges a $7 fee for day use, and $12 per night for camping.
- Quiet hours are rigorously enforced from 10 P.M. to 7 A.M.
- Dogs are not allowed on public beaches and must be leashed elsewhere in the park.
- Fishing requires an Arizona state license as well as a Colorado River stamp.

Further Information: Lake Havasu State Park, 1801 Highway 95, Lake Havasu City, AZ 86406; 928-855-2784.

Other Areas of Interest

Topock Gorge, known as the "little Grand Canyon," lies just north of the park in the Havasu National Wildlife Refuge. Call the U.S. Fish & Wildlife Service at 760-326-3853 for more information.

Balance Rock Cove

Distance Round-Trip: 6 miles

Estimated Hiking Time: 3 hours

Elevation: 2,800 to 3,000 feet

Maps: USGS Lake Havasu City South

Caution: This hike has exposed areas and requires route-finding skills.

Directions: From Lake Havasu City, drive south on U.S. 95 and turn right into the SARA Park (around mile marker 175). Follow signs to the trailhead.

This hiking route passes through a slot canyon—SARA Park Wash Crack in the Wall, affectionately called "the Crack"—at the south side of Lake Havasu City and ends at the shores of Lake Havasu. The hike starts at the SARA (Special Activities Recreation Area) Park **[1]** amid an amalgam of rock textures, colors, and strata where mountain slopes swoop down and then crumble into shallow canyon walls mortared with rubble-filled conglomerate. The eclectic geologic brew creates some stunning scenery and a compatible landscape as a desert bighorn sheep habitat.

At about mile 0.5, a large cairn signals that the route leaves the drainage and takes off on one of the several social trails outside the wash that explore the hillsides. Stick to the trail that parallels the wash. The trail eventually rejoins the wash just when the canyon walls start rising and narrowing, relinquishing their dark hues for salmon tinges. Beams of light burst through pin holes in the crumbly rock, and arches appear.

The canyon squeezes its pathway down to an arm's span **[2]**, then takes a moment to yawn widely into a small amphitheater before it sucks in its breath one more time and tumbles narrowly down a series of dryfalls into the Crack. Except for a seven-foot dryfall, all the drops can be easily negotiated. If the seven-

footer causes a problem, you can get around the Crack on an upper route. Remember the social trails? Go back to the rock cairn and take the path that climbs up the ridge.

If you opt to tackle the dryfall, simply continue through the Crack. As soon as you exit the Crack, you'll see a trail on the right that leads you to the upper route, then continues west to the lake.

The trail does a bit of a balancing act on the top edge of a ridge **[3]** (which may feel uncomfortably narrow if you suffer from vertigo) that tapers briefly to a foot wide and falls down 75-foot slopes on either side. This exposed stretch lasts only momentarily.

The unmaintained trail intersects with a couple more paths. At the first fork, where the trail looks stronger veering right, veer left. About a quarter-mile beyond, at the next fork, veer right. Soon you can see the blue-green waters Lake Havasu was named for.

A quick climb up the brow of a hill **[4]**, then down the other side, will land you at Balance Rock Cove **[5]**, a Bureau of Land Management shoreline campground where molten volcanic rock has created unusual rock formations, a diving rock, and shoreline ledges ripe for fishing bass. In late spring, the cove becomes a swallow rookery. In early mornings, bighorn sheep often walk the surrounding ridgelines on their way down to the lake for a drink.

If you stick around the campground, you'll have to pay the Bureau of Land Management a recreation site fee for day or overnight use. An Arizona fishing license is required if you plan to fish.

On the way back, you'll notice a large arch on a knob of a hill just south of the Crack. The arch makes a good landmark to head toward as you make your way back to the Crack. If you don't think you can climb up the seven-foot dryfall, simply follow the upper trail over the top of the Crack, then back down to the large rock cairn on the canyon floor.

Lake Havasu State Park

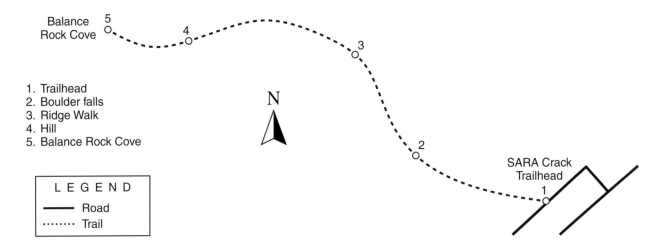

1. Trailhead
2. Boulder falls
3. Ridge Walk
4. Hill
5. Balance Rock Cove

LEGEND
—— Road
······ Trail

N

10. Kofa National Wildlife Refuge

- Find California fan palms growing naturally in a desert environment.
- See spreads of Mexican gold poppies on a springtime hike.
- Hike through a volcanic terrain full of strangely sculpted formations and arches.

Area Information

The Kofa National Wildlife Refuge is one of a few spots in Arizona that has native California fan palms. The trees are likely descendants of palms growing in the area during the last glacial eras in North America. These palms like a cooler clime than the desert provides, and do well nestled in canyon crevices in the refuge.

The 665,400-acre refuge has other unique features, too. A herd of about 800 bighorn sheep traipse the area's rugged Kofa and Castle Dome mountains. Though these rhyolite mountains, remnants of volcanic activity, don't have much elevation, they have the kind of precipitous landscape the sheep like. You might see a desert tortoise munching on plants in the springtime, or a desert kit fox traipsing among the desert hills.

The mountains contained some hefty caches of precious metals. In the early 1900s, prospectors established a number of mines in the refuge. The King of Arizona Mine, which inspired the name of the mountains (K of A), produced around $14 million.

The refuge keeps an undeveloped demeanor, inasmuch as trails are few and far between; most double as unmaintained backroads. The hillsides may be explored further on foot, but not by vehicle. Vehicles must remain within 100 feet of designated roads.

The best time to visit the refuge is late fall through early spring, when temperatures remain mild. During the summer, the temperatures linger around 110 degrees. After a wet winter, the wildflower displays can be spectacular. If you decide to visit the refuge in February, allow extra time to travel U.S. 95, which can back up with RV campers heading to this popular winter destination.

Directions: The refuge is located approximately 40 miles north of Yuma and 20 miles south of Quartzsite off U.S. 95 in western Arizona.

Hours Open: No restrictions.

Facilities: Primitive camping.

Permits and Rules:
- Mechanized vehicles and mountain bikes must stay on numbered roads.
- Carrying, possessing, or discharging firearms or explosives (including fireworks) is not allowed.
- Camping within 0.25 miles of water is prohibited; vehicles must remain within a 100-foot corridor of designated roads.
- Campfires are permitted using dead and downed wood only.
- Pets must be confined.

Further Information: Kofa National Wildlife Refuge, 356 West First Street, Yuma, AZ 85364; 928-783-7861.

Other Areas of Interest

Visit the town of Quartzsite, which hosts a gem and mineral show in February.

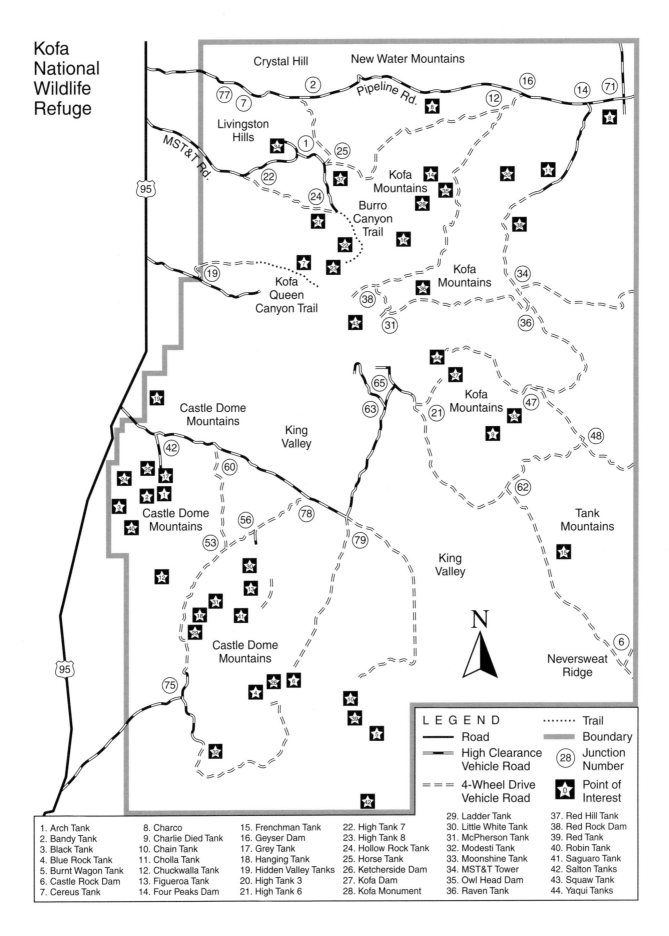

Kofa National Wildlife Refuge

Crystal Hill

New Water Mountains

Pipeline Rd.

MST&T Rd.

95

Livingston Hills

Kofa Mountains

Burro Canyon Trail

Kofa Queen Canyon Trail

Kofa Mountains

Kofa Mountains

Castle Dome Mountains

King Valley

Castle Dome Mountains

King Valley

Tank Mountains

Castle Dome Mountains

95

Neversweat Ridge

N

L E G E N D

....	Trail
——	Road
▓▓▓	Boundary
====	High Clearance Vehicle Road
(28)	Junction Number
= = =	4-Wheel Drive Vehicle Road
★	Point of Interest

1. Arch Tank	8. Charco	15. Frenchman Tank	22. High Tank 7	29. Ladder Tank	37. Red Hill Tank
2. Bandy Tank	9. Charlie Died Tank	16. Geyser Dam	23. High Tank 8	30. Little White Tank	38. Red Rock Dam
3. Black Tank	10. Chain Tank	17. Grey Tank	24. Hollow Rock Tank	31. McPherson Tank	39. Red Tank
4. Blue Rock Tank	11. Cholla Tank	18. Hanging Tank	25. Horse Tank	32. Modesti Tank	40. Robin Tank
5. Burnt Wagon Tank	12. Chuckwalla Tank	19. Hidden Valley Tanks	26. Ketcherside Dam	33. Moonshine Tank	41. Saguaro Tank
6. Castle Rock Dam	13. Figueroa Tank	20. High Tank 3	27. Kofa Dam	34. MST&T Tower	42. Salton Tanks
7. Cereus Tank	14. Four Peaks Dam	21. High Tank 6	28. Kofa Monument	35. Owl Head Dam	43. Squaw Tank
				36. Raven Tank	44. Yaqui Tanks

Kofa Queen Canyon 👢 👢 👢

Distance Round-Trip: 7.5 miles

Estimated Hiking Time: 3.5 hours

Elevation: 1,900 to 2,400 feet

Maps: USGS Palm Canyon

Best Time to Hike: November through March

Cautions: The route is a four-wheel-drive road that gets little vehicular traffic. The hillsides may be explored further on foot, but not by vehicle.

Directions: From Quartzsite, drive south on U.S. 95 about 19 miles to the signed turnoff for Palm Canyon; turn east (left); drive 3.2 miles to Road 19, then turn north (left); drive 4.3 miles to a parking area on the right. A high-clearance vehicle is required.

The hiking route in Kofa Queen Canyon is a four-wheel-drive road that leads to the Kofa Queen Mine, almost 4 miles into the canyon on the south side of the road. The rough road, rocky and rutted, gets little vehicular use and makes a good hiking route.

The route starts **[1]** as a cobbled wash braiding around islands of raised ground. During the spring, the roadsides and islands of ground in the road harbor colorful wildflowers after a wet winter. Look, especially, for sand blazing star and ghostflower. These yellow translucent flowers, one with reddish spots and the other with orange lines, appear mostly in western Arizona.

You might notice the colony of ocotillo climbing up the north ridge at about mile 0.5. Their clusters of red blossoms often appear when the weather warms up a bit. Let your eyes follow a series of needlelike peaks above the ocotillo to a formation that looks like a bent thumb, then just a bit farther to an arch.

By mile 1, just past an unusual brick-red outcropping, the roadway comes to an especially scenic area where an obelisk formation rises on the left and the canyon ridgelines rise to 3,500 feet **[2]**. As you pass the obelisk formation, look at the arch at the top of it and the window at the bottom. On the canyon walls, you can see needle-sharp spires rise off the south ridgetop, and rounded formations filled with arches rise on the north ridgetop.

At about mile 1.7, a dryfall pours down the north side of the canyon. A side canyon forms on the canyon's opposite side. The pouroff gives you a close look at how erosion has its way in the volcanic rock.

The canyon yawns wide enough **[3]** to allow a basin at about mile 2.3. The vegetation in the basin gets brushy with mesquite trees and jojoba bushes until the canyon walls quickly narrow again.

Vehicle travel ends **[4]** at mile 3, where a sign blocks further progress. The road, however, continues, albeit severely rutted and overgrown. You may continue following the road another 0.75 miles to the top of a ridge. The 360-degree panorama shows hillsides in every direction. In the spring, they may glow golden from Mexican gold poppies. When you have finished admiring the view, return the way you came.

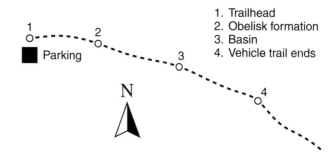

1. Trailhead
2. Obelisk formation
3. Basin
4. Vehicle trail ends

Burro Canyon 🥾 🥾 🥾

Distance Round-Trip: 9.4 miles

Estimated Hiking Time: 5 hours

Elevation: 2,200 to 3,400 feet

Map: USGS Livingston Hills

Best Time to Hike: November through March

Caution: The route is a four-wheel-drive road that gets little vehicular traffic, and hikers must share the road.

Directions: From Quartzsite, drive south on U.S. 95 about 11.2 miles to the unsigned turnoff for Refuge Road 24 just south of milepost 93; turn east (left) and drive 6.2 miles to Refuge Road 22 and veer right; drive 5.7 miles to the road's intersection with Refuge Road 24 and park. A high-clearance vehicle is required; a four-wheel-drive vehicle is recommended.

The four-wheel-drive road in Burro Canyon takes you to the De La Osa well placed deep in the Kofa Mountains during the cattle days. Now the well nourishes wildlife. As the canyon curls into the heart of the Kofa Mountains, it passes wildly eroded ridgelines, cuts a narrow corridor through ruddy rhyolite peaks, and wends around low-rising peaks.

The route starts **[1]** on the banks of a cross wash that runs over the road. The landscape's low-rising ridges only hint at the canyon they will develop into. The volcanic cliffs to the south show some character as they take on a dark brown cast. By mile 0.75, the wash starts to develop into a canyon as northern ridgeline walls oppose the southern sable-colored cliffs.

At mile 1.2, the canyon's north wall grows, and its south wall starts to approach the roadway, giving the canyon more definition **[2]**. Watch for a window rock on the top of the north wall. A bit farther, a slab of buff-colored rock stands out from the earthtones of the south wall. Then the surrounding cliffs start to develop an ostentatious pattern with brawny outcroppings, chunky strata of golden buff against toasty colors, alcoves dug into rockwalls, and erosion-carved spires.

By mile 1.4, the canyon walls start edging their way toward the road close enough to cast their shadow onto the route. After it passes a side canyon on its south side, about mile 1.6, the road squeezes between the narrowed canyon walls, entering a more shadowed environment. The scene takes a distinctive turn as the north wall's bedrock base becomes flush with the road, and globs of tuff ooze down the south walls.

By mile 2, the walls get close enough to allow you to scrutinize their erosion-carved features. Watch for stringy bushes of Bigelow ragged rock flower growing from cracks in the canyon walls.

The canyon walls retreat **[3]** when slopes form and start pushing them back at mile 2.3. After a wet winter these slopes get covered with Mexican gold poppies and Coulter's lupine. By mile 2.8, the south wall backs off and relaxes into a series of small mountains. You may notice faint paths crisscrossing the mountain slopes. These are trails beaten by bighorn sheep.

The road bends and heads into a cross wash at about mile 4.5. It snuggles inside the folds of the mountain as it wends its last 0.25 mile to the De La Osa windmill well where it dead-ends. When you reach the well, return the way you came **[4]**.

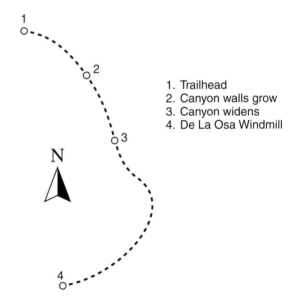

1. Trailhead
2. Canyon walls grow
3. Canyon widens
4. De La Osa Windmill

Central

Arizona's central region comprises an area below the Mogollon Rim in the north, the Salt River in the east, and the Gila River to Yuma County in the south and west. All of Maricopa and part of Yavapai, Pinal, and Gila counties lie in the region.

Topography

In the heart of Arizona, the central region, you find jagged swells of mountains, verdant valleys, and desolate-looking desert flats. Some of the state's most rugged and remote mountain ranges rise here. Between them, creeks and rivers carve a perennial route.

The rounded Bradshaw Mountains near Prescott, composed of schist and granite eroded into scenic shapes, were the state's treasure chest of precious minerals when thousands of prospectors converged to mine gold and silver ores in the late 1800s.

Moving south, Pine Mountain, a lonely island mountain, watches over the Verde Valley below it. Its solitary location makes it a harbor for game and a haven for hikers. The Mazatzal and Sierra Ancha mountains lie east of the Verde River. Both extraordinarily rugged and remote, these mountains brace the Tonto Basin, where the Tonto Creek flows from the Mogollon Rim into the Salt River.

Just south of the Salt River, the Pinal Mountains form a sky island range. Rich in minerals, animals, and vegetation, the mountains sustained Indians, miners, and farmers. Also below the Salt River, and east of Phoenix, the Superstition Mountains immortalized volcanic activity into its wild volcanic tuff landscape.

Finally, low-lying desert mountains and basins appear in the lower portion of the central region. This area is located in and around Phoenix.

Major Rivers and Lakes

The central region has a number of major lakes and rivers, as well as some notable creeks, though you wouldn't know it by the dry demeanor the region generally keeps. Life becomes concentrated around these water sources, attracting animals, birds, and humans.

One of the major tributaries in the state, the Salt River, has been made into a chain of lakes just north of the Superstition Mountains by a series of dams, the largest being Roosevelt Dam. From east to west, Canyon, Cherry, and Tonto creeks hang like fingers from a hand from the Mogollon Rim into the Salt River.

On the eastern end of the central region, the Verde and Agua Fria rivers travel south from the Mogollon Rim toward Phoenix and beyond into the latitudinal Gila River. Both of these rivers have dams that form lakes in the Sonoran Desert: Horseshoe Lake and Bartlett Reservoir on the Verde River, and Lake Pleasant along the Agua Fria River.

Common Plant Life

Plant life in the central region can range from ferns to cacti, depending on the location. In the region's mountainous terrain, you'll find ponderosa pine trees and Douglas fir on the mountaintops. Ponderosa pine trees and oaks live in the midrange elevations. Juniper and piñon pine trees settle into the high desert.

In the lower elevations of the Sonoran Desert areas around Phoenix, cacti reign: saguaro, prickly pear, barrel, pin cushion, cholla, and hedgehog. Paloverde and mesquite trees are the wood bearers. Creosote and a variety of prickly shrubs make up the bushes. After a wet winter, beautiful carpets of wildflowers appear.

Watercourses, however, will dramatically change the immediate landscape of an area. Monkey flowers and ferns decorate canyon walls. Moisture-loving trees, such as willows, cottonwoods, and sycamores, cling to banks of rivers and creeks. Bigtooth maple, velvet ash, Arizona walnut, and box elder trees grow in mountain canyons. These trees produce excellent fall color from mid-October to late November, depending on the elevation.

Common Birds and Mammals

Because of the strong network of watercourses in the central region, birds and mammals make a big show. The perennial waterways, such as the Verde and Salt rivers and Tonto, Cherry, and Canyon creeks, have their own ecosystems full of insects and birds. Animals, such as coyotes, mountain lions, javelina, and bobcats, come to their shores to drink. Bighorn sheep live in the craggy cliffs near the lakes pooled along the Salt River. Eagles gravitate to sections of the river, too, as well as along the Verde River.

Bears, mule deer, and mountain lions hang out in the highcountry of the central region. In the highest elevations, you'll find elk. Rattlesnakes appear all over the region, so be careful where you put your hands and feet.

Climate

Except for the highest elevations, which get snow in the winters, the central region has a mild winter climate. Its highcountry sees 90-degree days in the summer and cool nights. The desert regions will see triple digits throughout the summer.

Like all of Arizona, the central region takes part in the monsoon season. The highcountry, especially, can see rain on a daily basis from early July through mid-September. Watch for temperatures to drop 20 to 40 degrees during these fast and ferocious thunderstorms.

Best Natural Features

- Volcanic tuff ranges in the Superstition Mountains
- Razorback ridges of the Mazatzal Mountains
- Azure waters of dam-formed lakes
- Saguaro cactus forests on sunny hillsides in the lower elevations
- Spreads of wildflowers after a wet winter

11. Bradshaw Mountains

- Hike along scenic stacks of smooth granite boulders.
- Find prospector and cowboy remnants.
- Explore a verdant stretch of springs in the Grapevine Botanical Area.

Area Information

When mountain man Joe Walker found gold in 1863, the State of Arizona didn't even exist. Within a year, the wild and undeveloped locality, present-day Prescott, took on the characteristics of a boomtown hustling with prospectors, cowboys, merchants, painted ladies, and a constant influx of frontier folks.

This gold-hunting expedition was among the last of Walker's adventures. Walker's scouting reputation was legend. One mountain man claimed, "He don't follow trails, he makes 'em."

By the end of 1864, over 1,600 prospectors established mining camps in the granite mountains, panning in gold-rich streams and digging for veins of gold-bearing quartz. Like most mineral-related lifestyles, mining the Bradshaws had its heartbreaking moments. The rugged landscape posed as much danger as the resistant Yavapai Indians, who made their home along the mountain streams that lured gold prospectors.

Prospectors who made it through Indian attacks, greed, bitter winters, and meager water supplies had a good chance of striking it rich. The region was one of the richest mining areas in the state.

Though the gold fever played out by the first world war, the Bradshaws still coax a slight fever from modern-day prospectors who cherish their favorite creekside haunts. Prospectors need a permit to pan gold in the Bradshaws, except at a designated panning area on Lynx Creek between Lynx Lake and Walker.

Precious minerals were the rare commodity that drew thousands to the Bradshaw Mountains in the late 1800s. Now it's quiet remoteness. Much of the mountains' backcountry remains as rough-hewn as in the late 1800s. Trails lead hikers and mountain bikers (except in designated wilderness areas where mechanized vehicles are not allowed) into ponderosa pine forests, up craggy mountaintops with fabulous views, and down into oasis-like canyons harboring crystal pools. Along the way, you might find cowboy or prospector remnants. Please leave all artifacts where you find them.

Daytime temperatures stay reasonable in the mountains for much of the year, stretching the hiking season from spring through fall into winter on mild days.

Directions: From Interstate 17, drive 34 miles on Arizona 69 to the town of Prescott.

Hours Open: No restrictions.

Facilities: Camping, picnic areas, and restrooms at recreation sites.

Permits and Rules:
- Mechanized vehicles and mountain bikes must stay on designated roads and are not allowed in designated wilderness areas.
- In developed recreation sites, pets must be restrained on a leash no longer than 6 feet.
- Fireworks are prohibited.
- Fires must be attended at all times.
- Maximum stay is 14 days.
- Maximum group size is 10 people.

Further Information: Prescott National Forest, 344 South Cortez Street, Prescott, AZ 86303; 928-445-1762.

Other Areas of Interest

The Sharlot Hall Museum on West Gurley Street in Prescott gives you a look into the history of the area. Call 928-445-3122 for more information. A drive to Lynx Lake on Walker Road takes you to a favorite fishing spot that has boating, camping, and hiking. The Bradshaw Ranger Station has more information at 928-771-4700.

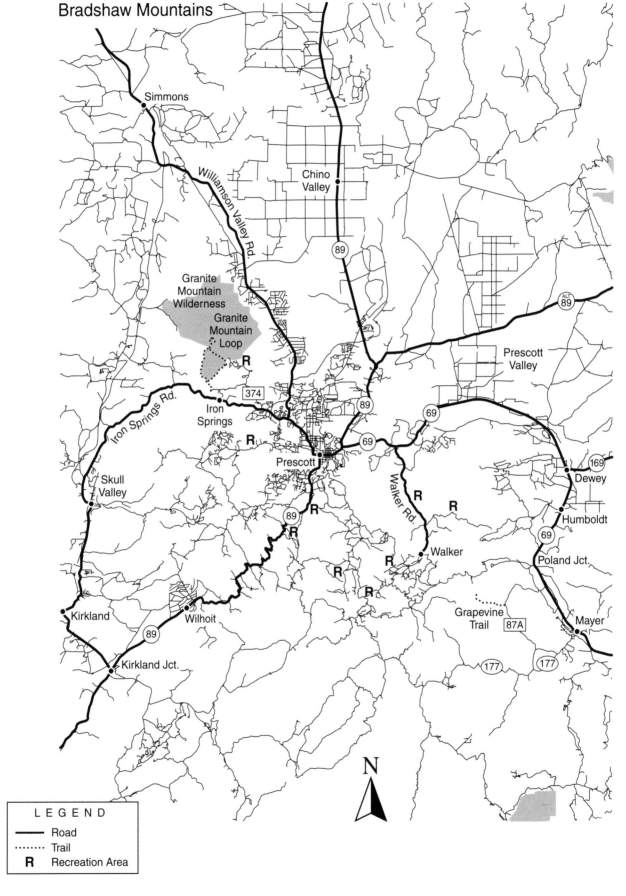

Bradshaw Mountains

Simmons

Williamson Valley Rd.

Chino Valley

89

ALT 89

Granite Mountain Wilderness

Granite Mountain Loop

R

Prescott Valley

374

Iron Springs

89

69

Iron Springs Rd.

R

Prescott

69

69

169

Dewey

Skull Valley

R

Walker Rd.

R

R

Humboldt

89

R

R

R

Walker

R

Poland Jct.

69

Kirkland

Wilhoit

R

Grapevine Trail

87A

Mayer

89

177

177

Kirkland Jct.

N

L E G E N D
- Road
- Trail
- **R** Recreation Area

Granite Mountain Loop

👢 👢 👢

Distance Round-Trip: 9.1 to 13.7 miles

Estimated Hiking Time: 4.5 to 7 hours

Elevation: 5,730 to 7,200 feet

Maps: Prescott National Forest, USGS Jerome Canyon

Caution: Peregrine falcons are on the federal list of endangered species; please view them with respect.

Directions: From Montezuma Street in downtown Prescott, drive north as it turns into Iron Springs Road (after 3.5 miles); continue north 1.7 miles past the turnoff for FR 374 (to Granite Basin Lake) and continue another 3.1 miles to the signed trailhead turnoff.

This hike links together three trails that take you into the Granite Mountain Wilderness. The trails pass a beautiful golden granite landscape of precipitous cliffs and erosion-smoothed boulders—a favorite haunt for rockclimbers and peregrine falcons.

The route starts out [1] on the Little Granite Mountain Trail, rising and falling among the granite ridges knobby with smooth boulders. The decomposed granite trail sees every ray of sunlight in this scrub oak-lined segment of the loop, so be sure to wear sun protection. Continue on the Little Granite Mountain Trail [2] as it intersects with the Clark Spring Trail at mile 1.3.

The trail travels northward, edging the western boundary of the Granite Mountain Wilderness. All the while, you get a fabulous panorama of the beautiful granite formations on Little Granite Mountain. At mile 2.6, continue past the path's intersection with the Upper Pasture Trail [3]. Then watch for Granite Mountain, the Granite Mountain Wilderness' high point, to come into view.

At the Granite Mountain Wilderness boundary [4], about mile 4.2, you can opt to hike 2.3 round-trip miles up to the Granite Mountain Viewpoint [5], or continue on the loop by turning right onto

Trail 261 toward Granite Basin Lake. The ancillary trail climbs 1,500 feet through a scenic spread of rock formations and boulders. The trail follows the boulder-strewn ridgetop to an overlook with fabulous views of Granite Mountain Lake and Prescott. The steep trail has dicey moments when the decomposed granite acts like tiny ball bearings and forces a skid or two on the downhill.

Back on the loop and Trail 261, the trail strolls through Blair Pass [6], a shady stretch of pines cradled by rockwalls decked with smooth boulders and columns of rock. The trail coasts on a gentle downhill along a wash until it intersects with the Clark Spring Trail at mile 6. Turn right onto the Clark Spring Trail [7] and follow trail signs closely.

The Clark Spring Trail takes you through a scenic wooded drainage, traveling up and down low-lying ridges through a pass between Two Rock Mountain [8] just south of the trail and Little Granite Mountain to the northwest. The trail joins with the Little Granite Mountain Trail at mile 7.8. Turn left onto the trail and hike back to the trailhead.

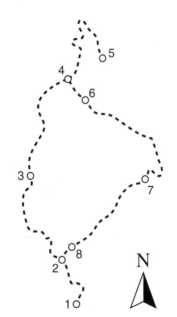

1. Trailhead
2. Clark Spring trail junction
3. Upper Pasture trail junction
4. Wilderness boundary
5. Granite Mountain viewpoint
6. Blair Pass
7. Clark Spring trail
8. Two Rock Mountain Pass

N

Grapevine Trail 🥾 🥾

Distance Round-Trip: 4 miles

Estimated Hiking Time: 2 hours

Elevation: 5,600 to 6,000 feet

Maps: Prescott National Forest, USGS Poland Junction

Caution: Watch for poison ivy along the trail.

Directions: From Prescott, drive east on Arizona 69 to unmarked FR 87 just past milepost 274, then turn right; drive about 0.4 mile past a fork in the road, then veer right at the next fork (mile 0.5) onto FR 87A; follow the road about 4 miles to its end. (At the driveway to a country home, about mile 2, the road quickly degenerates, and high-clearance vehicles are necessary.)

At the unsigned trailhead, marked only by a pile of rocks, the trail starts right along the Grapevine Creek drainage **[1]**. Depending on the time of year you hike the trail, the drainage will probably start out dry. By about mile 0.1, however, cascades suddenly sound, and lively flows of crystal water will start as quickly as they vanish, a pattern the creek follows until the trail nears its namesake springs farther upstream.

At about mile 1, watch for cairns that lead the trail across the creek **[2]**. Also watch for patches of poison ivy on the moist ground shaded by a mix of alder, Arizona walnut, willow, velvet ash, and cottonwood trees. The habitat is extraordinarily rich for the usually dry landscape of the Bradshaw Mountains. As the trail climbs several hundred feet above the creek, you may glimpse a few aspen in the drainage below.

The physical features of the drainage show the extreme dichotomy between the lush spring-fed environment of Grapevine Creek and the mountains' normal vegetation of manzanita and scrub oak, called *chaparral*. The drainage's north-facing slope has a forest of mixed conifers; the south faces a thick cover of chaparral. Both meet at the bottom in the extravagant riparian mix.

Near a fence line with signs demarcating property of the United States, a spring muddies the trail as it flows across the path toward the creek. Just below this spring lies the rest of Grapevine Springs, a cluster of about a dozen high-quality springs **[3]** that feed the Grapevine Botanical Area. The springs gush from under boulders and out of hillsides, feeding columbines, meadow rue, and canyon grape.

After you explore the area, with its picturesque cascades and lush vegetation, return the way you came.

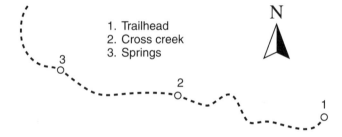

1. Trailhead
2. Cross creek
3. Springs

N

12. Pine Mountain Wilderness

- Hike along a cold mountain stream.
- See striking views of the Verde Valley and Bradshaw Mountains.
- Find remnants of early homesteaders.

Area Information

The Pine Mountain Wilderness, a couple dozen miles from the nearest town in the middle of nowhere, takes you far from modern civilization and gives you a true wilderness feeling. Remnants of homesteaders remain along the trails to remind you of antiquated lifestyles.

The trails in the 20,100-acre wilderness network around Pine Mountain, the highest point on the Verde River Rim. The central Arizona mountain rises like a verdant island in the middle of a hardscrabble landscape strewn with cobbles of lava, then stretches its eastern slopes down to the Verde River. Views from the Verde River Rim on the mountain's east face are striking.

Though it has few water sources, the mountain has rich stands of ponderosa pine and Douglas fir sprinkled with bigtooth maple trees. Trees on its upper reaches get twisted by the harsh elements.

The remoteness of this wilderness gives you a chance to see a variety of big game wildlife. It's not unusual to see bear scat along the trails. Trophy elk are common. Deer attract mountain lions.

The best time to hike the Pine Mountain Wilderness is from March through November. On a hot summer day in the desert, the mountain's cover of pines keeps a cool environment.

Directions: The Pine Mountain Wilderness is located approximately 75 miles north of Phoenix. Drive north on Interstate 17 to the Dugas interchange (exit 268); follow FR 68 17.8 miles to trailheads. The drive, which requires a high-clearance vehicle, will take about an hour.

Hours Open: No restrictions.

Facilities: Primitive camping, picnic area.

Permits and Rules:
- No mechanized vehicles or mountain bikes are allowed.
- In developed recreation sites, pets must be restrained on a leash no longer than 6 feet.
- Fireworks are prohibited.
- Fires must be attended at all times.
- Maximum stay is 14 days.
- Maximum group size is 10 people.

Further Information: Verde Ranger District, P.O. Box 670, Camp Verde, AZ 86322; 928-567-4121.

Other Areas of Interest

Take a tour of the experimental town near Cordes Junction, Arcosanti, designed by Italian architect Paolo Soleri. The goal of the town is to improve urban conditions while minimizing impact on the earth. For more information, call 928-632-6217.

Pine Mountain Loop 🥾 🥾 🥾

Distance Round-Trip: 9.6 miles

Estimated Hiking Time: 4.5 hours

Elevation: 5,200 to 6,814 feet

Maps: Prescott National Forest, USGS Tule Mesa

Caution: If you encounter any wildlife, stay far enough away that you don't interfere with their activity.

Directions: The trail starts at the Salt Flat trailhead at the end of FR 68. Starting out in a riparian forest along Sycamore Creek on the Nelson Trail **[1]**, this loop hike eventually climbs 1,500 feet up to the Verde Rim as it aims for its high point atop Pine Mountain. The gathering of Arizona walnut, Arizona sycamore, ponderosa pine, and Gambel oak trees at the trail's start weaves a cool cover of shade in the summer, then turns into a gold and russet canopy in the fall.

The trail follows Sycamore Creek, where trout break the ice-cold water's surface and fallen Arizona sycamore leaves steeping along the soggy banks release a spicy-sweet aroma. Bear signs, sometimes fresh enough to evoke caution, often blaze the trail.

An apple orchard at the Nelson Place, a homestead eroded down to a stone wall located in the first mile of the hike, draws the bruins. Elk, mountain lions, and deer also share the wilderness.

Shortly after the trail squishes through the spongy, spring-fed ground at the Nelson Place **[2]**, it enters the Pine Mountain Wilderness. The path separates from Sycamore Creek and starts to climb up to the Verde Rim. Ponderosa pine and Gambel oak trees provide immediate shade; but within a mile, bigtooth maple trees make a surprise staccato appearance along the steep slopes of the drainage. An anomalous stand of aspen waits in a crevice near the top of the rim.

At the Verde Rim Trail **[3]**, mile 4.3, turn right and head toward Pine Mountain. At about mile 4.6, watch for an ancillary footpath on the left. The steep path takes you up a ragged route to the top of the mountain **[4]**. A walk through a jumble of basalt boulders leads you to the edge of the mountain, where you get a 360-degree panorama with Horseshoe Lake in the south, the rugged Mogollon Rim in the east, the Verde Valley to the north, and the Bradshaw Mountains in the west.

Back on the main trail, which continues its edge walk along the Verde Rim, the vegetation has a dwarfed image. Buffeted by the weather, the oaks and pines grow gnarled and short. At mile 5.2, turn right onto the Pine Mountain Trail **[5]**.

Now more protected and secure, the forest trees grow to their natural height. View the Bradshaw Mountains in the west as the path zigzags down the mountain. The path meets back with the Nelson Trail **[6]** at about mile 6.4. Turn left onto the Nelson Trail and retrace your steps another 3.2 miles back to the trailhead.

Pine Mountain Wilderness

1. Trailhead
2. Nelson Place
3. Verde Rim trail
4. Pine Mountain
5. Pine Mountain trail
6. Nelson trail

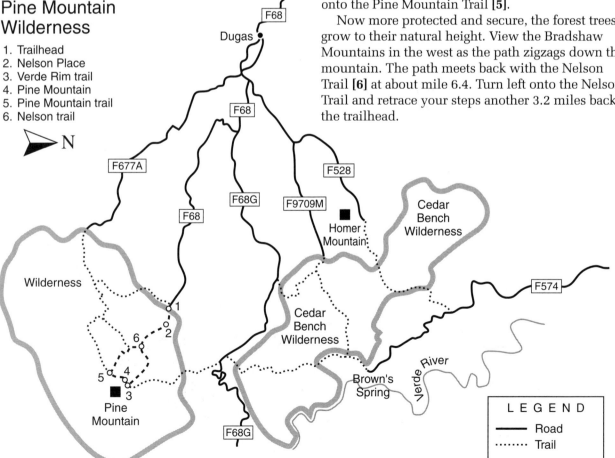

13. Agua Fria National Monument

- View petroglyphs from the Perry Mesa culture.
- Hike the scenic flow of the Agua Fria River.
- Find remnants from prospectors.

Area Information

One of Arizona's newer national monuments, the Agua Fria National Monument will appeal to hikers who like an adventure. There are no maintained trails in the monument. If you want to explore, you're on your own.

Hikers can canyoneer in the Agua Fria River or in several of its rugged side canyons. Mesa-top hikes cross lava-cobbled grasslands where pronghorn antelope, mule deer, white-tailed deer, and javelina hang out.

The 22-mile stretch of the Agua Fria River between Cordes Junction and Larry Canyon, just north of Black Canyon City, has been nominated for Wild and Scenic River status, which would ensure the protection of this unique wilderness.

Besides a habitat of the endangered bald eagle and pronghorn antelope, the monument contains one of the largest complexes of archaeological history in central Arizona. Parts of the monument are listed on the National Register of Historic Places.

The Agua Fria was home to a variety of prehistoric and historic American Indian cultures called the Perry Mesa Tradition Indians. The culture contains characteristics of Salado, Sinagua, Hohokam, and Anasazi peoples. They inhabited the area between 1,200 and 1,450 years after the birth of Christ. The Indians built three- and four-story pueblos, dug terraced farms on the canyon walls, and built satellite farm stations all over the mesa. Then they suddenly moved on to other parts of central Arizona.

The area is also rich in Anglo history. In the late 1800s, the river was home to miners and cowboys. Gold seekers ferreted for the precious ore along the river bottom, and cowboys grazed cattle along the grassy mesas.

The Civil Air Patrol and ground-based site stewards vigorously patrol the cache of history scattered in the area and are often successful in catching pillagers. Courts do not hesitate to slap hefty fines on lawbreakers who steal or deface rock art or ruins.

The best time to hike this monument is from November through March. Extreme temperatures in the summer could cause health risks, as the river, which dries to muddy pools, will not be available to refresh you.

Among all the danger and beauty the Agua Fria National Monument holds is an untamed atmosphere that can be as comfortable as it is enticing to hikers looking for a bit of adventure. If there's a part of the Wild West that hasn't yet been tamed, hikers will find a good dose of it on the Agua Fria.

Directions: Located 40 miles north of Phoenix east of Interstate 17.

Hours Open: No restrictions.

Facilities: None.

Permits and Rules: The Archaeological Resource Protection Act and state antiquity laws protect ancient and historic ruins. Anyone found excavating, collecting, defacing, or removing an artifact can be fined $500 to $250,000 and imprisoned up to five years. If you see a relic from a historic or ancient culture, you may inspect it, but you may not take it.

Further Information: Bureau of Land Management, 21605 North 7th Avenue, Phoenix, AZ; 623-580-5500.

Other Areas of Interest

Visit Black Canyon City just south of the monument off Interstate 17 and browse the little shops lined up in rustic Western-town style. The old mining town of Crown King, located about 30 miles west of the monument at the top of the Bradshaw Mountains, had its heyday in the late 1800s when the Crown King Mine produced around $2 million in gold.

Agua Fria River 👢 👢 👢 👢

Distance Round-Trip: 4 miles

Estimated Hiking Time: 4 hours

Elevation: 3,100 to 3,200 feet

Maps: BLM Bradshaw Mountains, USGS Bumble Bee

Best Time to Hike: November through March

Cautions: This hike follows no trail, and it requires rockhopping, boulder climbing, and wading. A swatch of private land drapes across the Agua Fria just west of Perry Tank Canyon, and segments of private land interrupt the southern portion of the river near Black Canyon City.

Directions: From Interstate 17 and the Badger Springs exit (252), head east on a dirt road to a parking area. High-clearance vehicles are recommended.

This hiking route takes you through a scenic segment of the Agua Fria River. Experienced hikers will find the route mildly challenging, but fun. If you feel uncomfortable during any part of the hike, you should turn back.

From the parking area **[1]**, follow a beaten path as it rambles through Badger Springs Wash to the Agua Fria River **[2]**. During wet weather, ephemeral springs fill the gravelly wash bottom. The Agua Fria River, about mile 0.5, makes a good turnaround point for an easy day hike, especially if you have limited hiking experience. To continue on the adventure, turn right to head down the river.

Depending on recent precipitation and snowmelt, the route may have you immediately wading. Other-wise, low water levels allow you to hop boulders along the river's edge.

After the first bend, about mile 0.75, you will crisscross the river by rockhopping or wading the stream **[3]**. The route enters a scenic area where saguaro cactus mix with spired rocks poking out from the canyon walls. During wet weather, cascades race down stair-step paths of rocks worn smooth by the indomitable flow of water.

By mile 1, the rust-colored canyon walls rise several hundred feet above the river. Intermittent boulder slides pour into the river, forcing you to climb over and squeeze between water-smoothed boulders. You may have to climb up the canyon walls to sidestep deep pools, such as the one at Perry Tank Canyon **[4]**, about mile 1.5.

This side canyon, tumbling into the Agua Fria drainage from the east side of the river, may have cascades of water flowing down it in wet weather. A pool that lingers most of the year at the foot of the side canyon often requires climbing a bit up the main canyon's walls to get around it.

As you pick your way along the rugged walls, watch for mining paraphernalia—water pipes poised on stone stacks and cable and metal braces. The relics remain from the Richinbar Mine, located just above on the western rim of the canyon.

The deeper you travel into the canyon from Perry Tank Canyon, the more its atmosphere takes on a wild and remote feel. Pouroffs require minor scrambling to maneuver around, and boulder hopping becomes common. If you continue down the river past mile 2, you will cross private property owned by the Richinbar Mine that extends down to the canyon floor **[5]**.

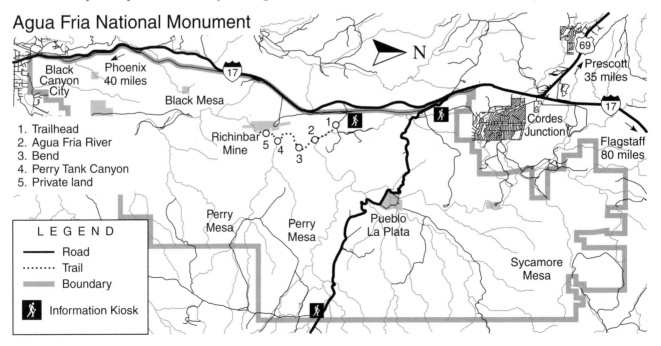

Agua Fria National Monument

1. Trailhead
2. Agua Fria River
3. Bend
4. Perry Tank Canyon
5. Private land

L E G E N D
——— Road
········· Trail
——— Boundary
🚶 Information Kiosk

14. Hassayampa River Area

- Hike a secluded side canyon.
- Climb to a 360-degree view of central Arizona.
- Hike in one of the richest gold-mining areas in the state.

Area Information

The Hassayampa River area had all the ingredients for a lucky strike back in the late 1800s. The area produced some of the biggest placer strikes and gold lodes in the state. The miners' creed—"If ya stumble on a rock, don't cuss it—cash it!"—could have started along Wickenburg's Hassayampa River.

Along the Hassayampa just north of Wickenburg, gold hunters plucked $100,000 in gold nuggets right off the ground of Rich Hill, the largest placer strike in Arizona history. The Vulture Mine, just south of Wickenburg and a few miles west of the river, produced enough gold ore to make it one of the richest lodes in Arizona's history. These nuggets helped convince Washington D.C. to grant Arizona its territory status.

Miner lore claimed the Hassayampa River turned men into liars. This stemmed from the propensity of prospectors to give misleading information about their claims or exaggerate the claims' actual worth. The prospectors blamed their deception on drinking water from the Hassayampa River. They said once anyone drank its water, he couldn't tell the truth anymore.

Besides a proclivity to produce gold and liars, the Hassayampa River also has a penchant for ducking underground in certain sections, leaving its riverbed dry as a bone as it continues a subterranean flow. With that in mind, a sign on the bridge over the sandy Hassayampa River bed in the town of Wickenburg says "No Fishing."

The best time to hike around the Wickenburg area is late fall through early spring, before temperatures rise to uncomfortable and dangerous heights. Fall and spring hikes along the Hassayampa River will see more birds. After a wet winter, wildflowers show in March.

Directions: From Phoenix, drive northwest on U.S. 60 to the town of Wickenburg.

Hours Open: No restrictions.

Facilities: Camping, picnic areas, restrooms.

Further Information: Bureau of Land Management, 21605 N. 7th Avenue, Phoenix, AZ 85027; 623-580-5500.

Other Areas of Interest

The Hassayampa River Preserve, located on the east end of Wickenburg off U.S. 60, attracts hundreds of birds to its riparian paths. A checklist of 229 species have been sited. For more information, call 928-684-2772.

Hassayampa River Area

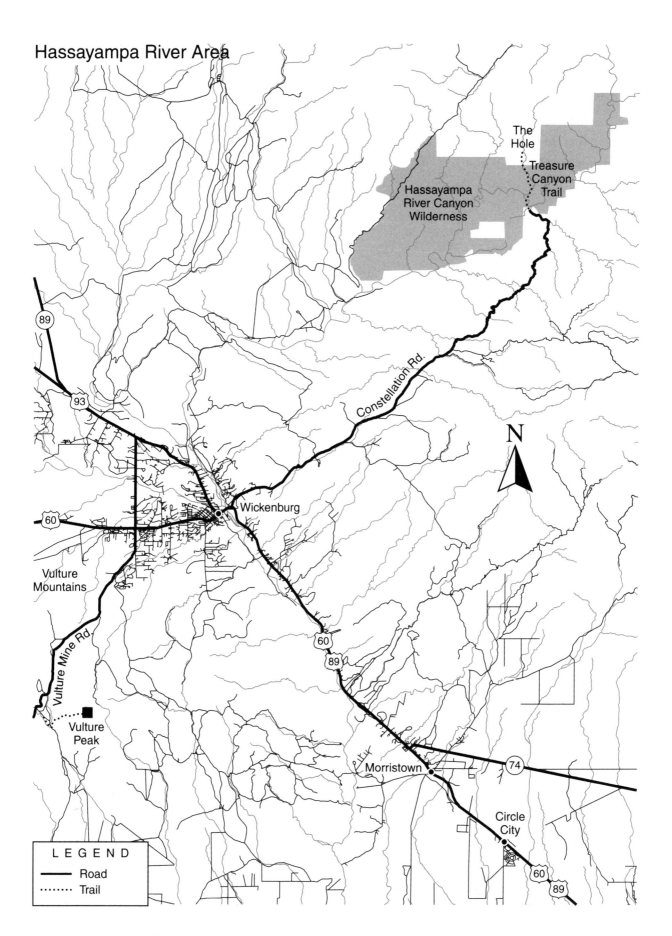

The Hole

Treasure Canyon Trail

Hassayampa River Canyon Wilderness

89

93

Constellation Rd.

60

Wickenburg

60

89

Vulture Mountains

Vulture Mine Rd.

Vulture Peak

N

Morristown

74

Circle City

60

89

LEGEND

——— Road

········· Trail

Vulture Peak Trail 🥾🥾🥾🥾

Distance Round-Trip: 4 miles

Estimated Hiking Time: 2.5 hours

Elevation: 2,480 to 3,660 feet

Maps: USGS Vulture Peak, Arizona and Vulture Mine, Arizona

Cautions: The last 0.7-mile stretch climbs 700 feet to the trail's end. Healthy hikers should bring sufficient water supplies to keep well hydrated.

Directions: From Wickenburg, drive west on U.S. 60 to Vulture Mine Road and turn south (left); drive 6.4 miles to the signed trailhead turnoff, then turn east (left); drive 0.4 miles to the trailhead.

Some of Arizona's richest gold mines can be seen from the top of Vulture Peak, but you have to work for the view. Though the trail follows a generally level course the first 1.3 miles, climbing over and down a few moderate hillocks, the last 0.7 mile starts a nonstop climb up 700 feet to a saddle where the maintained trail ends. An additional 240 feet of hand-over-foot climbing boosts you up an unmaintained path in a chute to the top of the peak.

The trail starts on a level course in a cholla-bursage community **[1]**. At mile 0.25, the path dips into the Syndicate Wash **[2]** and views its erosion-scarred cliffs on the climb out. The landscape takes on a corrugated look where small ridges divided by gulches rise and fall around major ridgelines. The trail climbs up and down several of these ridges before starting its austere ascent up to Vulture Peak.

Once it climbs a rounded ridge, the trail descends through a saguaro cactus forest, then back up another ridge. After a short break on a saddle, the trail continues the climb.

At about mile 0.7, the trail heads into a charming crevice that fills with wildflowers, such as Coulter's lupine, bladderpod, Mexican gold poppies, and mustard evening primrose, after a wet winter. A tangle of ocotillo arch their red-tipped wands over the path as it bends southward and drops gradually along a wash worn in many spots to bedrock.

As the trail takes its first steps into the wash, turn left to follow the path. Continue in the wash until a large cairn guides you out. The trail crosses a four-wheel-drive road and heads toward another large cairn into a narrow arroyo.

The trail climbs out of the arroyo at about mile 1 and heads toward its alternate trailhead at the end of a four-wheel-drive road **[3]**. Just past the trailhead, mile 1.4, the path starts its nonstop climb up Vulture Peak.

From here the path climbs 700 feet in 0.7 mile. This makes a good turnaround point for you if you're not ready for the climb. But if you want to see a 360-degree view of the area, are physically fit, and have enough water, continue on the Jeep track as it heads for the peak.

As the road narrows to a single track, it takes on an austere demeanor, picking through rocky slopes and high-stepping boulders. At about mile 1.7, the trail squeezes between a saguaro cactus and a grotto, then hugs the mountainside often shaded by a precipitous rockwall.

The trail becomes more demanding as it nears its end, and it makes its final heave onto a saddle between jagged peaks **[4]**. If you suffer from vertigo or don't feel up to a challenge to reach the top of the peak, return the way you came. Otherwise, continue on a hand-over-foot climb up the 240-foot chute to the top of Vulture Peak **[5]**.

Once on top, you get a 360-degree view of the area. You might get a bit of entertainment from swifts slicing the air with their aerial acrobatics or military jets doing wing rolls past the peak or dipping close enough for a quick buzz. When you've seen enough, carefully return the way you came.

1. Trailhead
2. Syndicate Wash
3. Alternate trailhead
4. Saddle
5. Vulture Peak

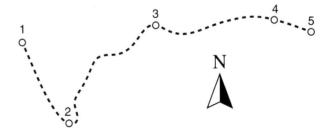

Treasure Canyon 👢 👢 👢 👢

Distance Round-Trip: 3 miles

Estimated Hiking Time: 3 hours

Elevation: 2,080 to 3,100 feet

Maps: USGS Wagoner, BLM Bradshaw Mountains

Cautions: The rocky and sometimes overgrown canyon bottom makes hiking slow. After wet weather, crossing the Hassayampa River may require wading. Water 3 feet deep traveling at 3 feet per second will knock an average-sized man down. Do not cross the water if it rises too high or is flowing too swiftly.

Directions: From the eastern edge of Wickenburg on U.S. 60, turn north on Constellation Road. Drive 8.4 miles to a fork and veer left toward the Williams Ranch. Drive about 8 miles to the parking area near the sign-in registry stand. A high-clearance vehicle is required.

The hike to Treasure Canyon starts **[1]** right in the drainage near the parking area. You may notice paths climbing out of the drainage, but continue in the wash as it heads northwest to the Hassayampa River. The wash passes benches where the Williams Ranch keeps horses for guests from around the world who stay at the ranch.

The wash meets up with the Hassayampa River at about mile 0.2. A signpost indicates a route heading eastward. This route will follow the river upstream into the Hassayampa Wilderness. To get to Treasure Canyon, however, follow a roadway across the river **[2]**, then veer left at a red and white "Route" sign that leads you up a bench along the north side of the river. The path weaves around a gallery of mesquite on the bench, then at about mile 0.3 drops off the bench back down to the river.

Pick your way along the riverbed, a mix of sand, gravel, and rocks, next to the north canyon wall. Treasure Canyon opens up on the north side **[3]** at about mile 0.5. The Bureau of Land Management has

developed an old cowboy trail that starts on the west side of Treasure Canyon. The route climbs through a classic Sonoran Desert landscape to the rim of Treasure Canyon, where it peers into the canyon. The route, traveling sections of State Trust land that require a permit, heads northward into the rugged Weaver Mountains. You can see Seal Mountain, the mountain that appears on the Arizona state flag, rising northeast of the trail.

You may take the trail that climbs along the canyon, or you may hike right in the canyon. This hike travels the more scenic route, directly into the canyon.

Once in Treasure Canyon, also called Mystery Canyon, the noisy flow of the Hassayampa River evanesces. If you hike during a wet winter, the canyon has a peaceful stream that traces a mossy path through the canyon system.

Deeper in the canyon, about mile 1, the walls rise high enough to give the canyon a cocooned feeling. Emerald pools nestle along ragged outcroppings. A gathering of cottonwoods provides a refreshing riparian cover along the narrow canyon bottom. As closed off as the canyon becomes to the outside world, its own ecosystem of birds, butterflies, turtles, garter snakes, trees, and water bustles with life.

The old cowboy path that started at the Hassayampa River rambles right above this area along the rim of the west wall. At mile 1.5, a 12-foot pouroff (The Hole) marks the end of this hike. Return the way you came.

1. Trailhead
2. Cross river
3. Treasure Canyon

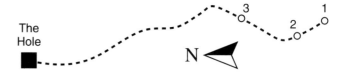

15. Hell's Canyon Wilderness

- Experience solitude on rugged trails in a wilderness only 30 miles from Phoenix.
- Have a chance meeting with a wild burro.
- Hike through a volcanic terrain full of strangely sculpted formations and arches.

Area Information

Hell's Canyon Wilderness has many geological features with reference to the underworld, such as Big Hellgate, Little Hellgate, Hellgate Mountain, and Lucifer's Gate. But the 9,200-acre wilderness looks more like a piece of heaven tucked into the scenic Hieroglyphic Mountains just northwest of Phoenix than a hellish scene. Remote and wild with unsigned trails, this wilderness is best explored by experienced hikers.

Prehistoric sites found in Hell's Canyon Wilderness indicate the Hohokam Indians made their home in the area. Remnants of ranching and mining, economic mainstays of the past, make an occasional appearance. But the wilderness has a rough-hewn, jagged topography that makes cultivation a challenge. Raspy canyons twist through the dips and heaves of the ruddy rhyolite terrain. Saguaro cacti, some centuries old, gather on the mountain slopes.

Mountain lions, mule deer, and javelina are common residents that add to the untamed persona of the wilderness. Also, a herd of about 225 burros roam the area. They travel in groups of 7 to 11 burros. Though they offer a cute and unusual experience, the burros have a feisty side—especially the jacks. If they feel as though they're cornered, they may kick or bite. The Bureau of Land Management manages the burros under the Wild Horse and Burro Act.

You may see burros in the wilderness, especially on the Burro Flats Trail, or you may hear their bray. More likely, you will only see their hoofprints. The prints, and those of other animals, may be the only ones you'll see on your hike in this wild and remote wilderness.

The wilderness may show some Hades-like characteristics in the summertime, when temperatures rise to the 110-degree range. With that in mind, the best hiking time is from late fall to early spring.

Directions: From Interstate 17 north of Phoenix, drive west on Arizona 74 about 11 miles and turn north (right) onto Castle Hot Springs Road.

Hours Open: No restrictions.

Facilities: None.

Permits and Rules: No mechanized vehicles or mountain bikes are allowed in this wilderness.

Further Information: Bureau of Land Management, 21605 North 7th Avenue, Phoenix, AZ; 623-580-5500.

Other Areas of Interest

You can see Lake Pleasant from high points along the trails in the wilderness. You can see it up close if you take Castle Hot Springs Road to the Lake Pleasant Regional Park entrance about a mile north of Arizona 74.

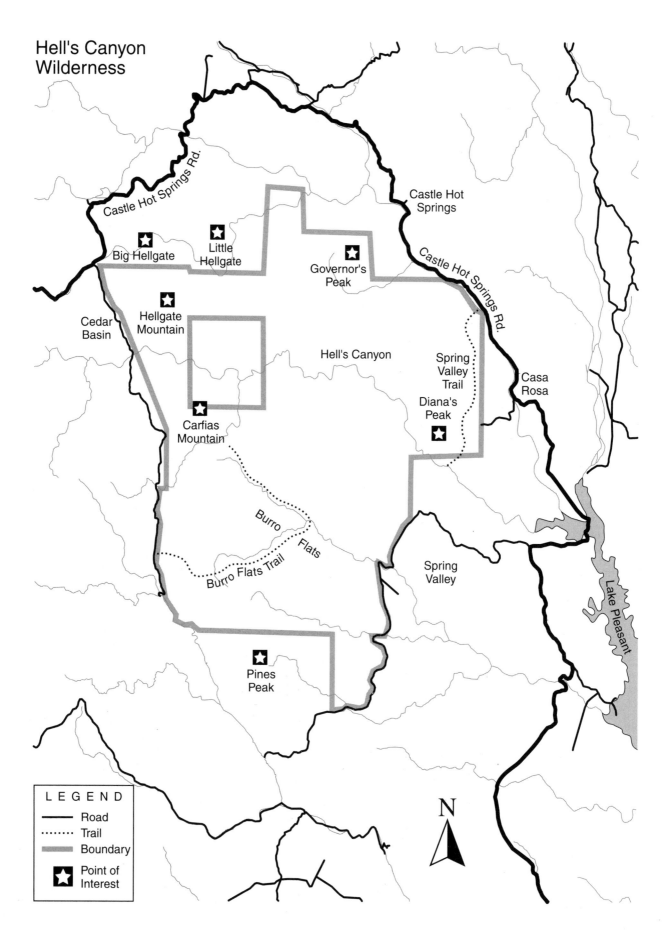

Hell's Canyon
Wilderness

Castle Hot Springs Rd.

Big Hellgate

Little
Hellgate

Castle Hot
Springs

Governor's
Peak

Castle Hot Springs Rd.

Cedar
Basin

Hellgate
Mountain

Hell's Canyon

Spring
Valley
Trail

Casa
Rosa

Diana's
Peak

Carfias
Mountain

Burro   Flats

Burro Flats Trail

Spring
Valley

Lake Pleasant

Pines
Peak

LEGEND
—— Road
······ Trail
—— Boundary
⭐ Point of
Interest

N

Burro Flats Trail 👢 👢 👢

Distance Round-Trip: 6 miles

Estimated Hiking Time: 3 hours

Elevation: 2,640 to 2,920 feet

Maps: USGS Governors Peak

Best Time to Hike: November through April

Caution: The trail has no signage and occasionally requires route-finding skills.

Directions: On Castle Hot Springs Road, drive 0.9 mile and veer left; drive 4.2 miles to unmarked Cedar Basin Road and turn south (left); drive 3.2 miles to the unmarked trailhead on the east side of the road. You will need a four-wheel-drive vehicle on Cedar Basin Road.

The trail starts on an old road **[1]**, faint in the beginning, traveling a landscape that dips and heaves between a network of washes. After climbing its first hill, the trail gives you a view of significant trail landmarks: a looming mesa on the north side of the path, and the rounded "3651 Mountain," the wilderness' highest peak, directly to the east.

The path heads east along an erosion-torn drainage. The trail watches how the drainage, about 100 feet below, digs into ruddy bedrock and then bends south, finally parting company with the trail.

The trail continues heading east, and coasts into a basin at about mile 0.75, then meets the drainage again. During wet weather, the areas near the drainage may have thick vegetation that you should walk through with caution. If you have a hiking stick, poke ahead of you to check for snakes.

At about mile 1.4, the canyon narrows. Eroded volcanic tuff outcroppings surround the path and create a wild and remote atmosphere. The trail crosses over to the south side of the drainage. Watch for a prominent outcropping right along the south side of the trail. It has several jagged knobs and the tiniest arch on its north edge.

Just past the outcropping, at about mile 1.5, the trail overlooks a precipitous slope. A bit farther, the path drops to the canyon floor. The trail wavers back and forth across the drainage again, then finally settles on the south side of the drainage until it reaches Lucifer's Gate **[2]** at about mile 2. The trail zigzags across the drainage once more, following cairns as it picks through the rocky crossings, and eventually heads north across Burro Flats.

At about mile 2.3, the trail follows cairns across a meadow, then rises and falls over the flats' rolling terrain **[3]**. A thick forest of saguaro cactus spreads across the flats. During the spring, poppies and owl clover dot a grassy cover.

A moderate climb up a red-hued hill gives you a look at Horse Creek to the north just below a golden rockwall. Another climb has the trail paralleling a jagged ridge on the southern trailside. If you hike during the spring, you may smell the perfumed yellow blossoms on bush penstemon.

The trail drops to its end into Horse Creek **[4]**. You may continue on the Horse Creek Trail 1.5 miles back to Cedar Basin Road, then head south 1 mile to your vehicle; or you may return the way you came.

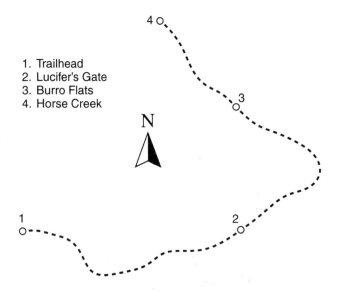

1. Trailhead
2. Lucifer's Gate
3. Burro Flats
4. Horse Creek

Spring Valley Trail 🥾 🥾 🥾

Distance Round-Trip: 4 miles

Estimated Hiking Time: 2 hours

Elevation: 1,800 to 1,920 feet

Maps: USGS Governors Peak

Directions: Drive 5.2 miles on Castle Hot Springs Road to a stop sign, then turn northwest (left); drive 5.2 miles to a signpost marked "Trail" just north of a cattle guard and under a power line. Park, then cross Castle Creek (normally dry) to the trail directly opposite the "Trail" signpost along the road.

As you cross the Castle Creek drainage to its west bank, head directly across from the trail sign near the parking area to hook up with the trail. The trail begins on the west bank at a metal registry **[1]**, then immediately climbs out of the drainage onto a ridge. When the trail tops out, take a moment to look at the jagged reddish-brown ridgelines all around. The wild topography adds to the hike's remote atmosphere.

At about mile 0.5, the trail parallels a wall of golden volcanic tuff on its left **[2]**, then begins a pattern of traveling up and down low ridges separated by drainages. During March, after a wet winter, spreads of owl clover and Mexican gold poppies lay carpets of color on the hillsides.

At mile 1.2, after teetering across a narrow rise between a tank and a wash, twisting into a wash, and picking through a rocky slope, the trail enters a small basin at the bottom of a ruddy ridge etched by erosion. Healthy colonies of saguaro cacti deck its slope.

Following its typical pattern, the trail runs up and down ridges, taking breathers in small basins. At mile 1.6, the trail tops a ridge that gives you a stunning panorama of Garfias Canyon **[3]**, a major east-west drainage in the wilderness. Bold volcanic mountains spread across the western horizon. Lake Pleasant shimmers behind you in the east. As the trail tumbles down the rocky slope into the canyon, golden outcroppings jut from the ruddy mountain walls, and saguaro cacti march down from the mountaintop across the trail.

The trail lands on a grassy bench filled with mesquite trees. After a short meander through the trees, the path ends at the canyon's streambed **[4]**. You may continue up the canyon for another 6.5 miles to the Garfias Wash Trailhead, or return the way you came.

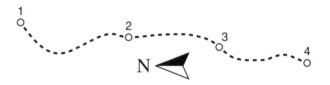

1. Trailhead
2. Volcanic wall
3. View of Garfias Canyon
4. Canyon floor

16. Lake Pleasant Regional Park

- Hike desert trails overlooking cool lake waters.
- Picnic under lakeside ramadas.
- Fish for eight different species of fish in secluded lake coves.

Area Information

Before the Waddell Dam was built across the Agua Fria River in 1925, the Sonoran Desert landscape's sear demeanor prevailed along the riverbanks. The river only flowed after rains and snowmelt, when its crystal clear water skipped along the bouldered riverbed and swirled in pools. As the water receded, pools stagnated with algae and the free flow of water turned to greasy muck.

Making a living in the volcanic mountains along the river demanded much from those who tried. Prospectors had their work cut out for them in the wild and rugged river drainage in their search for precious minerals. Numerous prospecting holes in the lower Agua Fria, near Lake Pleasant, tell about prospectors' vain search for gold.

If mining made a hard occupation on the Agua Fria, eking out a living fell right behind. The lower Agua Fria drew the down-and-out during the Depression, because the National Homestead Act of 1862 allowed people to own a tract of land. However, they not only had to live there, but had to cultivate the practically untamable turf for five years. Government inspectors visiting the homesteaders often winked at their farming attempts.

Since the completion of the New Waddell Dam (in 1995, to replace the Waddell Dam riddled with vertical cracks), the Agua Fria now pools with the Colorado River water via the Central Arizona Canal into gorgeous Lake Pleasant. The hard life of the pre-dam days of profitless prospecting and hardscrabble farming has been replaced by recreation.

Sweat equity goes into boating, fishing, swimming, biking, and hiking. Water sports reign in the late spring to early fall. Hiking and biking (unless you plan to hike to the lake to take a swim) are best done in late fall through early spring, when mild temperatures prevail. As soothing as the lake makes the desert seem, make sure you wear sun protection and watch for rattlesnakes and scorpions.

Directions: The park is located about 30 miles north of Phoenix. Take Interstate 17 north to the Carefree Highway exit and turn left (west) onto Arizona 79; drive 10.6 miles to Castle Hot Springs Road and turn right; drive 2.1 miles to Lake Pleasant Regional Park.

Hours Open: No restrictions.

Facilities: Campgrounds, semideveloped campsites, lakeside camping, boat launch, marina, visitors center, gift shop, hiking trails.

Permits and Rules:
- Maricopa County charges a $5-per-vehicle admission fee.
- Quiet hours in effect from 10 P.M. to 6 A.M.
- Pets must be leashed.
- No glass bottles allowed.

Further Information: Lake Pleasant Regional Park, 41835 N. Castle Hot Springs Road, Morristown, AZ 85342; 928-501-1702.

Other Areas of Interest

The Pioneer Arizona Museum, located 12 miles north of Phoenix off Interstate 17, gives you a look into the lifestyle of pioneers in the 1880s.

Pipeline Canyon Trail 🥾 🥾 🥾

Distance Round-Trip: 3.6 miles

Estimated Hiking Time: 2 hours

Elevation: 1,702 to 1,920 feet

Maps: USGS Governors Peak

Caution: The trail is closed at Dirty Shirt Cove (unless you care to swim the cove) during high water in the early summer months. Installation of a bridge is planned for the near future.

Directions: Drive on North Park Road about 3 miles to the southern trailhead. To arrange a shuttle at the northern trailhead, continue on North Park Road to its end.

Pipeline Canyon, a side canyon of the Agua Fria River now pooled into Lake Pleasant by the Waddell Dam, hooks into the lake after taking a meandering path through the desert. The Pipeline Canyon Trail follows part of its convoluted path to its end at Lake Pleasant. Even though the trail traverses a sear desert landscape, the hike takes on an interesting personality from the mix of azure lake water, volcanic cliffs, and saguaro cactus forests along the path.

The trail starts on a hilltop **[1]**, peering into the rugged and twisted route of Pipeline Canyon. It then cuts across a west-facing slope that fills with wildflowers after a wet winter: magenta owl clover, blue Coulter's lupine, yellow brittlebush, and Mexican gold poppies.

At mile 0.1, the trail enters a saguaro forest. These cacti bloom in May, when temperatures usually run too hot for a daytime hike. If you want to see the saguaros in bloom, take an early morning or sunset hike to beat the heat and to get the best look at the blossoms. The flowers start to open in the late afternoon, then remain open for 24 hours. Dawn and dusk will allow you to see them at their fullest before they wither with the daylight.

The trail follows Pipeline Canyon as it curls below, veering east around a bend toward the lake and plodding along the slope's north face. The path makes a gradual descent to Dirty Shirt Cove **[2]**. At about mile 0.5, the trail crosses the cove and continues heading north with the canyon. The path curves away from Lake Pleasant at about mile 0.8 and travels between two ridgelines.

The trail rises and falls with the rumpled desert terrain, scraping against piles of basalt boulders and watching forests of saguaro cacti marching up the eastern ridgeline. At mile 1.5, the trail drops into a wash **[3]**, then winds around inside it. Watch for desert lavender bushes that like to hang out along the drainage bottom.

You can see the lake once again when the trail leaves the wash behind and starts to drop downhill to the northern trailhead. If you haven't arranged a shuttle at the trailhead **[4]**, return the way you came.

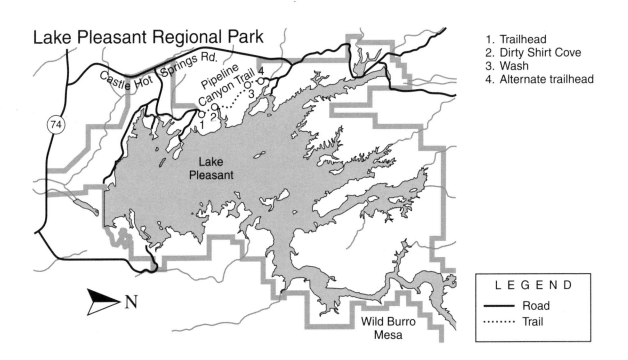

1. Trailhead
2. Dirty Shirt Cove
3. Wash
4. Alternate trailhead

Lake Pleasant Regional Park

Castle Hot Springs Rd.

Pipeline Canyon Trail

Lake Pleasant

Wild Burro Mesa

N

LEGEND
—— Road
········ Trail

17. Cave Creek Recreation Area

- Hike trails with a remote atmosphere right next to Arizona's largest city.
- See decades-old mine adits.
- Ride horseback on a classic Sonoran Desert landscape.

Area Information

The 2,922-acre Cave Creek Recreation Area got its name from nearby Cave Creek. The creek starts as a small stream in the hills to the northeast and flows southwesterly for 25 miles before reaching the next-door town of Paradise Valley south of the recreation area. The stream got its name from an overhanging bluff that forms a wide cavern right around the town of Cave Creek.

While Cave Creek flows east of the recreation area, Apache Wash cuts right through it. The wet-weather drainage carves scenic chasms in the rugged mountains. The name *Apache* comes from one of the tribes of Indians that lived in the area, the Tonto Apaches.

The Tonto Apaches held a notorious reputation. They had an unpredictable nature that made them difficult to capture. But the Cavalry did quell the Indians. About the time they did, mining came on the scene.

A remarkable variety of minerals brought prospectors to the area, which precipitated the development of dozens of mines. Earlier prospectors scratched for higher minerals, like gold, silver, and copper, but ended up digging for whatever they could find. Hikers will come across an occasional mine while hiking on park trails. The Maricopa County Park District does not allow entry into any of these mines. Fences and warning signs restrict any approach to the adits.

Though most of the mines in the area never paid off, a clay mine just west of the Go John Trail did. Lelia Pearl Irish claimed her mine in 1946 and marketed its clay powder as an elixir for good health under the Mineral Springs label. A spoonful of Mineral Springs clay in a glass of water held the promise of a cure for mankind's ailments.

Eleven miles of trails network around the recreation area for hiking, mountain biking, and horseback riding. Trails vary in length (from 2 to 4.8 miles) and in difficulty (from easy to difficult). Winter is the best time to hike the trails, but morning hikes in the warmer months work well, too.

Directions: Cave Creek Recreation Area is located about 15 miles north of Phoenix. Take Interstate 17 to the Carefree Highway exit; drive east to 32nd Street and turn north (left); drive 1.5 miles to the park entrance.

Hours Open: Park hours are 6 A.M. to 8 P.M. Sunday through Thursday, and 6 A.M. to 10 P.M. Friday and Saturday. Trails close at sunset.

Facilities: Washrooms with showers, RV camping, camping, horse staging area, picnic areas.

Permits and Rules:

- Maricopa County charges a $3-per-vehicle-entry fee, or $1 per person for entry on foot, horseback, or bicycle.
- Camping permits are necessary, and range from $8 to $15 per night.
- Dogs must be leashed.
- Firearms are not allowed in the park.
- Fires are allowed only in designated areas.

Further Information: Cave Creek Recreation Area, 37019 N. Lava Lane, Cave Creek, AZ 85331; 623-465-0431.

Other Areas of Interest

The Pioneer Arizona Museum, located 12 miles north of Phoenix off Interstate 17, gives you a look into the lifestyle of pioneers in the 1880s.

Go John Trail 👢 👢 👢

Distance Round-Trip: 4.8 miles

Estimated Hiking Time: 2.5 hours

Elevation: 2,150 to 3,000 feet

Maps: USGS Cave Creek

Caution: Do not enter the mines along the trail.

Directions: From the park entrance, drive 1 mile and turn left (north) onto Tonalita Drive; continue 0.2 mile to the signed trailhead. Follow the signs 1 mile to the signed trailhead.

The Go John Trail, named for the peak just east of the mountain it contours, travels a loop through a rugged landscape full of the charm and untamed beauty of the Sonoran Desert [1]. Heading east on the loop, the trail dips in and out of several gulches in a short span. At mile 0.3, the trail intersects with the Jasper Trail [2]. Continue straight on the Go John Trail.

As it climbs out of a draw, the trail bends to the left, climbs a bit, rests a little, then continues uphill. At the top of the hill, you can see Black Mountain poke its dark head between eastern peaks. Just ahead, the trail passes through a scattering of quartz. The mountains in the recreation area are networked with veins of quartz. Quartz was one of several

indicators prospectors considered when scouting for gold. At one time the area had over 50 mines.

The trail begins a long, gradual venture down the eastern face of the mountain, where the vegetation turns shrubby with jojoba, ratany, and fairy duster bushes. At about mile 2, the trail bends to the left and starts its ramble on the backside of the mountain [3]. A cozy remoteness surrounds the trail as all sights and sounds of the civilized world disappear and the Sonoran Desert wraps itself around the path.

Several mine shafts appear along the north face, where miners searched for higher minerals like gold, silver, and copper. However, they settled for the jasper, chrysocolla, and cinnabar the mines produced. Hikers are not allowed entry into any of the mines along the trail or hillsides. Fences and warning signs restrict approach to the adits.

A forest of saguaro cacti covers the hillsides along this section. In order to see their milky white blossoms, which appear in May, you should hike in the early morning.

By mile 3.7, the trail starts another gradual drop into a wash, then veers left into the shadow of canyon walls. The trail makes a long, steep climb out of the wash, topping out on a ridge at about mile 4.2. The ridgetop shows an almost 360-degree view [4]. Then the path drops sharply down the other side through another shrubby mix and lands back at the trailhead and your vehicle.

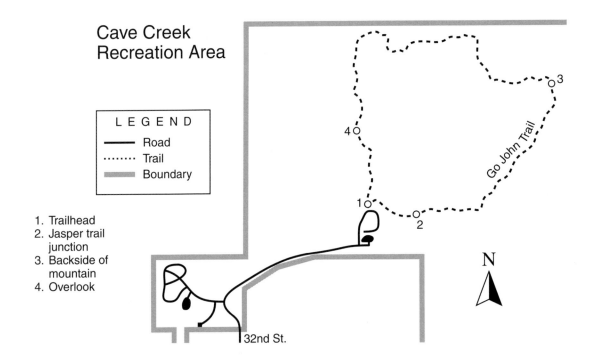

Cave Creek
Recreation Area

LEGEND
— Road
····· Trail
▬▬ Boundary

1. Trailhead
2. Jasper trail
   junction
3. Backside of
   mountain
4. Overlook

Go John Trail

32nd St.

N

18. White Tank Mountain Regional Park

- Hike in a remote county park trail system next to Phoenix.
- View petroglyphs etched by Hohokam Indians.
- Ride trails especially built for mountain bikers.

Area Information

The White Tank Mountain Regional Park, the largest of the Maricopa County parks, has 26,337 acres lying west of Phoenix. The freestanding White Tank Mountains, with their ragged ridges vaulting from the desert floor 1,400 feet to just over 4,000 feet above sea level, divide the eastward Phoenix Basin from the western Hassayampa Plain. The inner folds of the range have deeply carved canyons.

The mountains get their name from a natural process created by floodwaters. Occasional heavy rains pushed flash flood waters through the canyons and onto the plain. The torrents tumbled down chutes and dropped off ledges as they raged through the mountain. Along the way, they have scoured out a series of depressions, or *tanks,* in the white granite rock.

These tanks played an integral part in attracting the Hohokam Indians who lived in the mountains from 500 to 1100 A.D. Eleven archaeological sites have been identified in the regional park, mostly lying in canyons. The sites include sherd areas and villages.

The Archaeological Resource Protection Act and state antiquity laws protect ancient and historic ruins. Anyone found excavating, collecting, defacing, or removing an artifact can be fined $500 to $250,000 and imprisoned up to five years. If you see a relic from a historic or ancient culture, you may inspect it, but you may not take it.

Lying in a desert life zone, the regional park is best hiked from November through March. Desert tem-peratures exceed 100 degrees in the summer. No matter what time of the year you hike the park, take plenty of water and wear sunscreen and a hat.

Directions: The park is located 15 miles west of Peoria on West Olive Avenue.

Hours Open: 6 A.M. to 8 P.M. Sunday through Thursday, and 6 A.M. to 10 P.M. Friday and Saturday.

Facilities: RV camping, camping, washrooms, picnic areas, horse staging area, visitors center. A multiple-use 10-mile competitive track allows challenging, strenuous, high-speed outdoor recreation. The tracks are designed for cross-country runners and joggers, fast bicyclists and racers, and trotting/galloping equestrians and endurance riders.

Permits and Rules:
- Maricopa County charges a $3-per-vehicle entry fee, or $1 per person for entry on foot, horseback, or bicycle.
- Camping permits are required. Cost of permits ranges from $2 to $15 per night.
- Dogs must be leashed.
- Firearms are not allowed in the park.
- Fires are allowed only in designated areas.

Further Information: White Tank Mountain Regional Park, P.O. Box 91, Waddell, AZ 85355; 623-935-2505.

Other Areas of Interest

The city of Glendale, located 10 miles east of the mountains, makes an interesting stop. You can visit the 100-year old Sahuaro Ranch or the Bead Museum, then shop for antiques (Glendale is known as Arizona's antique capital). For more information, call 623-930-2957.

Waterfall Trail 👢 👢 👢

Distance Round-Trip: 2 miles

Estimated Hiking Time: 1 hour

Elevation: 1,520 to 1,700 feet

Maps: USGS White Tank Mountains

Caution: The second half of the trail is difficult, with steep grades and loose rocky surfaces that can be a challenge for inexperienced hikers.

Directions: From the park entrance, drive 2 miles to Waterfall Canyon Road, then turn west (left); drive 0.5 mile to the parking area.

The Waterfall Trail, known for its panels of Hohokam rock art and a 30-foot waterfall at its end, provides a scenic route to view a blend of nature and culture. The trail starts [1] on a barrier-free tread and has several benches on which to rest or just relax and take in the quintessential Sonoran Desert landscape filled with paloverde trees, bursage bushes, and a variety of cacti.

The Hohokam rock art begins at about mile 0.4 in an area called Petroglyph Plaza [2]. About 200 petroglyphs are visible on an assortment of panels around the trail. The Hohokams etched the panels by chiseling through the dark-colored desert varnish down to the natural light gray color of the park's granite rocks. Archaeologists believe the panels were a means of communication depicting what the Indians saw and what they wanted, as if they were illustrating a prayer or a desire.

Several benches gather around a mound of boulders filled with rock art at mile 0.5. This marks the end of the barrier-free segment of this trail. From here, the trail bends north, then starts its climb up the canyon.

The path parallels a boulder-filled wash, then swings away from it back toward a bouldered canyon slope on the opposite side of the wash. Watch for more panels of rock art pecked on the boulders jumbled along the slope. At about mile 0.75, the trail once again looks inside the wash, then climbs to a natural platform filled with rock art [3].

The last section of trail hops on, and squeezes through, a jumble of rocks and boulders [4]. As it nears the crook of the canyon, the path becomes shadier and moister. The spindly bushes hanging on the erosion-smoothed walls are Bigelow ragged rock flower.

The trail curls into the chasm and ends at a ribbon of a waterfall that splatters down the smooth silver- and toast-colored wall of granite into a pool [5]. Return the way you came.

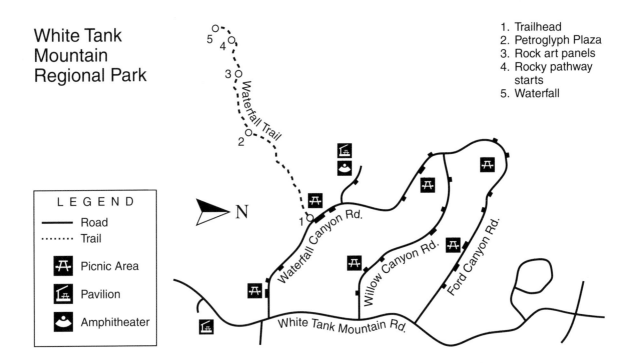

White Tank
Mountain
Regional Park

1. Trailhead
2. Petroglyph Plaza
3. Rock art panels
4. Rocky pathway starts
5. Waterfall

Waterfall Trail

N

LEGEND
—— Road
······· Trail
🏕 Picnic Area
🏛 Pavilion
🎭 Amphitheater

Waterfall Canyon Rd.
Willow Canyon Rd.
Ford Canyon Rd.
White Tank Mountain Rd.

19. South Mountain Park

- Hike along the spine of a mountain range.
- Visit the largest municipal park in the United States.
- View ancient petroglyphs.

Area Information

The nation's largest municipal park has some of the most unique natural and historical features found in a city. Hidden Valley has a curious collection of boulders strewn around the ground. Fat Man's Pass has you squeezing through a fissure formed by water. Petroglyphs inscribed by Hohokam Indians appear all around the park. And the Marcos de Niza Rock is said to have explorer Father Marcos de Niza's inscription on it claiming the area for Spain.

The 16,500-acre park has three parallel ranges that spread across its boundaries with 61 miles of trails for horseback riding, hiking, and mountain biking. The higher (and older) western end is composed of gneiss and is said to be 1.7 billion years old. The eastern end of the mountains is intrusive granite. Desert varnish, a dark patina formed by minerals and microorganisms, appears to cover the rocks like paint. The mountains contain gold that attracted prospectors who left testimony to their presence by a number of mines dug in the mountainsides.

You might see an assortment of reptilian inhabitants in the park, such as desert tortoises, rattlesnakes, Gila monsters, horned lizards, geckos, and chuckwallas. And you can usually catch a glimpse of a fleeing jackrabbit, cottontail rabbit, or ground squirrel.

Occasionally you might see mice, ringtailed cats, coyotes, javelina, and kit foxes.

Located in the lower Sonoran Desert, the park feels scorching temperatures in the summer. The best time for hiking runs from late fall to early spring; early morning hikes are best during the summer.

Directions: Located approximately 10 miles south of downtown Phoenix on Central Avenue.

Hours Open: The park opens every day at 5:00 A.M. and closes at 11 P.M. Road access to the mountaintop closes at 9:00 P.M.

Facilities: Picnic areas, horse staging area, washrooms, activity complex, South Mountain Environmental Education Center.

Permits and Rules:
- Dogs must be leashed.
- Fires allowed only in designated areas.
- No camping allowed in the park.

Further Information: South Mountain Park, 10919 S. Central Avenue, Phoenix, AZ 85040; 602-534-6324.

Other Areas of Interest

Visit the Department of Mines and Minerals in downtown Phoenix to learn about some of the mines in the South Mountains. For more information, call 602-255-3795. You can learn about the Indians who lived in the park at the Heard Museum, also in downtown Phoenix. For more information, call 602-252-8344.

South Mountain Park

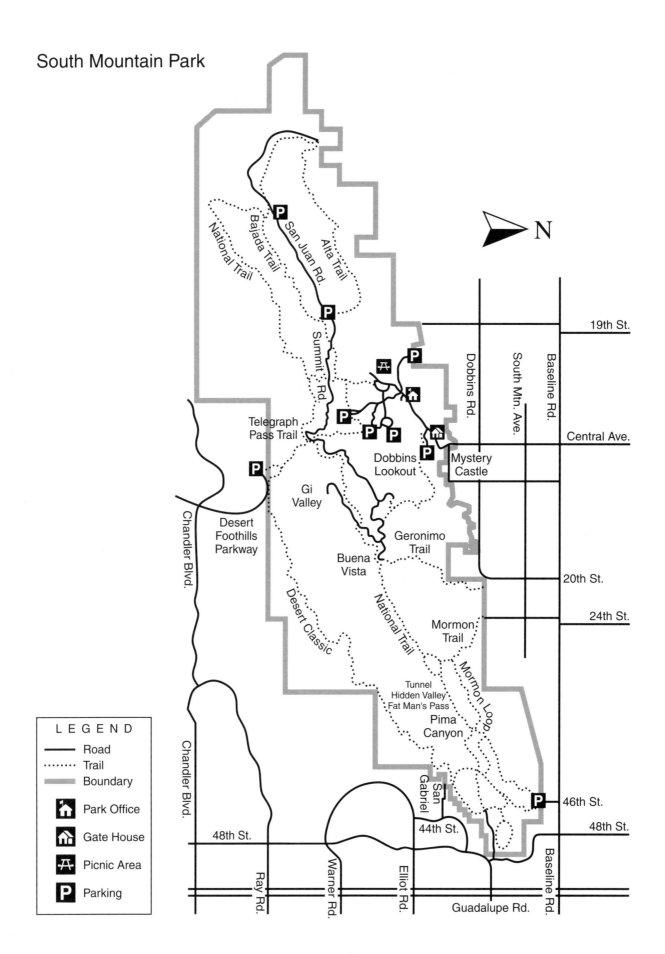

LEGEND

— Road
...... Trail
━━ Boundary
🏠 Park Office
🏠 Gate House
🛆 Picnic Area
P Parking

National Trail
Bajada Trail
San Juan Rd.
Alta Trail
Summit Rd.
Telegraph Pass Trail
Gi Valley
Desert Foothills Parkway
Chandler Blvd.
Desert Classic
Buena Vista
Dobbins Lookout
Geronimo Trail
National Trail
Mormon Trail
Mormon Loop
Tunnel
Hidden Valley
Fat Man's Pass
Pima Canyon
San Gabriel
Dobbins Rd.
South Mtn. Ave.
Baseline Rd.
Mystery Castle
Chandler Blvd.
Ray Rd.
Warner Rd.
Elliot Rd.
Guadalupe Rd.
Baseline Rd.
48th St.
44th St.
46th St.
48th St.
24th St.
20th St.
Central Ave.
19th St.

N

Bajada Loop 👢 👢 👢

Distance Round-Trip: 8 miles

Estimated Hiking Time: 4 hours

Elevation: 1,460 to 2,526 feet

Maps: USGS Lone Butte

Caution: Sections of this hike descend steep grainy sections of trail that may compromise your footing.

Directions: Drive west on San Juan Road 1 mile to the Five Tables Picnic Area; turn left and park in the parking area on the right.

In the early 1970s, the trail that runs the length of South Mountain Park and a segment of the 130-mile Sun Circle Trail that circles the Phoenix metro area was designated as a National Recreation Trail in the National Trail System. This trail, named the National Trail, runs from one end of the park to the other, curling around the western end of the range.

The National Trail runs 14.3 miles, and would take a shuttle to comfortably hike. This route takes you up the Ranger Trail to the western, and higher, section of the National Trail to far-reaching vistas and past several mines, then loops with the Bajada Trail on the lower slopes of the range.

The Ranger Trail, where this hike begins **[1]**, was named by a ranger for the rangers in South Mountain Park. The trail gets an easy start on a flat course on the desert floor. By about mile 0.3, near the junction with the Bajada Trail, the trail begins its 1,100-foot climb up the Gila Range **[2]**.

Gangly creosote bushes; hedgehog, barrel, and saguaro cacti; and ironwood and paloverde trees fill the rising landscape; the city of Phoenix sprawls in the distant north. At about mile 0.5, the trail takes a hairpin right to meet the Summit Road that winds to the mountaintop **[3]**.

After you cross the road, watch for a colony of brittlebush and cholla cactus that gathers around the trail and continues with the trail as it climbs its way to the mountain's ridgeline. The brittlebush will bloom yellow daisy flowers around March. The cholla has a habit of breaking off in small sections covered with inch-long needles that land in or near the trail. Be careful one doesn't hook onto you as you pass.

The last quarter-mile on the Ranger Trail makes several switchbacks to its end at its intersection with the National Trail on top of the ridge at mile 1.4. Turn right onto the National Trail **[4]**.

The National Trail treads along the spine of the mountain, giving you fabulous views to the south. At about mile 3.4, the trail starts to rise and fall over

intermittent peaks while gradually dropping. The trail flips over to the north side of the ridge for a while to give you a change of view.

When the trail switches back to the south side of the ridge, watch for mine adits, remnants from when prospectors burrowed for gold, that gape along the way. The Max Delta gold mine in the South Mountains attracted prospectors to dig the mines this trail passes. The Max Delta had an extraordinarily high-grade gold, as well as silver and copper, and reaped its owners 6,000 ounces of gold, 4,000 ounces of silver, and even some copper.

At about mile 3.8, the trail starts a more serious descent. Watch your step as the trail skids down rocky segments. The path settles down as it parallels a gulch and takes its time winding down to the floor. As the trail digs into the gulch, it takes on a cozy remoteness with the mineral-smudged walls cocooning the path.

At about mile 4.5, the trail bends north, climbs up a saddle, then heads back down to the desert floor and the Bajada Trail at mile 4.75. Turn right onto the Bajada Trail **[5]**.

The slight grades and dips into shallow washes reflect the rumpled nature of a bajada, after which the trail was named. Bajadas have alluvial accumulations from runoff draining off a ridge. This porous soil becomes a cache of wildflowers after a wet winter.

At about mile 6.5, the middle of the Bajada Trail, the trail climbs up the mountain slope to its high point at 1,700 feet, then drifts back down to the San Juan Road to parallel it. At about mile 7.75, the trail brings you back to the Ranger Trail **[6]**. Turn left onto the Ranger Trail, which brings you back to the parking area and your vehicle.

1. Trailhead
2. Bajada trail junction
3. Cross Summit Road
4. National trail
5. Bajada trail
6. Ranger trail

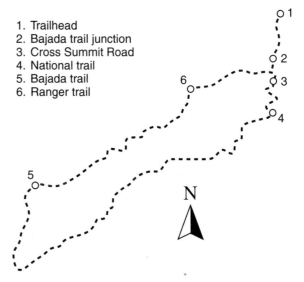

Alta Trail 🥾 🥾 🥾

Distance Round-Trip: 9 miles

Estimated Hiking Time: 4.5 hours

Elevation: 1,320 to 2,394 feet

Maps: USGS Lone Butte

Directions: From the park entrance, drive 2.5 miles on San Juan Road to the trailhead.

The Alta Trail has you climbing up the northwest ramparts of South Mountain Park. As it travels along the ridgetop, you get far-reaching views of the Phoenix Valley while experiencing the rugged and remote atmosphere of the ridge's north face.

The trail starts [1] on the desert floor as a neat path edged with hand-placed rocks. As the trail heads toward a ridge, it travels an easy rise on an almost imperceptible grade through Lower Sonoran vegetation of creosote bushes, barrel cacti, and buckhorn cholla cacti. At mile 0.3, the trail meets the base of the ridge and starts a rigorous climb. As the path climbs the south face of the ridge, watch for views to the northeast of the Four Peaks in the Mazatzal Mountains.

Brittlebush likes the rocky slopes the trail climbs, but saguaro cacti, looking for moisture, hang out in the drainage below. A stone bench cut into the trailside by the Civilian Conservation Corp at about mile 0.7 gives you a chance to rest if necessary and take in the scenery [2].

The path follows a tight pattern of switchbacks up to about mile 1, where it settles down a bit and climbs on a moderate slant. Watch for an overlook [3] at about mile 1.1 on the south side of the trail. The trail finally tops out on the ridge by about mile 1.4 and offers an extraordinary view: it looks at the jagged peaks along the ridge lined up to the west, highrises in the central corridor of Phoenix clustered in the northeast, and a patchwork of farms to the northwest.

The trail follows along the very edge of the ridgetop, switching sides from north to south and back from time to time. At about mile 1.9, the trail drops just below the ridgetop and travels along the rocky cliff on the north face [4]. The path follows the contour of the mountain, wending in and out of crevices and then cresting on peaks, all the while keeping an eye on the northern panorama.

The path finally climbs back onto the ridgetop at about mile 2.75, then starts down the south face, descending around Maricopa Peak [5]. The trail heads up the slope of Maricopa Peak as if to top it, but stays just below it. From there, the trail switchbacks down the ridge toward its alternate trailhead at the end of San Juan Road. You may take the National and Bajada (see page 71) trails back to the Alta Trail trailhead for a 9.5-mile loop, or return the way you came.

1. Trailhead
2. Stone bench
3. Overlook
4. Trail drops below ridge
5. Trail descends ridge

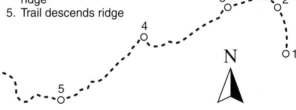

20. McDowell Mountain Preserve

- Hike scenic ridgelines in the Maricopa County park system.
- See spreads of wildflowers after a wet winter on a springtime hike.
- View the aftermath of the Rio Fire.

Area Information

When Hohokam Indians lived in the area near the confluence of the Salt and Verde rivers (until 1450 A.D.), they built a system involving farming, river irrigation, and hunting and gathering techniques. McDowell Mountain Preserve contains the remains of several such hunting and gathering sites within its boundaries.

After the Hohokam, the Apaches came. They lived under a system of hunting, gathering, and raiding. The Tonto Apaches wreaked havoc among settlers in the area, provoking the government to set up Camp McDowell a few miles southeast of the mountain park along the west bank of the Verde River in 1864. With the military presence, settlement in the valley flourished.

Maricopa County created McDowell Mountain Park in 1958 to set aside the scenic mountain area. The 21,099-acre park is considered one of the most scenic. However, a lightning strike from a dry thunderstorm on July 7, 1995, dramatically changed the looks of the lovely mountain park when it started the Rio Fire. Over 500 firefighters from Arizona, California, Nevada, New Mexico, and Idaho battled the Rio Fire in 110-degree heat.

The Rio Fire ended up turning 20,000 acres of Sonoran Desert into blackened skeletons of paloverde and mesquite trees, saguaro cactus, and jojoba bushes. The landscape is now in the process of repair and regrowth.

The park offers over 40 miles of hiking, mountain biking, and horseback riding trails that range in length from 0.5 mile to 15.3 miles, and in difficulty from easy to strenuous. The best time of the year to hike these trails is from late fall through early spring. Early morning hikes in the hotter weather, when daytime temperatures can top 110 degrees, work well, too. Be sure to bring plenty of water and wear sunscreen and a hat no matter when you hike these desert trails.

Directions: The preserve is located 15 miles northeast of Scottsdale in Fountain Hills. Take Shea Boulevard east to Fountain Hills, and turn left (north) onto Fountain Hills Boulevard; drive 4 miles through Fountain Hills, where the road changes to McDowell Mountain Road. Go another 4 miles to a signed turnoff for McDowell Mountain Regional Park entrance.

Hours Open: Park hours range from 6 A.M. to 8 P.M. Sunday through Thursday and 6 A.M. to 10 P.M. Friday and Saturday. Trails close at sunset.

Facilities: Washrooms with showers, RV camping, camping, horse staging area, picnic areas. A three-loop competitive track provides mountain bike riders, as well as joggers and equestrians, a variety of obstacles to test the riders' skills. The track has steep inclines, swooping turns, technical descents, and rugged terrain.

Permits and Rules:

- Maricopa County charges a $3-per-vehicle entry fee, or $1 per person for entry on foot, horseback, or bicycle.
- Camping permits are necessary; these cost $15 per night.
- Dogs must be leashed.
- Firearms are not allowed in the park.
- Fires are allowed only in designated areas.

Further Information: McDowell Mountain Regional Park, 15612 East Palisades Dr., Fountain Hills, AZ 85269; 480-471-0173.

Other Areas of Interest

Visit Out of Africa, a theme park in north Scottsdale just south of the McDowell Mountain Park. For more information, call 480-837-7779. The park features animals in nine unrehearsed educational shows each day.

Scenic Trail Loop 👢 👢 👢

Distance Round-Trip: 3.4 miles

Estimated Hiking Time: 2 hours

Elevation: 1,800 to 2,011 feet

Maps: USGS Fort McDowell

Caution: Summer hikes should be done in the early morning hours, with plenty of water.

Directions: From the park entrance, drive 3.3 miles to Shallmo Drive and turn right; drive .75 miles to the Pemberton trailhead.

The route starts on the Pemberton Trail **[1]**, then veers right at mile 0.1 onto the Scenic Trail. Right away, the path heads for a valley wedged between low ridgelines. Classic Sonoran Desert vegetation of saguaro and barrel cacti, bursage, and a variety of bushes that flower in the spring fills the landscape. During dry times, the bursage bushes will look like a tangle of sticks. After a decent rain, and during wet winters, the bush sprouts triangular leaves. Its lackluster green flowers can be troublesome for those with allergies.

The path weaves back and forth, and sometimes inside, a gravelly wash where brown signposts will direct you. By mile 1.2, the trail crosses the wash one more time, then rises up the rocky slope of the north ridgeline. The trail rounds the mountain to its east side at about mile 1.4, where you'll get a look at the devastation left by the Rio Fire in 1995 **[2]**.

The fire, which burned hot and quickly, burned two-thirds of the mountain park. Though the fire burned only the outside of most of the saguaro cacti, this charring weakened the saguaros. Many of the cacti succumbed to infections because of the stress of the fire. They continue to become diseased, fall, and die.

The mountain park did experience a positive result from the fire. Though covered with black snags and charred saguaro cacti, the burn area now produces beautiful spreads of wildflowers after a wet winter. This slope, in particular, gets a dramatic spread of Coulter's lupine. The pea flower blooms spread an indigo blanket across the whole slope.

The trail heads west on a comfortable climb up the mountain and gives you a look into the valley in which it started out. The trail tops out at about mile 1.6 and continues along the mountain's backbone **[3]** through a congregation of brittlebush, which produces a yellow daisy-like flower.

Before the trail veers west, take a moment to enjoy the almost 360-degree panorama surrounding you. The Weaver's Needle pokes out of the Superstition Mountains in the southeast, the Four Peaks rise in the east, the Mazatzal Mountains heave and dip like a tumultuous sea in the northeast, and Thompson Peak rises in the southwest.

The trail does a little give-and-take with the elevation following the mountain's rumpled terrain for the next half-mile, then starts its gradual descent to the valley floor, about mile 2.3. At the trail's juncture with the Pemberton Trail, about mile 2.8, turn left onto the Pemberton Trail **[4]**, which takes you back to the trailhead and your vehicle.

McDowell Mountain Preserve

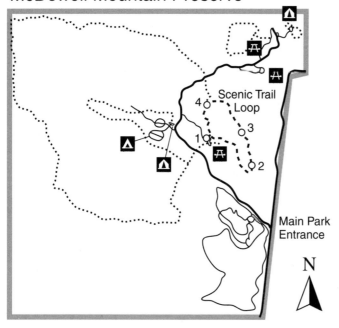

1. Trailhead
2. Rio fire
3. Mountaintop
4. Pemberton trail

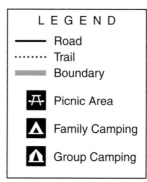

L E G E N D
——— Road
········ Trail
▬▬▬ Boundary
⛺ Picnic Area
▲ Family Camping
▲ Group Camping

21. Usery Mountain Recreation Area

- Tread land where nefarious characters hung out.
- Hike up to a wind cave.
- See exceptional views of the eastern Phoenix Basin.

Area Information

The 3,648-acre Usery Mountain Recreation Area features a quiet piece of desert on the eastern edge of the Phoenix Valley. The low-rising mountains, home to plants and animals of the Lower Sonoran Desert, create a pleasant atmosphere on the edge of the city. You would never know from its tranquil attitude that one of the West's more nefarious characters used the area as his stomping grounds at the turn of the 20th century.

King Usery, a rancher turned bank robber and horse thief, hid in this desert landscape for about 15 years. The notorious Usery lived off the land between Usery Mountain and Pass Mountain to avoid the Pinkerton Detective Agency, the investigators of choice in the old West.

The Usery Mountains have a more docile history, as well. Usery Pass provided an access for Mexican and Basque sheepherders traveling between the lowlands of the Salt River Valley to the highcountry north of Mount Baldy in the eastern end of Arizona.

The park has a compact trail system of a handful of trails ranging from 0.9 to 7.1 miles long. Each one takes you through scenic areas of the desert with varying difficulty.

The best time to hike the mountain park is from November through March. Summer temperatures reach triple digits. When you hike these trails, be sure to take plenty of water and wear sun protection, no matter how long the trail or what time of the year you hike.

Directions: Usery Mountain Recreation Area is located about 18 miles northeast of Phoenix. From Phoenix, take U.S. 60 to Ellsworth Road exit 191; drive north 6.4 miles to Usery Park Road and turn right (east) to the park entrance.

Hours Open: Park hours range from 6 A.M. to 8 P.M. Sunday through Thursday and 6 A.M. to 10 P.M. Friday and Saturday. Trails close at sunset.

Facilities: Camping, RV camping, picnic area, horse staging area, washrooms with showers, and an NFAA five-star archery range.

Permits and Rules:
- Maricopa County charges a $3-per-vehicle entry fee, or $1 per person for entry on foot, horseback, or bicycle.
- Camping permits are required; cost of permits ranges from $8 to $15 per night.
- Dogs must be leashed.
- Firearms are not allowed in the park.
- Fires are allowed only in designated areas.

Further Information: Usery Mountain Recreation Area, 3939 N. Usery Pass Road, Mesa, AZ 85207; 480-984-0032.

Other Areas of Interest

Saguaro Lake, located about 20 miles northwest of the recreation area along the Bush Highway, has fishing, boating, camping, and swimming.

Wind Cave Trail

Distance Round-Trip: 3.2 miles

Estimated Hiking Time: 3.5 hours

Elevation: 2,030 to 2,850 feet

Maps: USGS Buckhorn

Caution: Watch for bees in the wind cave.

Directions: From the park entrance, drive 1.1 miles to Wind Cave Drive and park.

The Wind Cave Trail climbs up the granite slopes of Pass Mountain to a wind cave in the strata of volcanic tuff across its top. This craggy strata of tuff gave the mountain its nickname of "Scarface."

The trail starts **[1]** on a flat, but by mile 0.25 it begins a nonstop climb up the mountain. The path looks into a couple of deep washes on either side as it starts on a reasonable grade. After a wet winter, you may see deep red flowers on chuparosa bushes and the bright orange-gold of Mexican gold poppies. You may catch a whiff of desert lavender, too.

The trail dips in and out of the wash on the left, then borders the one on the right before squeezing through basalt boulders around mile 0.5. The trail winds around more raspy basalt boulders, stepping over, atop, and around them on the way to the wind cave. At mile 0.6 the trail takes a more serious attitude toward the climb, and by mile 1 it's switchbacking up the mountain.

The path meets the mountain's face at about mile 1.3 **[2]** and walks across the rockface to the wind cave. Once the trail reaches the wind cave **[3]**, look for mabrya hanging from the walls of the cave. This vine, usually found only in central Arizona, clings to moist ledges and alcoves. Watch, too, for bees tending to their hives near seeps in the rock.

The panorama from the wind cave gives fabulous views of the valley. When you spot Usery Mountain—the mountain with "Phoenix" spelled in huge white letters with an arrow pointing toward the city—you get a better idea of where King Usery (see page 75) used to hang out. After you get through taking in the sights from the wind cave, return the way you came.

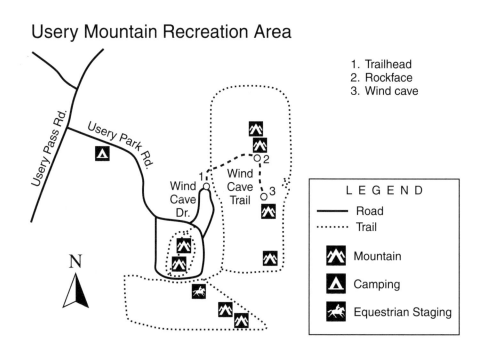

Usery Mountain Recreation Area

1. Trailhead
2. Rockface
3. Wind cave

LEGEND
——— Road
········ Trail
Mountain
Camping
Equestrian Staging

22. Superstition Mountains

- Visit mountains full of history, legends, and lore.
- Hike sections of the Arizona Trail.
- Enjoy panoramic views of a landscape formed by volcanism.

Area Information

The Superstition Mountains' attractive rough-hewn scenery and forbidding aura have created a charisma that still has some people wondering about them. Stories of people stumbling on headless skeletons, unexplained disappearances, and murders add to the mountains' mystique.

German prospector Jacob Waltz, nicknamed "the Dutchman," immortalized the mountains with tales of his Lost Dutchman's Mine. Waltz had a propensity for disappearing into the Superstition Mountains for a few weeks at a time, then reappearing in Phoenix with extraordinarily pure gold nuggets.

The Dutchman claimed an 18-inch-thick vein of gold "lies in the shadow of the Needle" (referring to a formation called the Weaver's Needle). Several people mysteriously disappeared when trying to follow Waltz to his gold source in the mountains. Though treasure seekers have searched for decades (illegally since 1964, when the Tonto National Forest stopped administering mining permits in deference to the National Wilderness Act), no one's found this phantom mine. But wars, feuds, and murders stemmed from the gold seekers' greed.

Before the Dutchman came on the scene and created fodder for most of the legends about the mountains, Apache Indians liked to hang out in the distinctive ridges. The Indians constantly wrangled with Mexican prospectors.

Now that prospecting is a thing of the past, the mountains have settled into a backyard wilderness that draws over 30,000 hikers each year. They predominantly hike the network of trails that traverse the peculiar geology formed by volcanism in the western end of the mountains. The burning ash that spewed from volcanoes 15 to 35 million years ago, scientists say, ran so hot that the ash welded together wherever it fell, creating spires, buttes, and mesas.

Three calderas formed in the mountains' western end when the volcanoes collapsed. Erosion carved their soft vulcanian rock into arches, alcoves, and caves.

The western mountains' strange terrain supports a varied flora. The quintessential Sonoran Desert vegetation fills with forests of columnar giant saguaro cacti, other assorted cacti, green paloverde trees, and ironwood trees. The eastern end of the mountains has a high desert landscape of pine and oak trees, cacti, and chaparral.

The best time to hike in the Superstition Mountains is from November through March. After a wet winter, springtime wildflowers produce prolific blooms in the lower elevations of the mountains.

As close as the mountains are to Phoenix, they still see deaths every year. Rockclimbers fall to their deaths, and inexperienced hikers get lost or, worse, die of exposure from the extreme desert heat. If you plan to hike in the Superstition Mountains, take plenty of water, stay on the trail, and don't hike farther than your level of endurance can safely handle.

Directions: The Superstition Mountains are located about 20 miles east of Phoenix near Apache Junction.

Hours Open: No restrictions.

Facilities: Horse staging areas and washrooms at some trailheads.

Permits and Rules:
- Some trailheads require a $4 pass for parking.
- Some trails are located in the Superstition Mountain Wilderness, where no mechanized vehicles or mountain bikes are allowed.
- In developed recreation sites, pets must be restrained on a leash no longer than 6 feet.
- Fireworks are prohibited.
- Fires must be attended at all times.
- Maximum stay is 14 days.
- Maximum group size is 10 people.
- The Archaeological Resource Protection Act and state antiquity laws protect ancient and historic ruins. Anyone found excavating, collecting, defacing, or removing an artifact can be fined $500 to $250,000 and imprisoned up to five years. If you see a relic from a historic or ancient culture, you may inspect it, but you may not take it.

Further Information: Mesa Ranger District, 26 North MacDonald, Mesa, AZ 85211-5800; 480-610-3300.

Other Areas of Interest

Stop at the Boyce Thompson Arboretum 13 miles east of Florence Junction to find out more about the vegetation you find in the mountains. For more information, call 520-689-2723.

Superstition Mountains

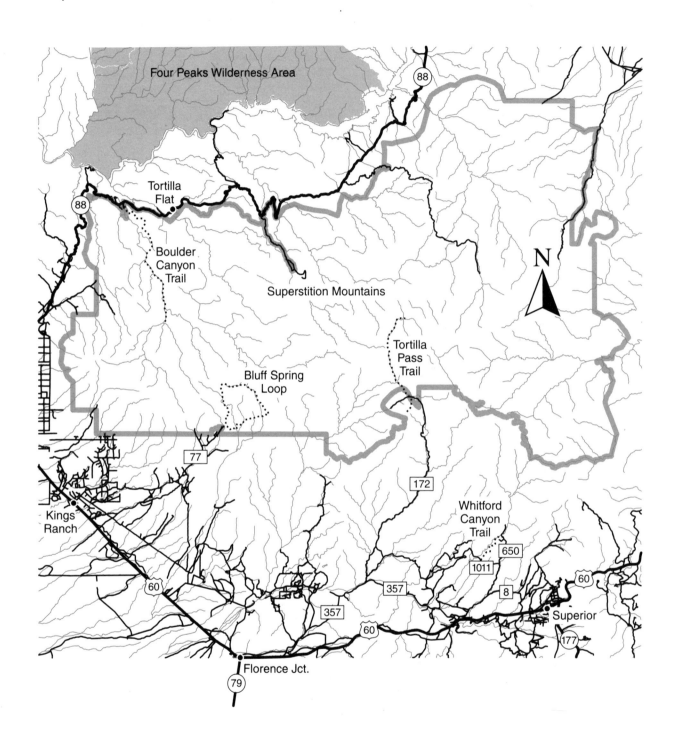

Four Peaks Wilderness Area

Tortilla Flat

88

88

Boulder Canyon Trail

Superstition Mountains

N

Tortilla Pass Trail

Bluff Spring Loop

77

172

Whitford Canyon Trail

Kings Ranch

650

1011

357

8

60

60

357

60

Superior

177

Florence Jct.

79

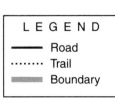

L E G E N D
— Road
······· Trail
━━ Boundary

JF-Rogers Canyon Trails to Angel Basin 👢👢👢

Distance Round-Trip: 10 miles

Estimated Hiking Time: 5 hours

Elevation: 3,250 to 4,600 feet

Maps: Tonto National Forest, USGS Iron Mountain

Directions: From Apache Junction, drive east on U.S. 60 to Queen Valley Road (about 2 miles east of Florence Junction) and turn north (left); drive 1.7 miles to Hewitt Station Road (FR 357) and turn east (right); drive 2.9 miles to FR 172 and veer north (left); drive 8.8 miles and veer west (left) toward the Woodbury Trailhead; drive 1.1 miles and turn north (right); drive 0.3 miles to the trailhead. High clearance vehicle recommended.

Heading north on the JF Trail **[1]**, the hike immediately climbs up a hill with a landscape on the verge of transitioning into the high desert vegetation so familiar to the eastern Superstition Mountains—barberry and catclaw bushes, prickly pear and saguaro cacti, and mesquite and juniper trees. The trail settles down to contour the rounded mountainside, then drops down to the Woodbury Trail **[2]** at about mile 0.5.

A metal windmill shines in the sunlight just north of this intersection. A tank may have cows milling around it. The JF Trail veers left along the northern edge of the tank, then follows along Randolph Canyon. At about mile 0.9, where a sign announces the Superstition Wilderness **[3]**, the path heads into a colony of sugar sumac bushes. The bushes' pink flowers bloom in February and March, then develop into berries. Indians used the fruit as a sweetener.

A couple of drainage crossings at about mile 1.5 have the trail rubbing shoulders with giant saguaro cacti. You might spot a cactus wren poking its head from a hole in a saguaro, or you might hear its grinding cry. Later, near Angel Basin, you might hear the raspy voice of the Stellar's jay.

The trail starts up a mile-and-a-half climb alongside an unnamed drainage to Tortilla Pass, taking a breather on a brief flat stretch at mile 1.7. When it

does level a bit, take a moment to peruse the panoramas of the ridgelines up close and mountains in the distance. Look for several rock arches and windows on a ridge northeast of the trail.

At about mile 3, the trail reaches Tortilla Pass **[4]** and intersects with the Rogers Canyon Trail. Continue north on the Rogers Canyon Trail.

The path climbs up a ridge to the head of another unnamed drainage and a panoramic view of where the trail will take you—Angel Basin in Rogers Canyon. You might notice the original trail blocked by branches on the right. It used to skid manically into the canyon. The reengineered trail safely takes its time switchbacking into the canyon. When it finishes the steep descent, about mile 4, the trail continues on a gradual descent to Angel Basin.

At about mile 4.5, the path picks through a streambed that has water during wet weather, weaving around erosion-chewed outcroppings. Watch for an arch just below the trail on the right. The last half-mile of the trail scrapes through several catclaw colonies; be careful of their thorns.

This hike ends when the trail enters Angel Basin **[5]**, a flat meadow surrounded by undulating golden volcanic cliffs. The stream in Rogers Canyon may have water, but you need to purify it if you plan to drink it. From Angel Basin, you may return the way you came, explore up the canyon on the Frog Tanks Trail, or head south on the Rogers Canyon Trail.

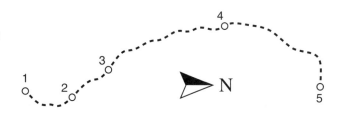

1. Trailhead
2. Woodbury trail junction
3. Wilderness boundary
4. Tortilla Pass
5. Angel Basin

Whitford Canyon 🥾 🥾

Distance Round-Trip: 3 miles

Estimated Hiking Time: 1.5 hours

Elevation: 2,500 to 2,700 feet

Maps: Tonto National Forest, USGS Superior

Caution: If you hike the canyon to see the saguaro cacti bloom in May, hike in the early morning to avoid the extreme heat typical of that time of the year.

Directions: Take U.S. 60 east toward Superior to just past mile marker 222; turn north (left) onto Hewitt Station Road, then immediately turn east (right) onto FR 8; drive 1.7 miles to a fork, then veer left onto FR 650; drive 2.8 miles to the trail access (look for a brown signpost on the left side of the road).

The Whitford Canyon section of the Arizona Trail, the approximately 800-mile-long trail that travels the length of Arizona, has a reputation as one of the most scenic sections of the central part of the trail. This hike travels a pretty pocket inside the Superstition Mountains where saguaro forests cover peach-tinged canyon walls and an ephemeral crystal stream skips under canopies of cottonwood trees.

The route starts **[1]** as you step off the road onto a grassy bench. Foot-high cairns lead you past a cross wash right into the canyon. The canyon walls take a ruddy tinge and squeeze together, forcing the path onto the canyon floor.

If you hike in March after a wet winter, dozens of species of wildflowers line the trailsides of the canyon. But even in the dry years, look for the plant canaigre, which looks much like its alternate name of wild rhubarb with its curly dock leaves and red stems.

A thick saguaro cactus forest spreads a prickly band on the canyon wall north of the stream. You can catch their creamy-white blossoms on an early morning hike in May.

When the trail crosses the stream **[2]** at about mile 0.25, look for a stone foundation—perhaps a prospector's or rancher's remnant—on the left just before you make the crossing. Once across the creek,

the trail pulls away from the shady stream habitat and enters the sun-soaked saguaro forest. This brushy section of trail has a variety of desert vegetation: jojoba bushes have oval leaves, bursage long triangular toothed leaves, and brittlebush smaller, sage-toned triangle leaves. You may smell the lanky desert lavender bush here, too.

The trail weaves back and forth across the stream a few times before sticking to the south side at about mile 0.4, passing through a mesquite bosque. Cottonwood trees stick streamside, and saguaro cacti stay on the slopes.

After two quick stream crossings, the trail starts up the northern slope **[3]** about mile 1. Cholla cacti mix with saguaro cacti as the path climbs the maroon-colored cliff chewed by erosion. The trail watches how the stream snakes along the canyon floor 100 feet below for a moment, then takes its time making its way back down to the canyon floor next to the stream again.

By mile 1.4, the trail crosses the stream and heads up the south ridge. An old unmarked mining road signals the end of this hike. When you reach the road, you may continue on the Arizona Trail, or return the way you came.

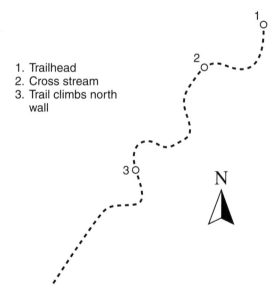

1. Trailhead
2. Cross stream
3. Trail climbs north wall

N

Boulder Canyon Trail 👢 👢 👢

Distance Round-Trip: 14.6 miles

Estimated Hiking Time: 7.5 hours

Elevation: 1,680 to 2,300 feet

Maps: Tonto National Forest, USGS Horse Mesa and Weavers Needle

Cautions: Minor route-finding skills are required for the second half of the trail. Hikers intent on going the trail's full length should plan an early start so they can finish before sunset during the shorter days of winter.

Directions: At Apache Junction, turn north on Arizona 88 and drive 15.8 miles to the trailhead across from the Canyon Lake Marina. Park in the marina parking lot at signs marked "Trailhead Parking." The parking lot closes from dusk to dawn.

The Boulder Canyon Trail immediately starts climbing up a ridge **[1]**, the east wall of La Barge Canyon that rises alongside of Canyon Lake. The lake is one of the string of reservoirs formed by damming the Salt River. The trail peers into the inlet of water into which La Barge Creek drains. After a mile-long climb, the trail rests at a viewpoint **[2]** showing off the tempestuous topography of the Superstitions to the south and the Four Peaks to the north.

The trail continues along a ragged ridgeline and eventually drops into La Barge Canyon. By about mile 3, the trail climbs up a pass **[3]** that opens up a route to the neighboring Boulder Canyon. Before the trail drops into the Boulder Canyon drainage, watch for a foundation of an old stone house. The home once belonged to a hermit who searched in vain for the Lost Dutchman's mine (see page 77).

At about mile 4, the trail meets up with the Second Water Trail **[4]**, which heads west out of the canyon. This hike, however, continues in Boulder Canyon. The trail generally wends along the dry creekbed piled with rocks and boulders, occasionally picking through the rocky drainage. When the trail makes drainage crossings, follow cairns stacked atop boulders or along the banks to help you reconnect with the path on the other side.

The rock-strewn trail will generally hamper progress through the canyon. Nevertheless, the slow going is worth it to experience the several scenic moments the trail offers as it travels through the wide and low-walled canyon.

The Calvary Trail **[5]**, about mile 5, makes a good turnaround point for a shorter day hike. The trail continues in the canyon, following a rock-ribbed route to its end at the Dutchman's Trail. During the last mile, pay especially close attention to cairns when crossing the drainage, as there are some dicey spots that can lead you off track close to the trail's end.

1. Trailhead
2. Viewpoint
3. Pass to Boulder Canyon
4. Second water trail
5. Calvary trail junction

Bluff Springs Loop 🥾 🥾 🥾

Distance Round-Trip: 9.5 miles

Estimated Hiking Time: 5 hours

Elevation: 2,280 to 3,210 feet

Maps: Tonto National Forest, USGS Weavers Needle

Directions: From Apache Junction, drive east about 12 miles on U.S. 60 and turn north (left) at the signed turnoff onto Peralta Road; drive about 8 miles to the trailhead. The Forest Service charges a $4-per-day parking fee.

This loop hike takes you around the Superstition Wilderness' jagged volcanic peaks, then drops you into two scenic canyons before returning to the trailhead. Starting on the Dutchman's Trail **[1]**, follow the well-plodded path as it hugs close to the edge of craggy outcroppings. As the trail climbs up a ridge, it dips into minor drainages that become pockets full of wildflowers in the spring after a wet winter. A number of social trails proceed from the ridgetop at about mile 0.4; veer left to continue on the Dutchman's Trail.

The trail starts a gradual descent down to the desert floor. You can see the Miner's Needle formation at the end of the ridge in the distant north as you descend the rocky path. Once the trail bottoms out, about mile 1, it heads west, dipping into more drainages. During wet weather, these drainages will have flowing streams.

At about mile 1.6, the trail enters a dense saguaro forest **[2]**. The path brings you right next to the multiarmed giants. In May, the cacti's tips will sprout large cream-colored blossoms in the late afternoon.

By about mile 2, the trail curves to the north face of the Miner's Needle **[3]** and shows how the saguaro forest sweeps across a large basin to the north. You can see the eye of the needle, an arch, when the trail reaches its western side.

Once past the Miner's Needle, the trail starts a several-hundred-foot climb up the Miner's Summit. When the trail crests the summit, about mile 3, you

get pretty panoramas of the Superstition range. After a downhill coast through a wide valley, turn left onto the Bluff Spring Trail **[4]**, about mile 4.

Now in Bluff Spring Canyon, the trail parallels and crisscrosses the Bluff Spring drainage. At the final crossing, about mile 4.7, be sure not to take the path heading south immediately opposite the trail; rather, travel the drainage for about 20 yards and take the path heading west. Once past this dicey jog, you will get a glimpse of the Weaver's Needle until the trail bends south to ascend a ridge and edge along the rim of beautiful Barks Canyon **[5]**.

The trail's journey through Barks Canyon passes some extraordinary scenery, from the spires jutting along the canyon's rim to far-reaching views of mountain ranges in the south. The trail eventually drops into the canyon at about mile 7.7, then climbs out over a series of ridges. The path scrambles steeply down solid rock and loose rubble during the last half-mile, then lands back at the trailhead.

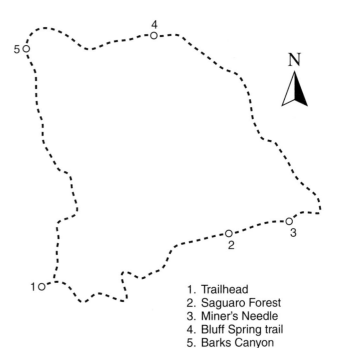

1. Trailhead
2. Saguaro Forest
3. Miner's Needle
4. Bluff Spring trail
5. Barks Canyon

23. Lost Dutchman State Park

- Picnic at the base of the fabled Superstition Mountains.
- See spreads of Mexican gold poppies on a springtime hike.
- Make an adventurous climb up a chute in the mountains.

Area Information

Named for the infamous gold mine fabled to lie in the Superstition Mountains, the 292-acre park sits right at the base of the mountains. Spreading across the mild-mannered foothills of the mountains, the park has a cozy network of trails for hikers of every level of experience.

The Lost Dutchman gold mine still intrigues people. The legend of the mine stems from the 1840s. As the story goes, a family from northern Mexico, the Peraltas, had mined gold in the Superstition Mountains. On their last prospecting expedition, however, they never made it out alive because Apache Indians ambushed them. The gold remained somewhere in the mountains.

In the 1870s, Jacob Waltz (the Dutchman) supposedly found the Peraltas' mine. Waltz did, indeed, show up with incredibly pure nuggets of gold each time he came back from a trip into the Superstition Mountains. The unsolved mystery is where he got the gold. Over 100 years after the Dutchman's death, the gold still has not been found.

The best time to hike the trails in the park is from November through March, when temperatures are moderate. The temperature for a day hike in the winter will hover around the 60s; in the summer, temperatures exceed 100 degrees. Trails in the park vary from easy nature trails to challenging climbs up the mountain. After a wet winter in the springtime, from around late February to the end of March, the park has one of the best displays of Mexican gold poppies in the state.

Directions: The park is located 5 miles north of Apache Junction off Arizona 88 at the base of the Superstition Mountains.

Hours Open: The park is open 365 days a year, from sunrise to 10 P.M.

Facilities: Visitors center, picnic areas with tables and grills, campground (no hookup available), restrooms, showers, group-use areas.

Permits and Rules:

- There is a $5-per-vehicle (up to 6 adults) admission fee.
- No ground fires or wood collecting in the park.
- Damage or removal of natural rocks, vegetation, or pubic property is prohibited.
- Pets must be leashed.
- Camping is allowed only in designated spaces with a maximum of 2 vehicles per campsite with up to 12 people.
- Quiet hours are enforced from 8 P.M. to 8 A.M.

Further Information: Lost Dutchman State Park, 6109 North Apache Trail, Apache Junction, AZ 85219; 480-982-4485.

Other Areas of Interest

If you like gorgeous mountain scenery and don't mind driving hair-raising mountain roads, drive the Apache Trail to Roosevelt Dam. The unpaved but graded road has hairpin turns and a narrow berth, and takes about 3-4 hours to travel through some of the most incredible desert scenery of saguaro-studded mountains, dramatic canyons, and jewel-toned lakes. On the way back, take U.S. 60 and stop at the Boyce Thompson Arboretum 13 miles east of Florence Junction. For more information, call 520-689-2723.

Siphon Draw Trail 🥾 🥾 🥾 🥾

Distance Round-Trip: 1.4 to 3.2 miles

Estimated Hiking Time: 2 to 3 hours

Elevation: 2,080 to 3,100 feet

Map: USGS Goldfield

Caution: The first 0.7 mile of this trail is steep, and the remainder requires hand-over-foot maneuvers over challenging terrain.

Directions: Follow the signs 1 mile to the signed trailhead. The Siphon Draw Trail takes you from the flat land of the desert floor up to a basin below the Flat Iron, the Superstition Mountains' western ramparts. Experienced hikers looking for an adventurous hike can continue past the slickrock to the top of the Flat Iron on an unmaintained foot path.

The trail starts **[1]** on a reasonable grade on an old road that heads toward the mountainside. During February and March, the bajadas that border the precipitous cliffs of the Flat Iron fill with colorful bands of wildflowers that start just after the Jacob's Trail junction **[2]**, about mile 0.3. The trail enters a yellow blanket of brittlebush streaked blue and gold with Coulter's lupine and Mexican gold poppy. The trailsides carry on with this intense coloration for over a half-mile until the trail becomes bouldered and starts high-stepping up the mountain.

The trail veers south to cross a section of the west face of the Superstitions, then jogs east again to enter the draw at about mile 1 **[3]**. The trail, engulfed by a strange mix of smoothly sculptured canyon walls and chiseled columns of ruddy tuff, continues its obsessive climb, picking through boulders, skirting ledges, and clamoring across slickrock. The maintained trail ends **[4]** on a basin piled with boulders in the shadows of a tangle of mesquite trees.

Just beyond the trail's end, the unmaintained path leaves the shadows and picks through a rock-ribbed ledge to a slickrock chute. Shuffle up the chute to a small platform. A waterfall may be active if there has been recent wet weather. If you are an experienced hiker who likes the challenge of exposed scrambling, you may follow the footpath another 0.9 miles to the top of the Flat Iron; otherwise, return the way you came.

Inexperienced hikers, or hikers uncomfortable with heights and exposed areas, should not attempt the last section of this trail. If you continue, your route becomes a dicey beaten path that climbs up steep walls; squeezes through, or climbs over, boulders; and scrapes past raspy patches of scrub oak. Cairns may guide you along the raucous path; and sometimes you have more than one path to choose from. Your route-finding skills must match your sense of adventure.

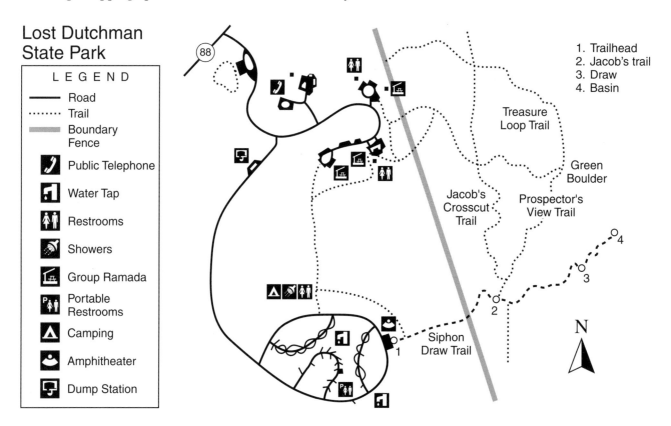

Lost Dutchman State Park

LEGEND

——	Road
....	Trail
▓▓▓	Boundary Fence
☎	Public Telephone
🔧	Water Tap
🚻	Restrooms
🚿	Showers
⛱	Group Ramada
🅿🚻	Portable Restrooms
⛺	Camping
🎭	Amphitheater
♻	Dump Station

1. Trailhead
2. Jacob's trail
3. Draw
4. Basin

Treasure Loop Trail

Green Boulder

Jacob's Crosscut Trail

Prospector's View Trail

Siphon Draw Trail

N

24. Bartlett Reservoir

- Experience the unique dichotomy of a sear desert at the edge of cool lake waters.
- Swim in secluded lake coves.
- Fish for bass and a variety of other fish.
- Picnic along a desert lake.

Area Information

Tucked between the New River and Mazatzal Mountains, the Bartlett Reservoir sits like a piece of azurite in the palm of the Sonoran Desert's hand. The granite mountainsides of the New River Mountains present golden slopes covered with stands of saguaro cacti, a variety of cholla cacti, and wands of ocotillo. Green-barked paloverde trees hang from outcroppings and collect in paths where runoff flows.

The area geology presents a scenic picture. Dikes form vertical intrusions jutting through ridges, and granite cliffs show curious shapes carved by erosion. On the east side of the lake, the Mazatzal Mountains rise in their tumultuous fashion, showing sheer cliffs, extreme uplifts, and razorback ridges.

The Verde River drainage drew a number of Indian tribes, including Hohokam, Sinagua, Apache, and Yavapai, along its banks. In the early 1990s, a large-scale archaeological excavation effort along the lower Verde River revealed exceptionally large sites.

The water continues to draw humanity, but now for recreation instead of survival—fishing, water skiing, hiking, and picnicking. After a wet winter, the trails fill with wildflowers.

You can visit the Bartlett Reservoir all year round. Its cool lake water can refresh you on the hot summer days that regularly reach triple digits. Winter brings mild days and cold nights. Whenever you do hike the area, always wear sunscreen and a hat.

Directions: The reservoir is located about 40 miles northeast of Phoenix. From Dunlap Avenue and Cave Creek Road in Phoenix, drive 33 miles north on Cave Creek Road; turn right (east) onto Bartlett Dam Road (FR 19) and drive approximately 14 miles to the pay station.

Hours Open: No restrictions.

Facilities: Campground, hiking trails, boat launch, picnic areas with tables and grills, washrooms.

Permits and Rules:
- The Tonto National Forest charges a $4-per-vehicle parking fee for 24 hours from the time of purchase at a self-pay station.
- In developed recreation sites, pets must be restrained on a leash no longer than 6 feet.
- Fireworks are prohibited.
- Fires must be attended at all times.
- Maximum stay is 14 days.
- Maximum group size is 10 people.
- The Archaeological Resource Protection Act and state antiquity laws protect ancient and historic ruins. Anyone found excavating, collecting, defacing, or removing an artifact can be fined $500 to $250,000 and imprisoned up to five years. If you see a relic from a historic or ancient culture, you may inspect it, but you may not take it.

Further Information: Cave Creek Ranger District, 40202 North Cave Creek Road, Scottsdale, AZ 85262; 480-595-3300.

Palo Verde Trail 👢 👢 👢

Distance Round-Trip: 7.6 to 9.4 miles

Estimated Hiking Time: 4 to 5 hours

Elevation: 1,840 to 1,940 feet

Map: USGS Bartlett Dam

Caution: The trail traverses terrain composed of decomposed granite that causes skids at steep sections entering and exiting washes. It's best to bring a hiking stick.

Directions: From the pay station, drive 0.2 miles to North Lake Road (FR 459) and turn left; drive 0.5 miles to Rattlesnake Cove and turn right; drive 0.8 miles to the trailhead. Follow the paved path at the north end of the facility to the fishing dock. The trailhead starts to the left where the paved path meets the dock.

To arrange a shuttle at SB Cove, drive about 3 miles farther on North Lake Road. You will come to a three-way stop at the Yellow Cliffs Boat Ramp. Go straight and continue through a parking lot to a short dirt road. Follow the dirt road to the beach parking areas. High-clearance vehicles are recommended, though not necessary.

The Palo Verde Trail, named for the green-barked trees that grow on the surrounding slopes, immediately climbs up a lakeside ridge. You get fabulous views of Bartlett Lake as the trail walks along high ground. After a wet winter, Mexican gold poppies,

wild heliotrope, brittlebush, and fairy dusters will color the hillsides.

The trail dips into a cove **(1)** and curls around its edges, a pattern the path follows for the length of the trail. Clusters of wildflowers that take advantage of the moist environment.

The trail rises and falls with the terrain into the next three coves. At about mile 0.5, the trail starts to parallel the lake. The dichotomy of cool lake water and sear desert creates an unusual twist. By about mile 1.25, the trail reverts to its propensity to drop into coves. One cove, at about mile 1.6, draws the trail away from the lake **(2)** as the path investigates the cove's inner folds. Keeping to high ground as it traces the cove, the trail gets to enjoy panoramas of the Mazatzal Mountains across the lake.

By mile 2.5, the trail crosses the cove's wash and heads for high ground again. When the trail tops out, it becomes sketchy in places, and you need to involve your route-finding skills by paying attention to cairns.

At mile 3, signposts in a wash indicate two trails **(3)**: straight or left. If you take the left fork, a 1.2-mile loop will veer you away from the lake and back to the trail. Continue straight to reach SB Cove.

On its way to SB Cove the trail meanders in and out of washes that have smooth granite boulders stacked curiously on top of one another. Because this part of the trail gets little use, trailside brittlebush, chuparosa, and globemallow bushes encroach into the path. If you have not arranged a shuttle when you reach SB Cove, return the way you came.

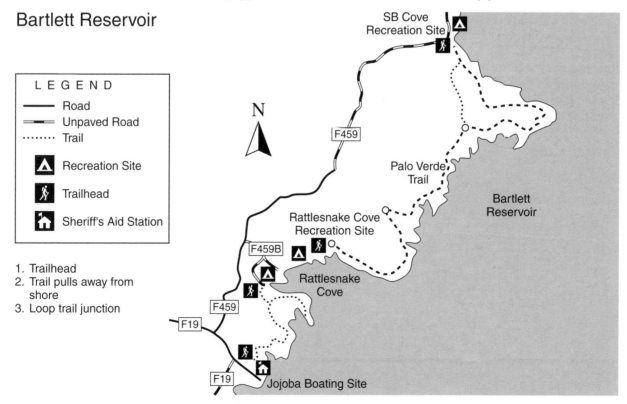

Bartlett Reservoir

L E G E N D
- —— Road
- ⇢ Unpaved Road
- .... Trail
- 🔺 Recreation Site
- 🏃 Trailhead
- 🏠 Sheriff's Aid Station

1. Trailhead
2. Trail pulls away from shore
3. Loop trail junction

25. Cave Creek Area

- Visit a rare desert riparian area.
- Hike through saguaro forests.
- Picnic along a perennial stream.

Area Information

The trails in the Cave Creek Area take you through a topographically diverse and culturally rich area. Several creeks and springs nourish the area, drawing a riparian cover of cottonwood, Arizona sycamore, willow, and velvet ash trees to their sides. These water sources attracted prehistoric, and historic, humanity.

Hohokam Indians farmed the area from about 450 to 1450 A.D. Their success at producing large crops and storing food gave these Indians plenty of time to play and create art. They invented a ball game that the Spanish explorers found Indians playing centuries later in Mexico. The Hohokam also developed a multi-designed clay pottery considered some of the best in Arizona during its time.

Known as the prehistoric merchants of the Southwest, the Hohokam bartered for colorful-feathered birds, seashells, and copper bells from Mexico. They created jewelry from the seashells and used the bird feathers for ceremonies. The men, rather than women, tended to wear the jewelry, and even wore face paint.

The land stayed silent after the Hohokam left, in a peculiarly mysterious manner, for about 400 years until ranchers and prospectors showed up. You can trace their historic activity from the corrals and mine adits that appear on trailsides and hillsides.

Trails that pull away from waterways pass through saguaro cactus forests and tortuous colonies of catclaw. In the higher elevations—the highest point is Skull Mesa at 4,560 feet—juniper trees turn canyon slopes and mountainsides nubby. Gatherings of cholla, prickly pear, and barrel cacti feel more comfortable in the lower elevations, starting at 2,500 feet.

The desert biome in which the trails travel makes fall through spring the best time for hiking. Summer temperatures exceed 100 degrees and scorch the exposed paths.

Directions: Drive north on Cave Creek Road in Phoenix to the town of Cave Creek. Continue on Cave Creek Road as it turns into FR 24. Drive north 12 miles to the Seven Springs Recreation Area.

Hours Open: No restrictions.

Facilities: Developed campground and restrooms at Seven Springs Recreation Area.

Permits and Rules:

- A $4-per-day parking permit must be purchased from electronic machines at the trailhead and displayed face-up on the vehicle dashboard.
- In developed recreation sites, pets must be restrained on a leash no longer than 6 feet.
- Fireworks are prohibited.
- Fires must be attended at all times.
- Maximum stay limit is 14 days.
- Maximum group size is 10 people.
- The Archaeological Resource Protection Act and state antiquity laws protect ancient and historic ruins. Anyone found excavating, collecting, defacing, or removing an artifact can be fined $500 to $250,000 and imprisoned up to five years. If you see a relic from a historic or ancient culture, you may inspect it, but you may not take it.

Further Information: Cave Creek Ranger District, 40202 N. Cave Creek Road, Scottsdale, AZ 85262; 480-595-3300.

Other Areas of Interest

Bartlett Reservoir, located at the end of Bartlett Lake Road, has fishing, boating, picnic areas, and hiking.

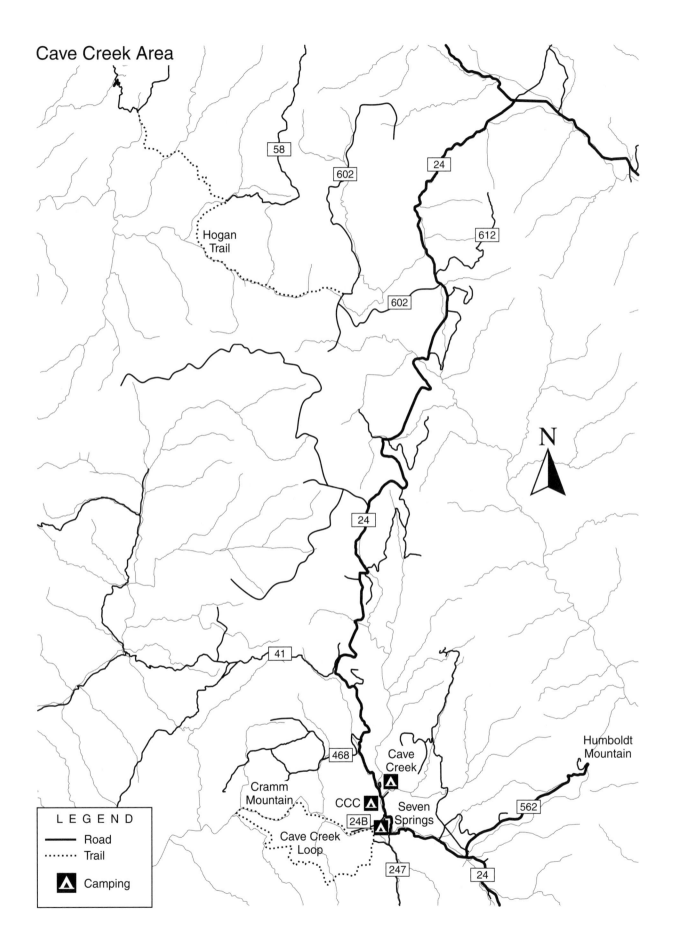

Cave Creek Area

Hogan Trail

58

602

24

612

602

N

24

41

468

Cramm Mountain

Cave Creek

CCC

Seven Springs

24B

Cave Creek Loop

247

562

24

Humboldt Mountain

LEGEND
— Road
...... Trail
🔺 Camping

Cave Creek Loop

Distance Round-Trip: 10 miles

Estimated Hiking Time: 5 hours

Elevation: 2,600 to 4,080 feet

Maps: Tonto National Forest, USGS Humboldt Mountains

Caution: Several creek crossings require rockhopping. A hiking stick will help your balance.

Directions: Pull into the signed trailhead lot on the west side of the road at the Seven Springs Recreation Area.

This route starts **[1]** on the Cave Creek Trail just north of the Seven Springs Campground, built in the 1930s by the Civilian Conservation Corp, a Depression-era work relief program. The campground, surrounded by a riparian cover of Arizona sycamore, velvet ash, and cottonwood trees, makes an oasis-like atmosphere in the middle of the desert. This environment joins you on the trail as it follows Cave Creek through an Upper Sonoran Desert life zone.

After traveling south a half-mile, the trail crosses FR 24B, drops into the creek drainage, then veers right to parallel the creek. At about mile 0.75, the trail intersects **[2]** with the Cottonwood Trail; continue straight on the Cave Creek Trail.

At mile 1, the Arizona sycamore trees triple in size and number. Huddled on an island delta where the creek forks, the forest reflects the abundant supply of water surrounding it. The riparian cover separates at mile 1.25 to show the surrounding mountains. Unlike the lushness of the creekbanks, these mountain slopes have a cover of scrubby desert vegetation such as mesquite trees, catclaw, prickly pear and cholla cactus, juniper trees, and shrub oak.

The trail passes through a metal green gate, then drops into the drainage next to a wall of willow trees at about mile 2. Immediately, the trail rockhops across the creek and picks through a rocky delta into the shady cover of velvet ash and Arizona sycamore trees.

With the trail now on the south side of the canyon, you can see saguaro cacti running up the sun-drenched northern slopes. Just before the trail passes a grassy bench with a primitive campsite, look for a crested saguaro on the north canyon wall. The crested [cristate] saguaros have a fan-shaped crown and make a rare occurrence.

After climbing a couple hundred feet above the drainage, the trail looks down on the treetops of Arizona sycamores and islands of gray boulders in the creekbed. At mile 2.8, the trail drops into the drainage, hops quickly across the creek, then climbs back above the creek on the north canyon wall where rust-colored outcroppings encroach on, and saguaro cactuses file past, its path.

At a signed trail junction **[3]**, about mile 3.6, turn left onto the Skunk Tank Trail. The trail starts a long climb up the slopes of Quien Sabe Peak. (The odd name *Quien Sabe* is Spanish for "who knows.") If you look back to the north, you can see a series of switchbacks climbing a peak in the near distance—the road to the Cramm Mountain mining operation. Closer to the trail, but still hundreds of feet away, you can see the rare beauty of Skunk Tank Canyon below.

The trail reaches the high point of the hike, and its intersection with the Quien Sabe Trail **[4]**, at about mile 6. An army of saguaro cacti march down the precipitous slopes that fall into narrow Skunk Tank Canyon. The trail takes a downward turn, passing through a scrub-covered area occasionally showing a verdancy of small stands of cottonwoods gathered in distant canyons.

At about mile 8.5, the trail intersects with the Cottonwood Trail **[5]**. Turn left on the Cottonwood Trail to continue on the hike.

The trail heads down to Bronco Creek and picks across it. The trail follows the creek back to the Cave Creek Trail, where you turn right and hike back to the parking area and your vehicle.

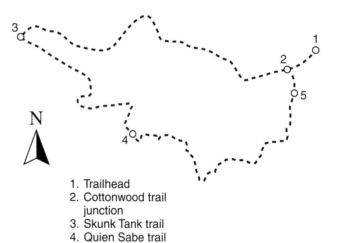

1. Trailhead
2. Cottonwood trail junction
3. Skunk Tank trail
4. Quien Sabe trail
5. Cottonwood trail

Hogan Trail 👢 👢 👢 👢

Distance Round-Trip: 13 to 15 miles

Estimated Hiking Time: 7 hours

Elevation: 3,700 to 4,200 feet

Maps: Tonto National Forest, USGS Cooks Mesa and Rover Peak

Caution: The trail may have overgrowths of catclaw. Watch for thorns when you pass through thickets.

Directions: From the Seven Springs Campground, drive 13.9 miles to FR 602; turn west (left) and drive 3 miles to the trail. A high-clearance vehicle is required. The road may be impassible in wet weather.

The Hogan Trail, located in a tucked-away section of the New River Mountains, crosses a variety of landscapes on its way to Hogan Cabin and Spring. As soon as the trail nestles into the Squaw Creek drainage, you can feel a remoteness that won't leave until you get back to your vehicle. That's not surprising, as the trail looks more like a wildlife thoroughfare, judging from hoofprints and pawprints, instead of a footpath.

The path [1] treks up and down rounded mountainsides where juniper trees make nappy appearances. The trail drops into the Squaw Creek drainage [2] at about mile 1.25 and follows right along it. During wet weather, the creek has a strong enough flow to have attracted Indians, and later homesteaders, along its banks.

During its ramble along Squaw Creek, the path passes through thickets of catclaw. This member of the pea family, also called *wait-a-minute bush*, will rip and tear at your clothes and skin if you brush against it; be careful during these stretches.

Goat Camp Spring, at about mile 3, is Squaw Creek's main attraction along the trail [3]. Flowing over polished granite dimpled with potholes and troughs, the creek cascades to a deep pool. You will have to pick your way over boulders and tall grasses in order to continue on the trail, which resumes on the same side along the creek.

Within a mile, the trail separates from the creek and heads toward an old corral [4]. This makes a good turnaround point for inexperienced hikers. The remainder of the trail requires some route-finding skills as the trail turns sketchy in a few places.

To continue on the trail, follow the path as it veers to the right of the corral and heads north, wending around peach-colored outcroppings as it climbs up a ridge, then drops down into Jacks Gulch. The path settles to a flat stretch along the gulch, then makes a sudden veer across the gulch [5] and heads west, about mile 5. If you come to a gate that leads to the Six Bar Ranch (private property) at FR 58, you have gone too far. Retrace your steps a short distance to hook up with the trail.

After crossing the gulch, the trail starts a long plod up a steep ridge. The rock-ribbed path tops the ridge and gives you an inspiring view of the mountainous area as it twists down the other side of the ridge. You can see signs of Hogan Spring in the distance where a stand of Arizona sycamore trees congregate.

The spring is named after a reclusive character named Hogan, who lived in a cabin near the spring. When the trail drops into the drainage, look for old man Hogan's tin-walled cabin tucked among the trees [6].

Once you reach the cabin, you may return the way you came or continue another mile across Middle Fork Creek to the trail's end at its intersection with the Squaw Creek Stock trail.

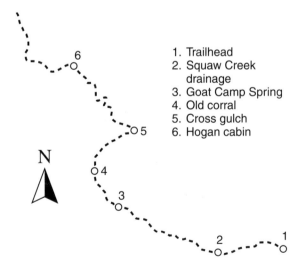

1. Trailhead
2. Squaw Creek drainage
3. Goat Camp Spring
4. Old corral
5. Cross gulch
6. Hogan cabin

26. Tonto Basin

- See mountain slopes turn gold from Mexican poppies in the spring.

- Hike through saguaro forests.

- Enjoy views of Roosevelt Lake from mountaintops.

Area Information

The Tonto Basin has always hosted humanity. Its compelling nature, created by a combination of ample water sources, rich spreads of grasses, and temperate climate, attracted several waves of inhabitants.

The Apache Indians roamed the basin's rugged landscape, cut by canyons and bordered by the Mazatzal Mountains to the west and Sierra Ancha Mountains to the east. Before them, the Salado Indians lived for hundreds of years and left pueblo-type dwellings.

When Anglos started homesteading the basin in the 1860s, the Apache Indians resisted. After a dozen years of brutal attacks from both sides, the U.S. Army prevailed. General George Crook wiped out the band of Tonto Apaches.

This opened the door to the Tonto Basin, and the cattlemen quickly moved in. Florance Packard, a cattleman who settled in the Tonto Basin area around 1875, related descriptions of the basin much different from what it looks like today. Packard described fields of grama grasses growing so high, the grasses brushed one's stirrups when riding through them. He spoke about creeksides full of timber.

Now only relict grasslands grow, mostly in inaccessible areas. And most of the old timber—felled for fuel, cut down to provide space for cattle to feed, or washed down the river—disappeared. The range, worn out and faltering from overgrazing at the turn of the 20th century, became only a memory after an 18-month drought in 1904.

In 1905, construction started on the Roosevelt Dam on the Salt River to help alleviate the moody flow of the river and provide water for irrigation. Historically, the Salt River's floodwaters would periodically wipe out settlements. During normal years, the river probably ran almost a mile wide and 5 to 6 feet deep. The Roosevelt Dam was built to preclude flooding and help resurrect the basin's productivity.

The winding Apache Trail, Arizona's first designated historic and scenic highway that provides a hair-raising journey from Apache Junction to Roosevelt Dam, was built as a service road to haul materials to the dam's construction site. Since its completion in 1911, the world's largest cyclopean-masonry dam has been expanded, covered with concrete, and has a hydrogeneration capacity of 36,000 kw.

You get beautiful views of the lake and the rugged mountains bracing the basin from high points on the basin's trails. The best time to hike the trails is from November through March, when temperatures remain reasonable. Summer temperatures rise to over 100 degrees. When hiking the area, wear sun protection and carry plenty of water.

Directions: The trail near Punkin Center can be accessed by driving north on Arizona 87 to Arizona 188; turn south on Arizona 188. Trails near Roosevelt Dam can be efficiently accessed from Globe by driving north on Arizona 188 to Roosevelt Dam. Taking the Apache Trail involves a drive of several hours.

Hours Open: No restrictions.

Facilities: Campgrounds, washrooms, picnic areas, boating, fishing, and boat launch available at Roosevelt Lake.

Further Information: Tonto Basin Ranger District, Highway 188, HCO 2 Box 4800, Roosevelt, AZ 85545; 928-467-3200.

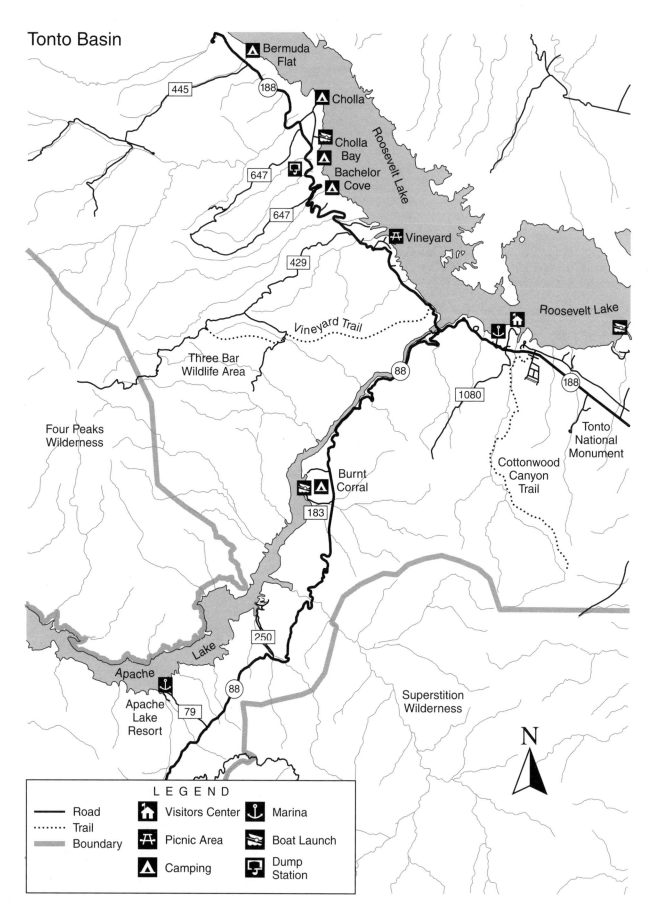

Tonto Basin

Bermuda Flat

Cholla

Cholla Bay

Bachelor Cove

445

188

647

647

429

Roosevelt Lake

Vineyard

Vineyard Trail

Three Bar Wildlife Area

Four Peaks Wilderness

88

1080

Roosevelt Lake

188

Tonto National Monument

Cottonwood Canyon Trail

Burnt Corral

183

Apache Lake

250

88

Apache Lake Resort

79

Superstition Wilderness

N

LEGEND

Road		Visitors Center	Marina
Trail		Picnic Area	Boat Launch
Boundary		Camping	Dump Station

Vineyard Trail 🥾 🥾 🥾

Distance Round-Trip: 11.8 miles

Estimated Hiking Time: 6 hours

Elevation: 2,200 to 3,600 feet

Maps: Tonto National Forest, USGS Theodore Roosevelt Dam

Caution: This trail travels in a desert environment. Warm-weather hikes should be done in the early morning hours only.

Directions: From U.S. 60, turn north (left) onto Arizona 88 just before Globe; drive 30 miles to Arizona 188, turn right, and immediately cross the bridge; drive 0.6 miles to a pulloff; park and cross the street, heading toward the end of the guardrail, where the trail starts at an unsigned trailhead.

The Vineyard Trail, part of the approximately 800-mile-long Arizona Trail, showcases an unusual side of Arizona: 25-mile-long Roosevelt Lake to the north and adjoining Apache Lake in the south. The Salt River strings the reservoirs together as it heads on a southwestern course. The trail starts out [1] with an eye on the azure lakes while traveling through a Lower Sonoran biome filled with saguaros and exquisite views of the surrounding peaks.

The trail begins with a demanding personality during the first mile, when it climbs 800 feet up Inspiration Point toward Vineyard Mountain [2]. Along the way, it passes by the ruins of Camp O'Rourke, where Roosevelt Dam's construction workers and their families once lived. As much effort as the trail demands, however, it lavishes returns in scenery. Once on the ridge, you get fabulous views of the lakes and the Four Peaks and Superstition wildernesses.

The trail continues along the ridge, passing Vineyard Mountain to the south, then heads deeper into the remote countryside of the Three Bar Wildlife Area. Cattle grazing is not permitted in this area, as the land is set aside exclusively for the study of wildlife.

The path takes its time winding between peaks and dipping in and out of draws. The sun-drenched slopes provide the perfect environment for an impressive saguaro cactus forest. An early morning hike in May will find the giant cacti blooming creamy fist-sized flowers.

At about mile 4.5, the trail [3] briefly joins FR 132, which is open to motor vehicles. Follow the well-placed Arizona Trail signs where the trail joins the road [4] and where it parts from it to keep on the trail.

Back on the hillsides again, at about mile 4.6, the trail heads gradually downhill to its end at FR 429. You may continue on the Arizona Trail, or return the way you came.

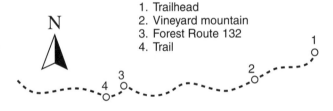

N

1. Trailhead
2. Vineyard mountain
3. Forest Route 132
4. Trail

Cottonwood Canyon Trail

👢 👢 👢

Distance Round-Trip: 12 miles

Estimated Hiking Time: 6 hours

Elevation: 2,300 to 3,800 feet

Maps: Tonto National Forest, USGS: Theodore Roosevelt Dam; Pinyon Mountain; Two Bar Mountain

Caution: Catclaw thickets might encroach into the trail in certain sections. Be careful while negotiating the bushes' thorns, which may snag clothes and skin.

Directions: Turn north (left) onto Arizona 88 just before Globe; drive about 28 miles to the signed Frazier Trailhead (located 3/4 mile east of the ranger station on the south side of the highway).

The Cottonwood Canyon Trail, part of the Arizona Trail, shows off Arizona's diversity as it travels from the lower canyon at Roosevelt Lake to its upper portion near the northern end of the Superstition Mountains.

The trail starts climbing up low ridges **[1]** and dips in and out of drainages. When it drops into Cottonwood Canyon, you can see how the forces of erosion have chewed through conglomerate walls, left boulders strewn along the streambed, and lodged twigs and limbs in the crevices of rocks from prior floods.

After a mild climb up the canyon, the trail brings you to Thompson Spring **[2]**, about mile 1. A stand of cottonwood trees gathers around a chain of pools floating with patches of watercress. Just beyond the spring, take a right turn onto FR 341 (which is open to motor vehicles).

The road climbs steeply up a ridge alongside Cottonwood Canyon, showing you the gorgeous outcome of volcanic activity. Copper cliffs, hollowed in spots by wind and water, look down the throat of the canyon, where jagged walls plunge out of sight into the canyon depths. From behind, views of Roosevelt Lake splay across the V of Cottonwood Canyon. The reward for the steep climb comes at about mile 3.2, when the trail tops out at a large metal tank, passes through a corral **[3]**, then reenters the canyon.

Waist-high cairns will guide you through this enchanting section of the canyon where the path crisscrosses Cottonwood Creek as it meanders under a riparian cover of cottonwood and Arizona sycamore trees. Just beyond the wooded cover, you can see saguaro cacti standing along the ruddy canyon walls.

At Cottonwood Spring **[4]**, about mile 5, a gathering of Arizona sycamore trees drip with grapevines at the base of the canyon's deep coppery cliffs. The trail eventually climbs out of the canyon to its end at FR 83. Return the way you came.

1. Trailhead
2. Thompson Spring
3. Corral
4. Cottonwood Spring

27. Four Peaks Wilderness

- Drive a scenic backroad up a distinctive central Arizona landmark.
- Hike with one of the largest concentrations of black bears in the state.

Area Information

You can see the Four Peaks for miles around. They stand, four peaks shoulder-to-shoulder, at the southern end of the Mazatzal Mountains. Each end peak eases a granite ridge slowly down to the desert floor. With the right light, the golden granite ridges turn as ruddy as a sunset can color them.

The geology of the peaks makes for stunning scenery along the trail. Granites and schists make up most of the mountains. Veins of quartz marbleize the peaks, and outcrops of shale form jagged edges.

The Four Peaks Wilderness covers 60,740 acres of the peaks. An almost 20-mile drive to the Lone Pine Saddle on a high-clearance road gives you a chance to see what the peaks are like up close. Along the drive, you pass through several different vegetative communities.

The rapid rise in elevation takes you from great stands of saguaro cacti; through a chaparral community full of piñon pine, Gambel oak, and manzanita; and up to stands of ponderosa pine trees. This quick change makes for interesting associations among the plants; species naturally found hundreds of miles apart might end up as neighbors on the Four Peaks.

The abrupt elevation changes also create a distinctive community of animals. Diverse, with little space to roam, the animals run the gamut from javelina, coyotes, ringtailed cats, and skunks; to deer, mountain lions, bighorn sheep, and bears. This area has one of the biggest concentrations of bears in the state. Watch, too, for scorpions, rattlesnakes, and centipedes in the desert biome.

Weather on the peaks can be just as varied as the vegetation and animal life. When the desert languishes in 100-plus temperatures in the summer, the upper part of the peaks relaxes in 80-degree days and cool nights. Winter rains on the desert strata bring snow to the peak tops. With that in mind, keep to the upper reaches from March through November, and the lower elevations from November through March.

Directions: The Four Peaks Wilderness is located about 40 miles north of Phoenix. From Shea Boulevard and Arizona 87, drive north on Arizona 87 about 16 miles to a signed turnoff for the Four Peaks.

Hours Open: No restrictions.

Facilities: None.

Permits and Rules:

- No mechanized vehicles or mountain bikes are allowed.
- In developed recreation sites, pets must be restrained on a leash no longer than 6 feet.
- Fireworks are prohibited.
- Fires must be attended at all times.
- Maximum stay is 14 days.
- Maximum group size is 10 people.

Further Information: Mesa Ranger District, 26 North MacDonald, Mesa, AZ 85211-5800; 480-610-3300.

Other Areas of Interest

Visit Saguaro Lake, one of the lakes you can see from ridgetops in the Four Peaks. To access the lake, turn east onto Bush Highway (located about 6 miles south of the turnoff for the Four Peaks) and drive about 5 miles to the lake. For more information, contact the Mesa Ranger District.

Four Peaks Trail 🥾 🥾 🥾

Distance Round-Trip: 12 miles

Estimated Hiking Time: 6 hours

Elevation: 5,800 to 6,800 feet

Maps: Tonto National Forest, USGS Four Peaks

Caution: The trail may have eroded spots where the Lone Pine Fire blazed.

Directions: Drive 19.7 miles to Lone Pine Saddle Trailhead. High-clearance vehicles are required, and four-wheel-drive vehicles are recommended. The road to the trailhead will take an hour to drive.

The path gradually starts **[1]** its contour around the Four Peaks as it heads along the northern flank of the mountain. Once shady with pines before the Lone Pine Fire in 1996, the path enters a corridor of charcoal skeletons: pines stand as charred stumps, and old oaks writhe in their nakedness. Nevertheless, bushes that were completely burned to the ground have already come back several feet high.

Though the largest fire in the history of the Tonto National Forest has given the trail a strange beauty, the trail has not relinquished its remote atmosphere or its fabulous panoramic views of the

Tonto Basin that come with the first mile as the trail heads to the eastern side of the mountain.

Just past the Amethyst Trail, the trail starts a long descent that eventually dips into Shake Spring **[2]** then climbs out to edge the sun-drenched mountain slope. Shake Spring may have water, especially after a wet winter.

Once the trail climbs out onto the mountain's eastern flanks, it travels along the slope toward its present end on Buckhorn Ridge. Scorched chaparral scrub remind you that this section saw the brunt of the blaze. Nevertheless, the views and scenery remain incredible. Outcroppings give way to the forces of erosion that chewed through them across the mountain's slope. The panorama to the east shows the rumpled terrain of the Tonto Basin sliding down to the blue waters of Roosevelt Lake.

By the time the trail gets to Black Bear Saddle **[3]**, about mile 5, you get a fabulous close-up view of the backside of the Four Peaks, along with a strong dose of remoteness. The Superstition Mountains' Flat Iron rises in the distant south.

The Forest Service's maintenance crew has reconstructed 6 of the almost 10 miles of the Four Peaks Trail. A sign stating "The Trail Is Not Maintained Ahead" **[4]** warns hikers that the trail will end in about a half-mile. At that point, you should return the way you came.

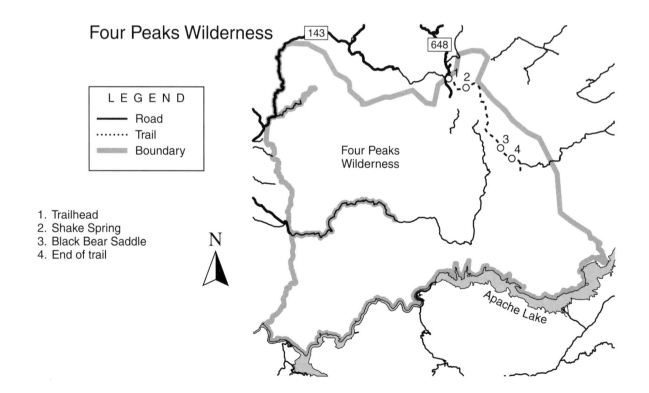

Four Peaks Wilderness

LEGEND
- —— Road
- ······ Trail
- ▬▬ Boundary

Four Peaks
Wilderness

1. Trailhead
2. Shake Spring
3. Black Bear Saddle
4. End of trail

N

Apache Lake

28. Mazatzal Wilderness

- Hike one of the less-visited wildernesses in the state.
- See exquisite views of central Arizona.
- Follow old cowboy trails.

Area Information

The Mazatzal Wilderness lies in the Mazatzal Mountains, one of the more rugged mountain ranges in Arizona. Wilderness trails can take you to places where you may not see another person for days, maybe weeks, depending on the trail. Because of the difficult terrain and remoteness, these trails work best for experienced hikers.

In typical Mazatzal topography, the mountains present a tumultuous display. Trails climb razorback ridges, peer into deep chasms, and mount craggy outcroppings. Canyon walls plunge dramatically and abruptly into rock-strewn streambeds choked with water-worn boulders. Ponderosa pines hang tenaciously on maroon walls where postwinter waterfalls tumble over cliff faces.

Regardless of their austere features, the mountains exude a comfortable atmosphere, much more amicable than their inhospitable landscape.

The mountains' usually staid high desert vegetation of piñon and juniper trees, laced with bushes that prick and tear at bodies and clothes, gets an eclectic touch when trails dip into or follow streams. Arizona sycamore trees gather near these reliable water sources. In the spring, wildflowers appear on trailsides and hillsides.

The mountains have seen many cultures, from prehistoric Indians to sheepherders and cowboys. Ranching remnants still prevail in the form of rickety wooden corrals and stone foundations of line shacks. Also, the trails in the Mazatzal Mountains (often cowboy paths) sometimes follow the cowboy tradition of taking the shortest distance between two points. This means some trails follow incredibly steep routes. Watch for deer, black bears, mountain lions, and javelina as you hike these paths. Also, be careful for rattlesnakes, which like to hang out in more remote sections.

The best time to hike the wilderness is spring and fall, although summer hiking is possible because of forests and riparian cover in canyons. However, temperatures can nudge into the 90s, and you should drink plenty of water.

The range's unusual name, which stems from a word from the Aztec culture in Mexico meaning "land of the deer," experiences some quirky pronunciations. One popular pronunciation is *mat-az-al*; another *mad-as-hell*. The correct one is *mah-zat-zail*. The mountains' name is a classic example of how Indian words often became convoluted because the "white eyes" (Anglos) didn't bother to learn the correct pronunciation.

Hours Open: No restrictions.

Facilities: None.

Permits and Rules:

- No mechanized vehicles or mountain bikes are allowed in wilderness areas.
- In developed recreation sites, pets must be restrained on a leash no longer than 6 feet.
- Fireworks are prohibited.
- Fires must be attended at all times.
- Maximum stay is 14 days.
- Maximum group size is 15 people.
- The Archaeological Resource Protection Act and state antiquity laws protect ancient and historic ruins. Anyone found excavating, collecting, defacing, or removing an artifact can be fined $500 to $250,000 and imprisoned up to five years. If you see a relic from a historic or ancient culture, you may inspect it, but you may not take it.

Further Information: Payson Ranger District, 1009 East Highway 260, Payson, AZ 85541; 928-474-7900 and Mesa Ranger District, 26 North MacDonald, Mesa, AZ 85211-5800; 480-610-3300.

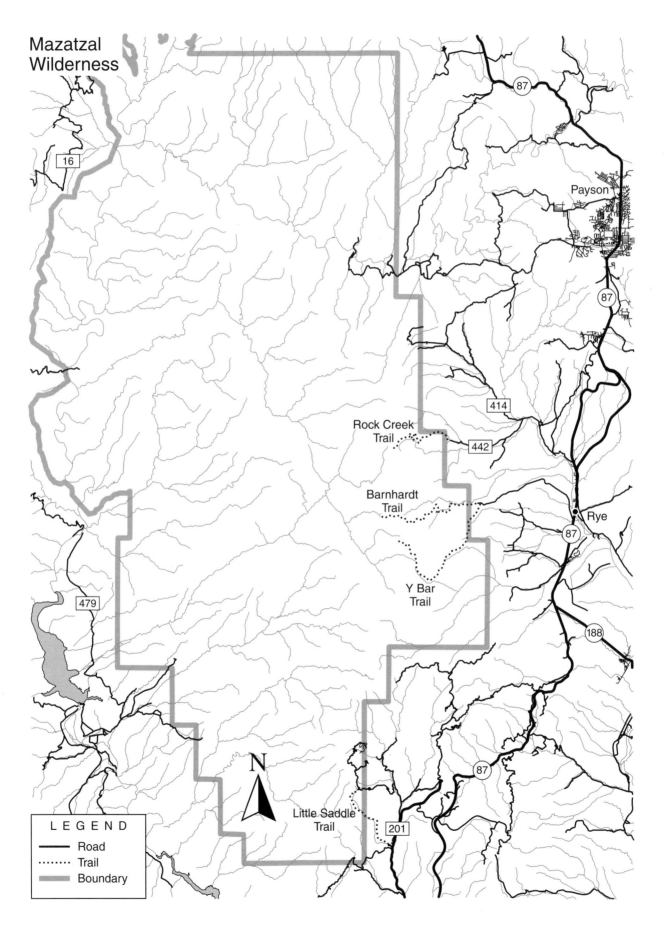

Mazatzal
Wilderness

16

Payson

87

87

414

Rock Creek
Trail

442

Barnhardt
Trail

Rye

87

479

Y Bar
Trail

188

N

87

Little Saddle
Trail

201

LEGEND
——— Road
········· Trail
▃▃▃ Boundary

Little Saddle Trail 🥾 🥾 🥾

Distance Round-Trip: 8 miles

Estimated Hiking Time: 4 hours

Elevation: 3,720 to 5,020 feet

Maps: Tonto National Forest, Lion Mountains

Cautions: Watch for snakes in the spring and fall.

Directions: Drive north on Arizona 87 about 32 miles and turn west (left) at the signed Sycamore Creek turnoff (past milepost 222) onto the old Arizona 87; drive 3.2 miles to the trailhead on the west side of the road. Park in the horseshoe pulloff on the east side of the road.

A Forest Service sign signals the start **[1]** of the Little Saddle Trail right along the old Arizona 87 highway. Within moments, the trail passes through a gate, then starts a moderate climb up a ridge. The trail shoulders along an unnamed drainage where Goat Spring [2] keeps a show of water in it even in dry weather. The moisture invites canyon grape, Arizona sycamore trees, and sugar sumac bushes to the trailsides.

After a pass through another gate, the trail comes to an intersection with the Sunflower Trail at mile 0.5, then continues climbing up a ridge. A contour across the ridge, past colonies of Schott agave plants, brings you to the unnamed canyon the trail will follow on its way to Little Saddle Mountain. If you hike during the month of May, you may catch the foot-high Schott agave in bloom when it sends up a three-foot stalk with a cluster of fragrant waxy yellow flowers. The plant's spine-tipped leaves, growing to about shin height, give the plant its appropriate nickname of *shindagger*.

As the trail descends into the canyon, you get a view of some stunning geology **[3]** a bit different than what the Mazatzal Mountains usually offer. Light conglomerate strata line the canyon slopes separated by green high desert vegetation of juniper trees and scrub oak. Cottage-sized boulders tumble trailside, directing the path's winding route.

By about mile 1.6, the trail drops into the streambed on the canyon floor. Wet weather will get the stream running, but several springs will form pools of water even in dry weather and force you to rockhop across the stream as the trail crisscrosses the drainage.

The path stays cloistered in the canyon bottom until about mile 2.1, when it comes up for air on the west wall. Now wider with lower walls, the canyon sees more sunlight. The trail still flirts with the streambed as it climbs with the drainage toward its head. The trail ascends to the upper reaches of the eastern wall. Jagged rocks vault along the trail and it steps over quartz boulders. The wide pine trees in the canyon are Arizona cypress trees.

The trail compromises its way back to the streambed that has risen to meet the path at about mile 2.7. The trail starts another climb, however, and leaves the drainage once and for all. When it tops out, look to the northeast, where colorful Little Saddle Mountain rises between two peaks.

The trail starts a pattern of climbing steeply, then catching its breath on a short, level stretch to its end. Watch for a distant panorama **[4]** that comes into view to the west of the trail at about mile 3.6, showing the rugged personality of the Mazatzal Mountains. At the end of this trail, you may continue on the Saddle Mountain Trail **[5]**, which travels 4.5 miles to the Story Mine; or return the way you came.

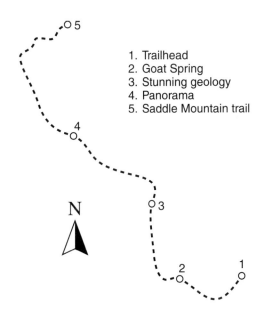

1. Trailhead
2. Goat Spring
3. Stunning geology
4. Panorama
5. Saddle Mountain trail

N

Barnhardt Trail 👢 👢 👢

Distance Round-Trip: 12.4 miles

Estimated Hiking Time: 6.5 hours

Elevation: 4,200 to 6,000 feet

Maps: Tonto National Forest, USGS Mazatzal Peak

Caution: This trail has long, steep grades.

Directions: Drive 47.2 miles north on Arizona 87 to the Barnhardt Trailhead turnoff; turn left and drive 5 miles to the trailhead. High-clearance vehicles are recommended.

The Barnhardt Trail, the most popular trail in the Mazatzal Mountains, takes you through spectacular scenery as it climbs up Barnhardt Canyon to the Mazatzal Divide. The trail starts **[1]** from the parking area in the company of a variety of oaks on a rocky path, then settles on a well-maintained footpath on the south wall of Barnhardt Canyon.

At about mile 0.5, the path picks through a rock-ribbed drainage jumbled with boulders at Garden Spring **[2]**, then begins an ascent up the canyon wall. Just past the wilderness boundary, you may catch glimpses of Barnhardt Creek several hundred feet below the trail through the line of bushes that start appearing along the path—cliff fendlerbush, deerbrush, sugar sumac, and quinine bush. Just below the trail on the downslope, you may notice stunning bursts of yellow-orange flowers from the flannel bush during a March hike. If you hike in May or June, agave will light up the canyon slopes with yellow flower clusters.

As the trail zigzags farther up the canyon, the tumultuous geology of the canyon at about mile 2.5 starts to grab your attention. The canyon's north wall shows pressured strata and jagged lifts of maroon cliffs. At about mile 3, the trail climbs **[3]** to a maroon-colored chasm pouring a stream of water that pools around and across the trail. During snowmelt, a spectacular waterfall cascades down a chute in the back of the chasm. The wet environment in the chasm supports moisture-loving flowers.

Look for tiny pink flowers in a loose cluster on alumroot nestled in the ledges on the chasm wall. The yellow blossoms on common monkey flower line the stream edges, and yellow columbine arches from the streamside. Also watch for poison ivy. Normally a one- to two-foot shrub, poison ivy can grow face-high here. The chasm makes a good turnaround point for a shorter day hike.

The exquisite trailside geology follows as the trail continues climbing up the canyon. The trail twists around outcroppings that provide scenic panoramas, and picks across a couple avalanches of rock. Continue past a trail intersection with the Sandy Saddle Trail **[4]** at about mile 4 as the path presses through a thick cover of manzanita bushes on a sun-soaked mountainside. Watch for mounds of claret cup cactus in this section. The sun-loving cacti grow close to the ground in clusters in rocky areas and bloom red flowers in March or April.

The trail cools off in forests of Gambel oaks and ponderosa pines as it dips in and out of minor drainages. You may catch sight of a stand of bigtooth maple trees at about mile 5. The trail contours a craggy slope just before meeting with the Mazatzal Divide Trail **[5]**. On the divide, you get fabulous views east and west of the mountains. From here, you may take the Mazatzal Divide Trail south and hook up with the Shaketree Trail (also known as the Y Bar trail) for a loop back to the trailhead (totaling about 15.5 miles), or return the way you came.

1. Trailhead
2. Garden Spring
3. Chasm
4. Sandy Saddle trail
5. Mazatzal Divide trail

Rock Creek Trail 🥾 🥾 🥾

Distance Round-Trip: 6.6 miles

Estimated Hiking Time: 3.5 hours

Elevation: 3,980 to 7,080 feet

Maps: Tonto National Forest, USGS Mazatzal Peak

Cautions: The trail crosses remote country. Watch for snakes.

Directions: Drive north of milepost 240 on Arizona 87, then turn west onto FR 414; drive about 4.8 miles and veer left onto unmarked FR 442; drive about 3.1 miles to a fork and veer left; drive 0.3 miles to the road's end at the trailhead. Four-wheel-drive vehicles are required.

The Rock Creek Trail made the Mazatzal Wilderness trail system on a rumor. The rugged and wild trail stayed clear of the Forest Service's knowledge until they started hearing rumors of it in the 1970s. The trail is too steep and rough for cattle, so the Forest Service doesn't quite know why it exists. Once you expend the effort on its torturous climb up into the heights of the Mazatzal Mountains, you may understand the Rock Creek Trail doesn't need a reason to exist other than to take you to its extravagant scenery and panoramas in its upper reaches.

The trail starts out **[1]** dipping right into its namesake, Rock Creek. The drainage, which runs with water during wet weather, draws oak and juniper trees to its side. True to its name, the watercourse has boulders and large rocks strewn around it.

The trail climbs out and stays on the north side of the drainage, climbing with the creek in a westerly direction up a ridge. The ridge's ruddy massif comes into view at about mile 0.5, giving you an idea of where the trail is heading.

Watch for wildlife as the trail continues along the stream. As a water source, Rock Creek may draw a variety of animals—deer, bears, mountain lions, javelina—to its side. If you do see any animals or snakes, give them enough space and the right of way.

A sign **[2]** at about mile 0.75 marks the trail's entry into the Mazatzal Wilderness. A few switchbacks later, traveling on a crest above Alder Creek to the north and Rock Creek to the south, the trail climbs into a section of chaparral. This brushy area has few trees and a thick mix of scrub oak and manzanita.

Bears like to munch on the manzanita berries. Watch for green catkins on quinine bushes after they bloom in February. Deerbrush displays sweet-smelling clusters of white flowers in late March and April.

The trail's pass through the sun-drenched chaparral can be particularly draining in the hotter months. Make sure you take extra water to accommodate you through this section.

The trail drones through the chaparral until about mile 1.8. The grade not only flattens a bit into a brief reprieve from the harsh climb, but it starts to nuzzle up to piñon pine trees that drop swatches of shade onto it.

The trail continues its climb into the upper reaches of the ridge by about mile 2.5 and winds around its ragged cliffs **[3]**. This is when you realize the trail needs no utilitarian reason to exist. If you're hiking in late March or early April, look for lousewort here, the first flowers to bloom in the highcountry. Watch, too, for pretty red flowers on claret cup cactus and magenta blooms on hedgehog cactus. Both cacti like to nestle in outcroppings.

Another steep climb takes you into dramatic maroon-colored cliffs where shindaggers and agave like to stuff themselves in crevices. During wet weather, you may hear water splattering below the trail. Stick with the trail as it takes you to the source, and this trail's end, at the intersection with the Mazatzal Divide Trail. The Hopi Springs form a chain of pools that drain down the slope **[4]**.

You may explore further in either direction on the Mazatzal Divide Trail, which runs a 29-mile north-south route in the mountains; or return the way you came.

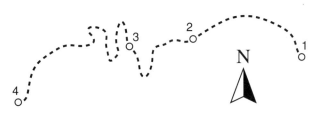

1. Trailhead
2. Wilderness boundary
3. Cliffs
4. Hopi Springs

Y Bar Trail (Shaketree Trail)

👢 👢 👢

Distance Round-Trip: 12 miles

Estimated Hiking Time: 6 hours

Elevation: 4,200 to 7,100 feet

Maps: Tonto National Forest, USGS Mazatzal Peak

Cautions: Talus sections along the trail make hiking difficult, especially on the downhill. If you plan a loop hike connecting the Barnhardt Trail (see page 100), hike up the Y Bar and down the Barnhardt.

Directions: Drive north on Arizona 87 about 47.2 miles to the Barnhardt Trailhead turnoff; turn left and drive 5 miles to the trailhead (high-clearance vehicle recommended). Of the three trailheads, take the far left one.

The trail begins **[1]** by plodding up the cobbled and grassy eastern slope of Mazatzal Peak. The high desert vegetation of agave, claret cups, and prickly pear cactus make a prickly show. During March and April, claret cups will bloom deep red flowers; the prickly pear opens fist-sized yellow blossoms in May; and the agave sprout tall stalks topped with clusters of yellow flowers in June.

At about mile 1, just before Gambel oaks start to offer shade, the rock-ribbed trail shows off stunning panoramas of surrounding ridges **[2]**. The Sierra Ancha Mountains form rows of ridges in the east, and the Superstition Mountains display curious formations in the southeast.

By mile 2, when the piñon pines appear, the trail dips into hairpin bends where drainages have dug into the rugged mountain slopes. If you hike the trail in late March, watch for the bright yellow flowers on flannel bushes and the fragrant white clusters on deerbrush at a drainage under a maroon outcropping.

The mountains start to show off their rugged characteristics at about mile 3 with an exceptionally scenic display of geology. The trail teeters along the side of the mountain in a sun-drenched spot that plunges hundreds of feet down into Shaketree Canyon **[3]**. The mountain's ruddy ridges spread scenically beyond.

The trail dips in and out of more erosion-carved drainages. At mile 4, colorful outcroppings peer down from the surrounding ridgetops as the trail bends north and pushes its way through scrub oak, sugar sumac, and manzanita bushes. The trail eventually rises to eye level with the ruddy ridgetops and ducks under a ponderosa forest.

At about mile 4.5, the trail drops into Windsor Spring **[4]**. A burn area along the drainage has kept the charred remains of a forest fire from several years past. The path takes to climbing again and enters an area full of slabs of bedrock and boulders on the west slope of Mazatzal Peak. The trail clatters across the bedrock and winds past the boulders.

The trail ends at the Mazatzal Divide Trail **[5]**, at mile 6. You may return the way you came, or continue about 3.5 miles on the Mazatzal Divide Trail, then hike 6.2 miles on the Barnhardt Trail back to the trailhead.

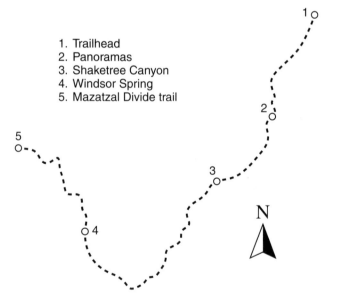

1. Trailhead
2. Panoramas
3. Shaketree Canyon
4. Windsor Spring
5. Mazatzal Divide trail

N

29. Mogollon Rim

- Explore the largest stand of ponderosa pines in the world.
- Hike along a remote crystal-clear stream.
- Follow game trails along a blue-ribbon trout stream.

Area Information

When Zane Grey first experienced the Mogollon Rim, his poetic prose met its match as he "saw a scene that defied words. . . . For wild rugged beauty; I had not seen its equal." So enthralled was he with his newfound piece of wilderness, Grey settled down in a cabin there to write novels with heroes and heroines who traipsed the rim's enchanting countryside.

The Mogollon Rim still casts a spell too mesmerizing for some people to untangle themselves from. You only have to see its forested ramparts where fluted limestone stacks on blushing sandstone outcroppings, fill your lungs with the pine redolence dripping in some of the cleanest air on the planet, or feel sealed in an envelope of silence in a remote section of the largest stand of ponderosa pines in the world to understand the rim's lure.

Whether you're looking for fossils, caves, emerald pools squeezed between several hundred foot high red rock walls, or a remote mountain stream in which to fly fish, the rim's got it. Like intense mood music that penetrates the soul, the sights, sounds, and smells of the rim's backcountry saturate the senses.

Tall, aromatic pines grow close enough to rub shoulders with each other, and each one seems to stretch taller than the one before it. Stands of bigtooth maples hang out around the creeks that babble and gush. Aspens take advantage of cool, moist crevices. Legend views from the rim's edge show off rows of razorback ridges from surrounding mountain ranges, their craggy details evanescing into a blue haze.

Some of the best trails on the rim follow creeks that flow from the side of the rim. Consequently, the hikes involve 1,700- to 2,000-foot climbs from their trailheads to their end. The hard work required to hike them is worth it. In the summer, lush colonies of roses, canyon grape, ferns, and wildflowers appear across the forest floor. Autumn ignites bursts of red, gold, and russet from bigfoot maple and Gambel oak trees.

While the pine forests are at their best on the Mogollon Rim, the weather is often on its worst behavior in the summer when daily monsoon storms rake across the escarpment, bringing wind, rain, or hail. The rim also has the second-highest incidence of lightning in the United States. With that in mind, you should bring rain gear and a synthetic jacket for extreme temperature drops, and stay away from high spots.

Directions: The Mogollon Rim is located about 90 miles north of Phoenix along Arizona 260 near Payson.

Hours Open: No restrictions.

Facilities: Picnic areas and washrooms; camping in recreation sites. Some trailheads have restrooms and horse staging areas.

Permits and Rules:

- In developed recreation sites, pets must be restrained on a leash no longer than 6 feet.
- Fireworks are prohibited.
- Fires must be attended at all times. During May, June, and early July, the forests may have campfire and smoking restrictions.
- Maximum stay is 14 days.
- Maximum group size is 10 people.

Further Information: Payson Ranger District, 1009 East Highway 260, Payson, AZ 85541; 928-474-7900.

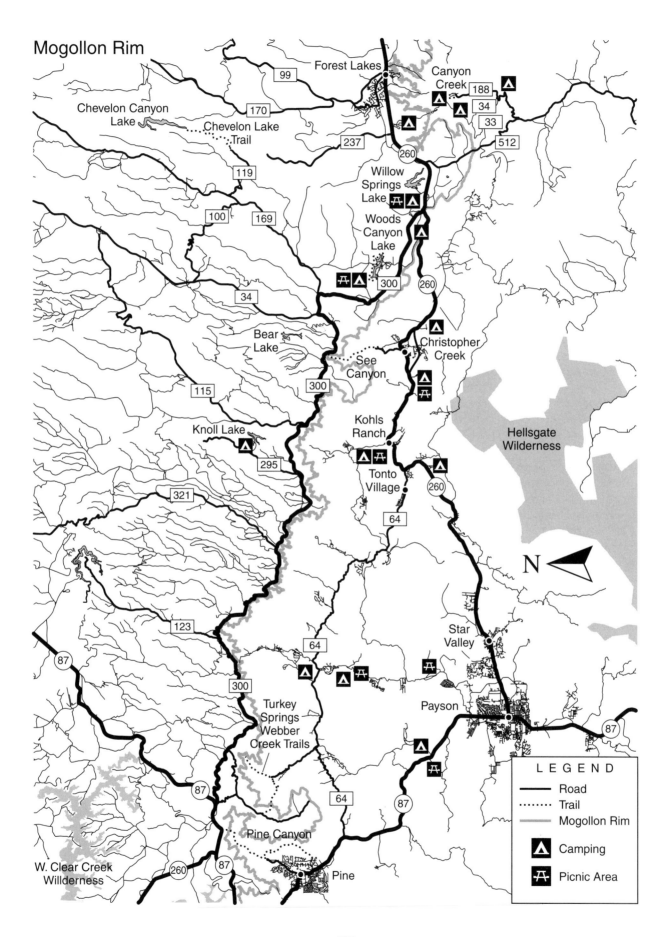

Mogollon Rim

Pine Canyon Trail 👢 👢 👢

Distance Round-Trip: 16 miles

Estimated Hiking Time: 8 hours

Elevation: 5,000 to 7,200 feet

Maps: Tonto National Forest, USGS Pine

Caution: The climb out of the canyon is steep and long. Make sure you have the necessary physical stamina if you plan to hike the whole trail.

Directions: From Payson, drive north on Arizona 87 about 1.1 miles past its junction with Arizona 260, then turn right (east) onto FR 6038; proceed through the gate (be sure to close it) 0.1 mile to the parking area at the trailhead. You may arrange a shuttle hike, leaving a vehicle at the signed trailhead just south of the town of Pine.

The trail starts as an old ranch road **[1]** in a ponderosa pine forest. The pines let in enough sunlight to attract a variety of wildflowers, and a roadside drainage collects enough moisture to harbor a bramble of wild raspberry bushes in the summertime. When the trail comes to a fork at about mile 0.2, veer right.

The trail climbs out of the drainage to a drier environment where manzanita bushes meet with Fendler's ceanothus along the roadsides. You can recognize the manzanita by its mahogany-colored limbs. At another fork, about mile 0.3, veer left. The trail drops toward the edge of the Mogollon Rim **[2]**, and by mile 0.5 takes a step over the edge to start its descent into Pine Canyon.

The trail zigzags below the rim down the south face of the Coconino sandstone canyon wall, picking through cobbles and hobbling down sandstone slabs while it shows off stunning views of the canyon system. Ledges of sandstone become rock gardens where Indian paintbrush and goldenbeard penstemon add striking red colors to the buff sandstone's blush. High desert vegetation of Parry's agave, manzanita, and scrub oak thrive in the sun-drenched environment.

As it passes the intersection with the Spalding Canyon Trail, about mile 1.5, the trail ducks under a forest of pines. Moist crooks gather colonies of poison ivy, so be careful. At mile 1.75, the trail intersects with the Cinch Hook Trail. Both of these side canyon routes climb about 1.5 miles back up to Arizona 87 on the rim.

By the time the trail reaches Pine Creek **[3]**, around mile 2, hardwoods that turn pretty colors in the fall join the pine forest. The trail follows alongside the creek, barely avoiding the soggy flow of Parsnip Spring **[4]** just before it junctures with the Temple Canyon route, about mile 3. This makes a good turnaround point for a shorter hike.

From here, the trail pulls away from the creek and starts its five-mile dry course, dipping in and out of shallow drainages along the south side of the rim through a forest of Gambel oak trees. You can see the town of Pine from several vantage points along the way.

After passing muddy Dripping Springs **[5]** surrounded by thorny locust trees at mile 6.5, the trail intersects with the Highline Trail at mile 7.7, then heads to its end near the town of Pine. If you haven't set up a shuttle, return the way you came.

1. Trailhead
2. Mogollon Rim
3. Pine Creek
4. Parsnip Spring
5. Dripping Springs

See Canyon 👢 👢 👢

Distance Round-Trip: 7.5 miles

Estimated Hiking Time: 4 hours

Elevation: 6,100 to 7,860 feet

Maps: Tonto National Forest, USGS Promontory Butte

Caution: This is a steep trail that has minor washouts in its upper half.

Directions: From Payson, drive east on Arizona 260 about 21 miles to FR 284; turn left (north) and drive 1.6 miles to the trailhead.

The See Trail—named for Charley and John See, the father and son who settled at See Spring around 1900—starts on the downhill [1] as it drops into the Christopher Creek drainage. A variety of deciduous trees—box elder, bigtooth maple, velvet ash, and Gambel oak—gather along the drainage. In the fall, these trees produce a collage of color. In the summer, a gathering of wildflowers converge on the creekbanks and the small clearing along the trail as it climbs out of the drainage.

The trail quickly exits the drainage and enters a wooded area that parallels the creek. The trees shelter a cover of bracken ferns and luxurious grass in the summer. When you come to a signed fork, veer left.

At about mile 0.5, the trail distances itself from the creek and starts its rigorous climb up the rim. The outflow from See Spring [2], about mile 1, usually has a crowd of cardinal flowers following its path in the summer. A bit farther, the trail makes its way back to the creek and makes its first of several creek crossings.

By mile 1.5, the trail sticks close to the creek drainage for the remainder of the hike, passing through thick covers of bigtooth maple trees. At this point, too, the trail becomes austere in its travels to the top. Trail washouts appear and the grade has intensely steep moments. One particularly confusing washout occurs at mile 2.5. Cairns indicate routes on both sides of the drainage. For the easier but still challenging route, cross the rock-ribbed creekbed and continue on the left side of the drainage.

At mile 3.25, the bigtooth maple trees relinquish their hold on the path to a forest of mixed conifers. Stands of aspens [3] grow among the evergreens covering the canyon wall.

The last half-mile of the trail continues up a rocky slope through a ponderosa pine forest that finally ends at FR 300. Return the way you came.

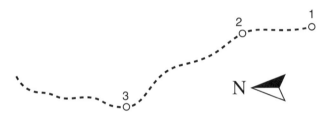

1. Trailhead
2. See Spring
3. Aspen stands

Turkey Springs and Webber Creek Trails 👢 👢 👢 👢

Distance Round-Trip: 11 miles

Estimated Hiking Time: 6 hours

Elevation: 5,400 to 6,640 feet

Maps: Tonto National Forest, USGS Pine Kehl Ridge

Caution: Watch for poison ivy along the trail.

Directions: From Payson, drive north on Arizona 87 to FR 300 and turn east (right); drive 0.1 mile to FR 218A and turn south (right); drive 1.3 miles to FR 218 and turn southwest (right); drive 2 miles to the trailhead.

The Turkey Springs Trail drops 2.5 scenic miles down the face of the jagged-edged Mogollon Rim to the East Webber Trail. The little-used East Webber Trail follows Webber Creek 3 miles to its source, where it flows out of the wall of the Mogollon Rim.

The Turkey Springs Trail starts [1] on an easy uphill grade to the edge of the Mogollon Rim, about mile 0.5. From there, the trail turns manic as it slides down a steep and rocky route switchbacking down the rim. The limestone columns bracing the rim wall blush with hematite or glow with golden hues, especially near a limestone formation called Balanced Rock.

At about mile 2, the trail slides into Turkey Springs [2]. At the springs, water drops steadily from a pipe into a wooden barrel-shaped tub. Indian fighter Colonel Thomas Devin and his troops might have tanked up here during their mission to subdue Indians around the 1870s.

The springs create a verdant corridor for the trail to pass through on its way to the East Webber Trail. Canyon grape drapes down trees; bracken ferns, the most abundant species of ferns in Arizona, carpet the ground; and bigtooth maple and Arizona walnut trees line the trail. At about mile 2.25, the trail crosses one drainage, then another, then hooks up with the East Webber Trail [3].

The East Webber Trail, not accessible from a road, is tucked away beneath the Mogollon Rim like an inside pocket of an exquisite suit. The trail, which follows the course of Webber Creek, bears the name of a homesteader who built his home along the creek.

The path passes through a forested domain where shadows reign. It starts in a forest of box elder, maintaining a gradual upward grade. Bigtooth maple trees start to appear as the trail rises.

After mile 4.5, the trail takes on a wilder nature, and its climb becomes more austere. Fallen logs lounge across the trail, healthy colonies of poison ivy brush against interlopers' legs, and the path takes to maneuvering through thick growths of bigtooth maple trees. Each time the trail crosses the copper-bottomed creek, it passes cascades, deep pools, or a spread of boulders as gray as a stormy sky.

Near the trail's end, the creek falls from cascades down a scenic section of bedrock surrounded by bigtooth maple trees. Then the path shortly disappears into an avalanche of boulders on the side of the rim. Return the way you came.

1. Trailhead
2. Turkey Springs
3. East Webber trail

Canyon Creek

Distance Round-Trip: 1.2 miles

Estimated Hiking Time: 1 hour

Elevation: 6,400 feet

Maps: Tonto National Forest, USGS OW Point

Cautions: This hike has no maintained trail and requires rockhopping. Wear footgear you don't mind getting wet. The OW Ranch, a working ranch on the hill just east of the creek, has existed for over 100 years. Please respect all signs designating private property.

Directions: From Payson, drive east on Arizona 260 about 31 miles and turn south (right) onto FR 512 (Young Road); drive 3 miles to FR 33 and turn east (left); drive 2.9 miles to FR 34 and turn south (right); drive about 2.2 miles and continue straight on FR 188; drive 2.3 miles to the Canyon Creek bridge and park.

Canyon Creek, a blue-ribbon trout stream tucked away on the eastern edge of the Tonto National Forest near the Fort Apache Indian Reservation, keeps a low enough profile so that you may see more signs of animals than people. The cool canyon environment, forested canyon walls, and grassy meadows stretching from the pristine creeksides produce a tranquil atmosphere.

When warm weather arrives, the creekbanks overflow with wildflowers, turning the creek into a sort of smorgasbord for wildlife. Animals tracks appear often along the creek. With that in mind, purify any creekwater before you drink it.

Look for a faint path on the eastern side of the parking area [1] to lead you to a gate that positions you next to the creek. Once inside the fence line on the creekbanks, spend some time enjoying the wildflowers. Mounds of locoweed paint the banks solid purple. Daisy-like Mexican hat adds rusty red in the meadow filled with purple wild geranium.

Horehound hugs rocky patches. White virgin bower vine twists around a willow surrounded by bergamot, Richardson's geranium, and larkspur.

As you walk along the creek, brown-eyed Susan, another daisy-like flower, stands around the creekwater that braids around clumps of grass. The slender plant with tiny pink flowers is willow weed. Watercress forms mats with white flowers in the water.

As you head upstream on game trails or the route of least resistance, you may find elk tracks sunken into the soft earth or catch a giant blue heron gliding silently overhead. A variety of songbirds will chatter and tweet in the surrounding trees.

At about mile 0.3, look for beaver dams stretched across the creek. Also look on the bench just north of the creek for an old rock corral. The corral, which looks like a long pile of rocks, was probably a holding corral. When ranchers were herding cattle, they'd "catch" them, then "hold" them in the rock corral.

As you near the Airplane Campground, about mile 0.4, look for a footpath [2] on the east side of the creek. The path squeezes into a forest environment lush with current and rose bushes, then exits the forest and passes through a sun-soaked meadow full of patches of field mint. This pink-flowered mint often exudes a strong scent when you crush its leaves or step on it unawares.

When you reach the campground area, you may continue upstream in Canyon Creek, or return the way you came.

1. Trailhead
2. Footpath near
   Airplane Campground

Chevelon Lake 🥾🥾🥾🥾

Distance Round-Trip: 6 miles

Estimated Hiking Time: 5 hours

Elevation: 6,500 to 7,200 feet

Maps: Apache Sitgreaves National Forest, USGS Weimer Point

Cautions: Chevelon Canyon has no trail.

Directions: From Payson, drive about 32 miles east on AZ 260 to FR 300, then turn left; drive 4 miles to FR 169, then turn right; drive 7.4 miles to FR 119 and turn right; drive 2.2 miles to the trailhead.

This hike will take you to a secluded trout stream where the wild side of nature has its way. If you plan to fish, Chevelon Lake is open to fly- and lure-fishing only. No live fish may be held; trout must be immediately killed and kept, or released.

The route starts [1] on the Telephone Ridge Trail, located at the end of FR 119. The trail steps right off the road and coasts through an open ponderosa pine forest on a slight downhill directly down to the rim of Chevelon Canyon, about mile 0.1. You get an exceptional view of the wide canyon and catch glimpses of Chevelon Creek as the trail starts a series of switchbacks down the western canyon wall.

The trail plunges below the cap of sandstone on the rim top, stepping past ledges and slabs on a sandy surface. Watch for creeping barberry nestled in the cracks and crevices of the sandstone. The foot-long plant blooms yellow clusters of flowers in spring and berries by summer; in autumn, its holly-shaped leaves turn fiery colors.

After ducking through a stand of oaks, the trail drops into a forest of ponderosa pines. A forest fire has left deadfall covering the canyon slope like sticks scattered pell-mell on the ground. Strong winds snapped the trunks of, or totally uprooted, charred ponderosa pine skeletons left standing from the fire. Ponderosa pine trees have mainly surface roots, making them prone to uprooting. When the trees crash to the ground, they sound like thunder.

At about mile 0.6, veer left with the trail into a crevice rather than following the social path that heads directly into the canyon. The maintained trail lets you down as easily as possible next to a stream in the cleft that flows in wet weather. When the trail turns into Chevelon Canyon, you get a look at the wild side of nature as the path picks through the collection of deadfall on the ground and wends around charred skeletons; some have a definite list, waiting for a gale to finish them off, and others stand stubbornly fixed.

The maintained trail ends at a primitive camp [2] on the banks of Chevelon Creek. A mix of alder, box elder, and willows grows along the creek. Ponderosa pine trees fill the canyon floor and mingle with the creek's riparian cover. Rockhop across the creek and head north toward Chevelon Lake.

Game trails provide the only paths to follow as you hike along the forested floor of the canyon. You may spot elk, white-tailed deer, or black bear. You can depend on seeing elk signs—hoofprints and droppings. In the spring, you may find a shed elk rack; in the fall you may hear their bugle. The elk like to munch the yellow clusters of pea flowers on the thermopsis plant appearing along the trail.

At about mile 2, the eastern canyon wall pushes you across the creek [3]. You can latch onto a beaten path if you walk toward the western canyon wall. At about mile 2.8, when you notice the bench narrowing as the west wall moves in, find a game trail that takes you through the alder thicket along the creekbank; and cross the creek again.

An unnamed side canyon [4] cuts through the eastern wall of the canyon at about mile 3. Watch how the creek suddenly deepens here; this is Chevelon Lake [5]. You may continue in the canyon for three more miles to Chevelon Dam, or you may return the way you came.

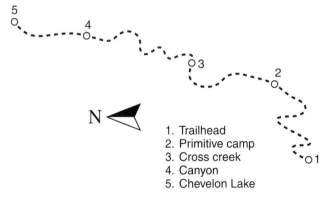

1. Trailhead
2. Primitive camp
3. Cross creek
4. Canyon
5. Chevelon Lake

Woods Canyon Lake 👢 👢 👢

Distance Round-Trip: 5 miles

Estimated Hiking Time: 3 hours

Elevation: 7,500 feet

Maps: Apache Sitgreaves National Forest, Woods Canyon

Caution: The unmarked path has faint spots; stay along the lake to follow the route.

Directions: From Payson, drive about 32 miles east on AZ 260 to FR 300, then turn left; drive 3.5 miles to FR 105, then turn right. Drive 0.75 mile to the Spillway Campground parking lot.

Woods Canyon Lake, shaped like a puzzle piece, lies almost horizontally on the Mogollon Rim. This loop hike traces the shore of the 52-acre lake. The route starts **[1]** at the Spillway Campground and heads north where you walk across the spillway. Fishermen gather on slabs of sandstone piled in the curve of the lakeshore, angling for rainbow trout.

After climbing briefly up a rock-ribbed slope, the trail settles down about 100 feet above the shore on a generally sunny route, always watching the lake through the ponderosa pines. You might spot pine cones that squirrels have nibbled to the core like corn on the cob.

By about mile .75, the trail drops to the lakeshore again and curls around a cove **[2]**. These inlets, secluded and quiet, often attract wildlife. You may spot a bald eagle on a tree limb or an eagle nest stuffed in a flat-topped pine tree. The eagles prefer trees with open branches that comfortably accommodate them for sitting and building nests. You might hear croaks from giant blue herons or, more typically, startle the skittish birds into flight. Kingfishers wait on snags, perusing the lake for a fish dinner. If you don't see elk and beavers, you will certainly see their signs.

The trail rises above the lake again by about mile 1.4. Pine needles covering the trail make the route sketchy, but the path never strays from the lake, and well-beaten areas show the way. A drainage at about mile 1.7 will have water cascading down it in wet weather. The path squishes across the flow that heads into the lake.

At about mile 2.1, the trail has you picking through a broken sandstone ledge **[3]** that eventually forms into a cliff. Though you always have sight of the other side of this narrow lake, the lake tapers substantially here to the width of a creek. The path winds through a thicker cover of pines, and often picks through sandstone jumbles of rocks or up ledges.

As the trail rounds an inlet on the northern tip of the lake **[4]**, about mile 3, the landscape transitions from a loose-knit cover of ponderosa pine and meadows on the dry side to a moist mixed-conifer forest. Watch for cairns to lead you across a marshy area full of wild strawberry, wild rose bushes, and tall brown-eyed Susan. As you head west, the lake evanesces to a threadlike stream at about mile 3.5. Cross the spongy meadow and follow the path as it heads east.

At a fork, you can veer either way. Both paths, well-defined and easy to follow, have unmistakable routes along, or just above, the lake. Gooseberry bushes drip with orange flowers in the spring and berries in the summer if the animals haven't plucked them.

The trail ends at the Rocky Point Picnic Area **[5]**, about mile 4.5. You can follow the road back to the Spillway Campground parking area, or make your way back on the lakeshore to finish the hike.

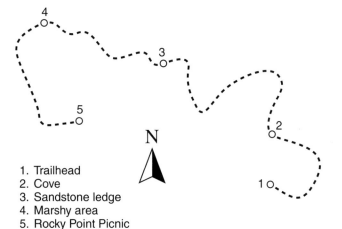

1. Trailhead
2. Cove
3. Sandstone ledge
4. Marshy area
5. Rocky Point Picnic Area

30. Sierra Ancha Mountains

- Hike up rugged and precipitous canyons.
- View exceptional displays of autumn color.
- Travel along refreshing creeks.

Area Information

Exceptionally rugged and scenic, the Sierra Ancha Mountains provide hikers with an aesthetic opportunity for a remote experience. Trails climb steeply up spired mountaintops, plod under hardwood forests shading cold mountain streams, and traipse along ridgelines above Indian ruins nestled out of sight in boxed canyons and precipitous cliffs.

The broad base of these mountains, uncut by canyons, inspired their name, which means "broad mountain" in Spanish. The Indian bands that hung out in the mountains, however, called them *Ewee-Tha-Quaw-Ai*, or "wide ranges of rocks." And this name correctly fits the mountains. You can find conglomerate, schist, shale, quartz, and limestone segments in the mountains.

The mountains tend to the dry side, with only an occasional show of springs and streams. All water must be filtered before you drink it. Trails along the handful of water sources provide great opportunities to see wildlife. Observant hikers might catch the sun glinting off the burnished back of a black bear as it lumbers up a canyon wall. Or they might watch a white-tailed deer spring off into the pine and oak forest that keeps the trail cool even in the midst of summer. Elk reside in the highest points of the wilderness, javelina in the lowlands.

Highcountry trails make good destinations in the summer, with their cool cover of pines. However, afternoon thunderstorms can bring discomfort, if not danger. Bring rain gear and a light jacket for extreme temperature changes during a storm, and watch for lightning. A hike down Cherry Creek is also refreshing in the summertime, but should be avoided during wet weather, when flash floods can threaten. Explore the lower high desert areas between October and April.

Directions: The Sierra Ancha Mountains are located in Gila County, 36 miles north of Globe and 15 miles south of Young. To access trailheads, drive north on Arizona 188 from Globe to Arizona 288 and turn north (right). High-clearance or four-wheel-drive vehicles are necessary to access some trailheads.

Hours Open: No restrictions.

Facilities: Reynolds Creek Campground located just outside the wilderness; picnic area at the Parker Creek Trailhead.

Permits and Rules:

- No mechanized vehicles or mountain bikes are allowed.
- In developed recreation sites, pets must be restrained on a leash no longer than 6 feet.
- Fireworks are prohibited.
- Fires must be attended at all times.
- Maximum stay is 14 days.
- Maximum group size is 15 people.
- The Archaeological Resource Protection Act and state antiquity laws protect ancient and historic ruins. Anyone found excavating, collecting, defacing, or removing an artifact can be fined $500 to $250,000 and imprisoned up to five years. If you see a relic from a historic or ancient culture, you may inspect it, but you may not take it.

Further Information: Tonto National Forest Pleasant Valley Ranger District, Box 450, Young, AZ 85554; 928-462-3311.

Other Areas of Interest

Roosevelt Dam, the world's largest cyclopean-masonry dam, lies just south of the wilderness on Arizona 288.

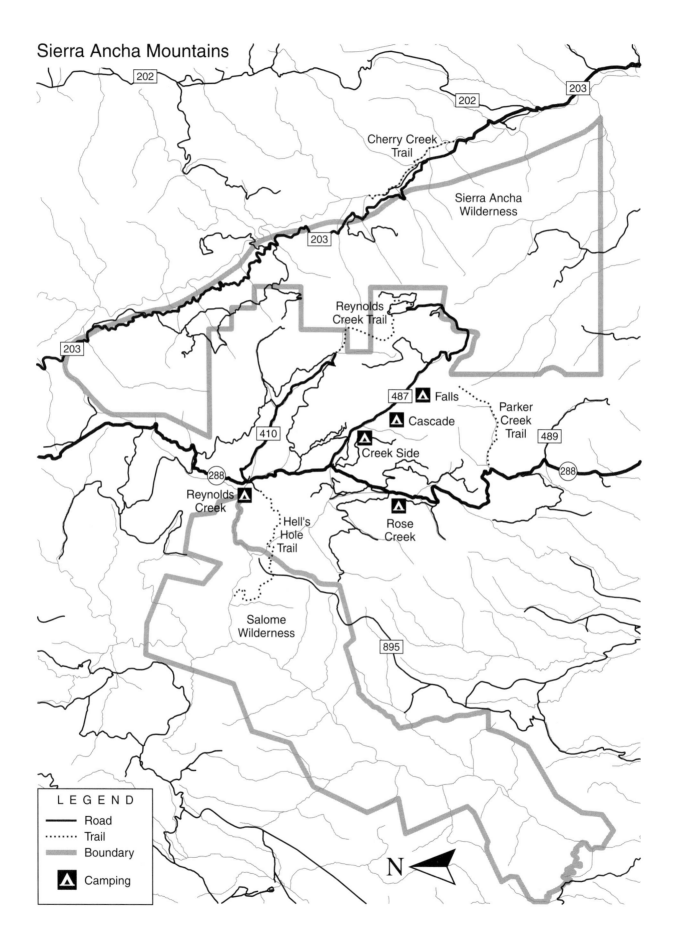

Sierra Ancha Mountains

202

203

202

Cherry Creek
Trail

Sierra Ancha
Wilderness

203

203

Reynolds
Creek Trail

487 ⛺ Falls

Parker
Creek
Trail

489

⛺ Cascade

410

⛺ Creek Side

288

288

Reynolds ⛺
Creek

Hell's
Hole
Trail

⛺
Rose
Creek

Salome
Wilderness

895

LEGEND
—— Road
······ Trail
—— Boundary
⛺ Camping

N

Parker Creek Trail 🥾 🥾 🥾

Distance Round-Trip: 6.8 miles

Estimated Hiking Time: 4 hours

Elevation: 5,100 to 7,000 feet

Maps: Tonto National Forest, USGS Aztec Peak

Caution: Watch for poison ivy, especially along the first 2.5 miles of the trail.

Directions: Drive 19 miles on Arizona 288, then turn east (right) at the signed trailhead turnoff; drive 0.1 miles and park.

This trail takes you up a relatively moderate climb to the head of Parker Canyon. The path passes through the Sierra Ancha Experimental Forest, where the Forest Service does research.

The trail gets its start **[1]** at the old Parker Creek Experimental Station Headquarters. The dark earth path climbs with Parker Creek under a particularly flourishing riparian cover. Uncharacteristically tall Arizona sycamore and oak trees coiled with canyon grape form a canopy over the canyon. During the summer, a cacophony of chirps and chatters from frogs and birds saturates the ground level, creating a primordial atmosphere.

The trail's strict beginning has you climbing steeply in segments during the first quarter-mile before it settles down to a moderate grade. During this heave, you get glimpses of the spired rock formations on the rim of the canyon through the tall riparian cover.

Switchbacks take the edge off the climb as the trail continues on the uphill. At mile 0.5, the trail over-looks a water gaging station in the creekbed **[2]**.

The trail enters a cover of ponderosa pine trees mixed with junipers. Creeping barberry lines the trail in clusters. You can tell where black bears have grubbed by the unearthed rocks lying askew along the trail.

A panorama near mile 1 overlooks the canyon **[3]** all the way down to the wending roadway where you started. Once past the scenic distraction, the trail levels out for a moment, then clatters across an avalanche of rock slabs at mile 1.5. After wet weather in the warmer months, look for colonies of alumroot on the forested edges of the rockslide.

The trail resumes its uphill course, and by mile 1.9 starts to rub shoulders with the eroded north canyon wall it glimpsed at the beginning of the hike. After crossing the creek **[4]** at mile 2.25, the path takes to switchbacking again until it tops off on the canyon rim. Right away you notice the effects of the 10,000-acre Coon Creek Fire of May 2000, which ended at this point **[5]**.

The trail quickly starts a downward trend to a saddle and junctions with the Rim Trail. The Coon Creek Trail, also at this intersection, is closed until the area stabilizes. You may continue on the Rim Trail, or return the way you came.

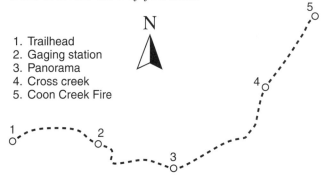

1. Trailhead
2. Gaging station
3. Panorama
4. Cross creek
5. Coon Creek Fire

N

Reynolds Creek Trail 🥾 🥾 🥾

Distance Round-Trip: 7.4 miles

Estimated Hiking Time: 4 hours

Elevation: 6,200 to 7,600 feet

Maps: Tonto National Forest, USGS Aztec Peak

Cautions: Creek crossings may require minor wading during snowmelt or after heavy rains. Part of this trail lies in the Sierra Ancha Wilderness, where mechanized vehicles and mountain bikes are not permitted.

Directions: Drive about 27 miles north on Arizona 288, then turn east (right) at FR 410; drive 3.7 miles to the trailhead. High-clearance vehicles are required for FR 410.

This trail takes you on a scenic route up a wooded canyon as it follows the course of Reynolds Creek. The riparian forest along the creek and springs makes a cool cover in the summer and a colorful one in the fall.

The trail starts **[1]** right along Reynolds Creek. During the summer, this section fills with wildflowers, and you may identify over two dozen in this area. At about mile 0.1, the trail crosses the creek. This entails squishing around thickets of long grasses and stepping across troughs eroded into bedrock.

Once on the other side, the trail starts a steady climb up the canyon under a forest of pines. For a while, the trail keeps its eye on the creek, then climbs more seriously above and away from it.

At about mile 0.6, the trail breaks from the tree cover and takes on a high desert persona as it brushes next to the eroded rim of the chiseled canyon wall. Mountain mahogany, agave, and cacti fill the trailsides. Reynolds Creek Falls **[2]**, which cascades during snowmelt and wet weather, comes into view at mile 0.75.

After a zigzag up the rockwall along a section called the Switchbacks, the trail levels off and follows the creek under a cover of hardwoods and pines. A creek crossing at mile 1.25 takes the trail to its

junction with the Center Mountain Trail **[3]**. Continue straight on the Reynolds Creek Trail.

Hardwood, fir, and pine trees shade you as the trail follows right along the creek. A rockwall at about mile 1.4 may display clumps of alumroot and other wildflowers in the summer. In the fall, this section becomes a kaleidoscope of color. Velvet ash and Arizona walnut turn yellow, and bigtooth maple trees flare every shade of red. At about mile 2, the trail enters an aspen stand in Knoles Hole **[4]**.

At mile 2.3, the path meets up with an old road, joins it, and levels out its grade a bit. Currant bushes form a brushy wall along the path. The trail takes to climbing again at about mile 2.75 as it veers left from the old road up a ridgetop, then starts down the other side of the ridge forested with firs and aspen. Cairns will lead you on a twisting route that drops through the forest. At mile 3.3, you can see an old ranch building **[5]** around which the trail makes a wide bend. The trail ends near the ranch at FR 487. Originally called the Murphy Ranch, the ranch has its new name, Haldi, on it.

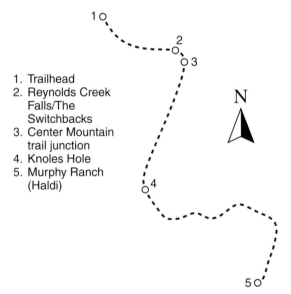

1. Trailhead
2. Reynolds Creek Falls/The Switchbacks
3. Center Mountain trail junction
4. Knoles Hole
5. Murphy Ranch (Haldi)

Cherry Creek

Distance Round-Trip: 2-plus miles

Estimated Hiking Time: One mile an hour

Elevation: 2,780 feet

Maps: Tonto National Forest, USGS Aztec Peak; McFadden Peak

Cautions: Watch for poison ivy and snakes. Hypothermia can threaten wet hikers in prolonged shady areas. Check the weather report for surrounding areas as a precaution to flash floods; be sure you have an exit route in case of rain.

Directions: From FR 288, drive about 7.5 miles and turn east (right) onto FR 203 (Cherry Creek Road); drive at least 7.5 miles to the Ellison Ranch, and park at a convenient location to the creek anywhere north of the ranch.

At the eastern edge of the Sierra Ancha Mountains, Cherry Creek runs a course as wild as the wilderness it traces. North of the Ellison Ranch [1], the creek veers into a remote atmosphere that becomes an oasis-like retreat from reality during the warm weather of late spring to early fall. There is no trail along the creek; rockhopping, wading, and bushwhacking through willow, piñon pine, and juniper trees is the common course.

Animals overwhelmingly outnumber humans here. Bears come down the mountain for a drink, deer bolt in thickets, and javelina packs roam the creekbanks. In the creek, fish and frogs dart across the open waters; turtles lounge near rocks mottled with moss; and crayfish lurk on the bottom, kicking up clouds of silt as they scuttle under rocks.

The course along Cherry Creek never lacks for boulders, rocky overflow areas, and tangles of willows. The boulders, pink as the wild rose blossoms arching across the creek's emerald waters in June, form swirls and cascades. Pools gather near rockwalls and wrap themselves around giant boulders and outcroppings.

The wildly eroded slopes of the Sierra Ancha Mountains make constant companions as they loom over the creek. A trained eye might spot a Sinagua Indian ruin tucked into a rugged side canyons or a relic hidden along the banks of the creek. If you do spot Indian signs, leave them where you found them.

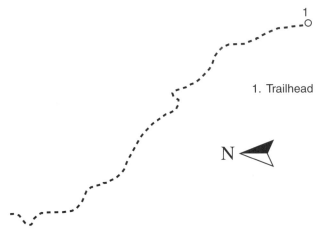

1. Trailhead

N

Hell's Hole Trail 🥾 🥾 🥾 🥾

Distance Round-Trip: 11

Estimated Hiking Time: 5 hours

Elevation: 4,200 to 5,500 feet

Maps: Tonto National Forest, USGS Aztec Peak

Caution: The final descent to Hell's Hole on Workman Creek is steep and treacherous.

Directions: Drive about 27.5 miles north on Arizona 288, then turn west (left) onto FR 284 near the Reynolds Creek Campground to the trailhead.

The trail starts [1] on a decomposed granite path that climbs several hundred feet up a saddle between Jack Mountain to the south and a smaller peak just north. The trail descends to a wooded mix of Arizona sycamore trees woven through pines, covering Workman Creek [2] at about mile 1.5. The creek got its name for a rancher in the area named Wertman; Workman is a misnomer.

Along the 600-foot climb out of this section of Workman Creek, you can see the extremely rugged topography of steep slopes, precipitous outcroppings, and jagged ridges of the wilderness to the north. The view disappears when the trail plateaus on a mesa at about mile 2.5.

The flat traverse across a mesa runs through a pygmy forest of piñon and juniper trees. Agave plants, which bloom deep yellow clusters of flowers, dot the landscape. The succulent plants bloom once in their lives during the months of May or June—some time around their 35th year—and then die. By mile 4, the path starts its last descent into the Workman Creek drainage (Hell's Hole) [3].

The trail drops unkindly, forcing you to pick your way through large rocks down the steep slope. The path alternates between long, lazy horizontal stretches and treacherously steep switchbacks. Overgrowths of scrub oak bushes and locust trees encroach the trail in areas. Watch that you don't get scratched by the inch-long thorns on the locust trees.

The trail finally lands on the banks of Workman Creek. Arizona sycamore and cottonwood trees shade the compact creek, a bit wider than a stream. Patches of poison ivy plants hang around the banks.

You may explore the creek (the confluence of Workman and Reynolds creeks lies about a quarter-mile upstream, and Salome Creek about a mile downstream), or return the way you came.

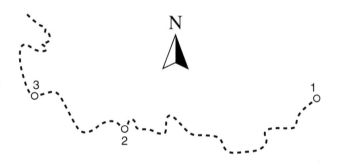

1. Trailhead
2. Workman Creek
3. Descent into Hell's Hole

31. Pinal Mountain Recreation Area

- Experience the dramatic vegetative changes on a sky island mountain.
- See an array of autumn color.
- Find remnants of mines and logging.

Area Information

The Pinal Mountains, which encompass the Pinal Mountain Recreation Area, rise abruptly from the desert floor, creating a vegetative wonder. A trail in the mountains can take you from cacti to aspen trees as it climbs several thousand feet in a handful of miles. The canyons that carve the granite slopes have drainages that pack with hardwood trees.

These drastic elevation changes mean the trails in the area involve some hard climbs up. Centuries ago, the extreme rises in elevation meant a large variety of game and extended harvests of crops for the Indians who lived in and around them.

Ancient Paleo and Archaic Indians used the slopes thousands of years ago. The Salado Indians swept over the slopes around 1440 A.D. and built several reservoirs in the mountains. They deforested the slopes so badly, the ridges eroded down to their farms at the base of the mountains.

By the time the miners came in the late 1800s, the Yavapai Indians lived in the foothills above Six Shooter Canyon and the Apache lived on the south and east sides of the mountains. Later, the Chinese used the Salado reservoir in Six Shooter Canyon to water their crops. They placed a gold screen in the flow to capture gold dust as the water traveled to the crops.

While hiking these trails, you may see abandoned mines. Gold kept prospectors hunting for mother lodes in the 1890s. During the Depression, some prospectors eked out a living on sparing sources of nuggets. You may also find remnants of sawmills. Timber businesses devastated the forests along with the impact from the Indians in the early 1900s. And once again, the trees have grown back.

Often, sky islands have strong concentrations of wildlife whose range becomes limited to the area of the mountains. In the Pinal Mountains, you may see signs of black bear or mountain lion along a trail, or catch a deer springing through a forest of pines. Ringtailed cats might raid your camp. In the upper reaches of canyon trails, you can hear the hauntingly sweet cry of the hermit thrush.

The best time to hike the mountains is March through November. Deep snow settles in the high country in winter, but the lower elevations may be comfortably hiked.

Directions: The area is located just south of Globe.

Hours Open: No restrictions.

Facilities: Recreations sites have campgrounds, picnic areas, and washrooms.

Permits and Rules:

- In developed recreation sites, pets must be restrained on a leash no longer than 6 feet.
- Fireworks are prohibited.
- Fires must be attended at all times.
- Maximum stay is 14 days.
- Maximum group size is 14 people.

Further Information: Globe Ranger District, 7680 S. Six Shooter Canyon Road, Globe, AZ 85501; 928-402-6200.

Other Areas of Interest

Besh-Ba-Gowah' Archaeological Park in Globe has the largest Salado Indian community site, making it one of the most significant finds of Southwest archaeology. Call 928-425-0320 for more information.

Six Shooter Trail 👢 👢 👢

Distance Round-Trip: 12 miles

Estimated Hiking Time: 6 hours

Elevation: 4,320 to 7,680 feet

Maps: Tonto National Forest, USGS Pinal Peak

Caution: Hikers not used to long climbs should do a shuttle and hike from the higher elevation down.

Directions: Heading west on Ice House Canyon Road, drive 1.8 miles to a stop sign and continue straight 2 miles to the end of the pavement; drive 0.5 miles to the CCC Camp picnic area and the Six Shooter Trailhead.

The Six Shooter Trail, located just north of Globe in the sky island Pinal Mountains, takes on an austere personality. Within 6 miles, the trail obsessively climbs almost 3,000 feet to transport you from scrubby chaparral mix along raspy mountain slopes to quaking aspen trees at its end near Ferndell Springs.

The trail starts **[1]** in the heat of the sun among the chaparral mix of manzanita and scrub oak bushes. When it drops into the Six Shooter Creek drainage **[2]**, about mile 1, the creek's riparian forest cools the path down. But the trail quickly climbs out of the oasis and heads back into the chaparral to make a steady ascent up the mountain. Along the way, panoramic views of Globe spread in the east.

By mile 2, the trail continues its nonstop climb under canopies of Gambel oak trees. In another mile, depending on which side of the canyon it's on, the trail deviates from a rugged trek through a high desert mix of agave, piñon, junipers, and cactus nestled on rocky outcroppings to a cool climb through a cover of conifers and Gambel oak trees.

Still climbing, the trail pulls away from the canyon's crevice and stabilizes as it enters a pine-oak forest **[3]** around mile 4. Granite boulders loll around the forest floor, tawny from pine needles and crisped oak leaves. Sometimes black bears leave trails of overturned boulders as clues they've grubbed along the path.

At mile 4.5, the trail becomes more animated as it joins an old mining road surrounded by a forest of hardwoods and mixed conifers. The road drops abruptly several hundred feet and levels off until it reaches one of the mountains' mine shafts **[4]** on the left side of the path. In the 1880s, a sawmill and cabin sat opposite the mine. The workers at the sawmill reportedly packed six shooters on their hips. Their propensity for six shooters gave the canyon its name.

The route takes to climbing again and struggles another mile toward Ferndell Spring. At about mile 5.5, the trail veers off the road onto a single track on the right and enters a forest that reflects a Canadian life zone full of mixed conifers and aspen trees. The trail ends about a quarter-mile beyond Ferndell Springs **[5]** at its junction with the Middle Trail just short of the top of Pinal Mountain in a crown of aspen. Return the way you came.

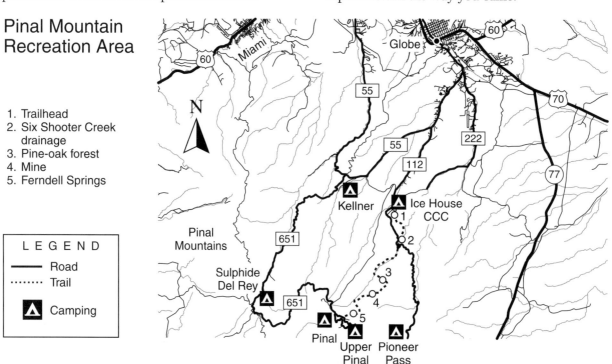

Pinal Mountain Recreation Area

1. Trailhead
2. Six Shooter Creek drainage
3. Pine-oak forest
4. Mine
5. Ferndell Springs

LEGEND
—— Road
······· Trail
🏕 Camping

South

The southern region of Arizona contains parts of Maricopa, Pinal, and Pima counties. The region includes the Tohono O'odham Indian Reservation, Organ Pipe Cactus National Monument, the Sonoran Desert National Monument, and part of the Cabeza Prieta National Wildlife Refuge.

Topography

Desert flats and low-rising mountains characterize the landscape of the southern region. Well off the beaten track, the main event in this region is nature—the Sonoran Desert at its wild best.

The view from the top of one of the several-thousand-foot-high mountains that rise in the southern region shows rows of desert ranges that rise like islands in a sea of desert. With any bit of wind, the desert dust kicks up a misty effect. This poetry suddenly fades when the harsh reality of the desert imposes itself.

Ranges, often composed of volcanic rock, rise quickly from the desert floor. Their steep grades demand stamina to climb them. Raspy ridgelines display the ongoing work of erosion caused by extreme weather conditions. Gullies show where torrents of rain gouged paths across the desert floor.

Canyons exhibit a sense of verdancy by default—any precipitation runoff from higher ground runs in and through them, giving them double portions of moisture compared with the rest of the landscape. Vegetation gloms onto any hint of water, such as an ephemeral spring or a pool of leftover rainwater. All this austerity produces an intense environment, but the desert's poetry always reappears.

Major Rivers and Lakes

The southern region, where a major water source is often a *tinaja* (a depression in bedrock that holds rainwater), is on its own regarding water. It has no surface rivers or lakes. This keeps the region at the mercy of the weather. It also emphasizes the importance of the Sonoran Desert's rainy seasons.

Common Plant Life

Creosote and bursage communities thrive in the southern region. In some of the most desolate-looking areas, such as the Rainbow Valley, the Cabeza Prieta, and the reservation, creosote makes a strong showing. Other desert denizens, such as saguaro cactus, a variety of cholla cacti, ocotillo, prickly pear, and barrel cactus, like to climb the bajadas. Along the washes, which collect precipitation, chuparosa, bursage, and desert lavender might meet; mesquite and paloverde trees offer their stingy shade.

At the bottom of the southern region, some Mexican cacti find a home in Arizona. As sun worshipers that prefer day-long sun and need year-long warmth, the organ pipe and senita cacti grow mainly in the Organ Pipe Cactus National Monument along the Mexican border. More comfortable in Mexico, where they get the warmth they love, these cacti tend to grow on south-facing slopes in the monument, where a deadly frost is less likely to occur.

If the winter's been good and supplied enough rain, a cover of wildflowers will color the landscape, giving the desert an absolutely gorgeous appeal. After the fanfare of the colorful herbaceous season ends (if there is one), the area gives its more common rendition of the desert in bloom when the cacti and heat-loving plants open their distinctive flowers. Many, such as the saguaro and organ pipe cacti and plants from the four-o'clock family and unicorn plant, prefer to flower in the cover of night. Other cacti glory in the sun, and their blossoms won't budge open until the sunlight touches them.

But the desert doesn't need color to evoke its drama. Even in the depths of a drought, when herbaceous plants have strawed and creosote leaves wither to the texture of dried leather, the desert keeps its fascinating allure.

Common Birds and Mammals

In a land where most of nature waits until the cover of dark to come alive, the term *common* takes a new meaning. Kangaroo rats, which never need to take a sip of water, bounce around the desert floor in the cool of the night. The rats' activity energizes their nocturnal predators, such as rattlesnakes, owls, and kit foxes.

Coyotes announce their presence with wavering howls. The mournful tones match the soulfulness of the mourning dove, which favors the morning to sing its song. The coyotes that haven't gotten their meal during the day will continue to hunt through the night.

Night pollinators follow the musky scent of night blossoms, which take on an exaggerated profundity in the denser molecules of the night air. Long-nosed bats flit around the columns of saguaro and organ pipe cacti. Hawk moths sip from desert wishbone bush, cacti blossoms, and sacred datura.

Climate

Compared with most deserts of the world, which are reduced to barren sand, cracked earth, and meager vegetation, the Sonoran Desert takes on an Eden-like persona. Most visitors communicate their surprise at how green the Sonoran Desert looks when they first encounter the land. The Sonoran's secret is its two rainy seasons.

In a perfect year, the winter rains begin in the desert right after Thanksgiving. Fronts from the Pacific Northwest sweep down low enough into the state to produce gentle, steady rains that last

several hours to several days, then move on. A couple weeks later, a new front moves in. This cycle continues through February, then occurs less frequently. Daytime temperatures on a sunny winter day hover in the 60s; at night they dwell in the 40s. A cold front will bring frost.

The second rainy season starts in July, when the moist air from the Gulf of Mexico rises and mixes with cold mountain air to create turbulent thunderstorms. The storms move from the higher mountains to the desert. Cloudbursts drop heavy rain. Summer temperatures during the rainy season stay between 90 and 110 degrees, the lower temperature appearing at night. In the dry summer season, temperatures often top 110.

During the milder spring and fall, daytime temperatures relax into the 80s. At night they bottom out in the 50s.

Best Natural Features

- Pristine Sonoran Desert vegetation, such as at Organ Pipe Cactus National Monument, the Cabeza Prieta National Wildlife Refuge, and the Sonoran Desert National Monument

- Saguaro forests that cover sunny mountain slopes, especially when they flower in May and June

- Far-reaching views from rugged ridgetops

- Carpets of wildflowers after a wet winter

32. Sierra Estrella Wilderness

- Explore the challenging terrain of a remote and rugged wilderness.
- Climb a peak composed of milk-white quartz.
- Experience a chance sighting of bighorn sheep.

Area Information

Rising out of the desert flats of the Rainbow Valley in the Sierra Estrella Mountains, the 14,400-acre Sierra Estrella Wilderness lies relatively close to the city of Phoenix, but with an out-in-the-middle-of-nowhere-feeling. The remote and rugged wedge of wilderness is surrounded by the Akimel O'odham Indian Nation.

The only trail in the 14,400-acre wilderness climbs steeply up Quartz Peak. True to its name, the mountain harbors a considerable amount of quartz riddled in the rocks and scattered about the trailsides. Though quartz often indicates the presence of precious metals, there are no mines in the wilderness. The absence of mining has preserved the pristine quality of the area.

A hike in the wilderness requires hiking experience and a well-conditioned body. Steep, unrelenting climbs demand strength and agility. Unclear sections that pick through boulders require route-finding skills. If you're an experienced hiker, the trail to Quartz Peak may end up as one of your favorites.

The precipitous and rocky terrain makes perfect stomping grounds for bighorn sheep. You will probably see signs from the small herd of about 40 sheep that roam the wilderness, and maybe catch a glimpse of one. A water catchment in Butterfly Canyon, the canyon just east of Quartz Peak Trail, helps keep the sheep hydrated. The Arizona Game and Fish Department has built up the sides of a natural dip in the slickrock at the bottom of the canyon. This catches the water flowing from the surrounding peaks. A lumber ramada protects the catchment.

When you hike this rigorous wilderness, plan to do so in the cooler months, from November through March. Temperatures well exceed 100 degrees in the hotter months. When you do hike, bring more water than you usually drink—you'll need it during and after the intense workout of climbing the mountain.

Directions: The wilderness is located about 15 miles southwest of Phoenix. Take Interstate 10 west to exit 126; drive south on Estrella Parkway/Rainbow Valley Road 20.2 miles, then turn east (left) onto Riggs Road; drive 9.3 miles and turn southeast (right) on an unmarked road; drive 1.9 miles and turn east (left) onto the trailhead road (should be marked); drive 1.9 miles to the trailhead. A four-wheel-drive vehicle is required.

Hours Open: No restrictions.

Facilities: Picnic area, restrooms.

Permits and Rules: No mechanized vehicles or mountain bikes are allowed.

Further Information: Bureau of Land Management, 21605 North 7th Avenue, Phoenix, AZ 85027; 623-580-5500.

Other Areas of Interest

The Casa Grande Ruins National Monument in Coolidge features the largest Hohokam Indian structure built. Call 520-723-3172 for more information.

Quartz Peak Trail 👢 👢 👢 👢

Distance Round-Trip: 6 miles

Estimated Hiking Time: 4 hours

Elevation: 1,550 to 4,052 feet

Map: Montezuma Peak, Arizona

Caution: The trail may require route-finding skills in some sections.

Directions: Drive southeast along the wilderness on an unmarked road 1.9 miles and turn east (left) onto the signed trailhead road; drive 1.9 miles to the trailhead.

The Quartz Peak Trail, the only established trail in the Sierra Estrella Wilderness, takes you into a rugged, remote niche in the desert where bighorn sheep like to hang out. The trail starts **[1]** on the floor of Rainbow Valley, then climbs 2,500 feet to the milk-white tip of Quartz Peak.

An old road brings you to a register box where you may sign in, then bends across the desert floor to a ridge at about mile 0.25. Quartz and mica-flecked rocks stacked into cairns guide you as the trail transitions into a single track onto the ridge. From here, the trail takes an austere turn as it starts up the low end of the ridge and rarely stops climbing. Fist-sized cobbles on the trail make for unstable footing.

Watch out for segments of cactus lying on the trail, too. The segments, covered with inch-long needles, drop from the teddy bear cholla along the trail. The needles have barbed tips that make them difficult to remove.

The trail gives you a chance to rest at about mile 0.5 when it switchbacks on a flat swatch of land that makes a scenic overlook, then contours the west side of the ridge on a nearly level course. At about mile 0.75, the trail starts climbing up the next level of the ridge. If you look back, you can see how the trail follows the spine of the ridge that rises in stair-step fashion.

By mile 1, the trail is in the throes of some serious climbing, making tight switchbacks and high-stepping up bulges of bedrock. The stiff arms of paloverde trees reach into the path. Saguaro cactus, ocotillo, and a variety of cholla cacti cover the slopes.

The halfway point **[2]** has a landing big enough to set up a small primitive camp. You can see the ragged ridgelines of the North and South Maricopa mountains in the distant west.

The path reaches the bouldery cap of the ridgetop at about mile 2. Jagged rocks and outcroppings, golden and streaked with a dark brown patina, jut along the trailsides. You can catch Quartz Peak showing itself during the trail's zigzag up the ridge. A bit farther, you can see notched Butterfly Peak to the right of Quartz Peak. As the trail nears Quartz Peak, the matrix of white quartz draped across it becomes more defined.

You will need good route-finding skills after the trail stops on a flat overlook at about mile 2.5 and starts picking through the boulders **[3]**. A beaten path and cairns will direct your scramble over and around boulders. This last segment may take over a half-hour to carefully climb up to Quartz Peak.

If you decide to make the scramble up Quartz Peak, enjoy the stunning views. Then return the way you came.

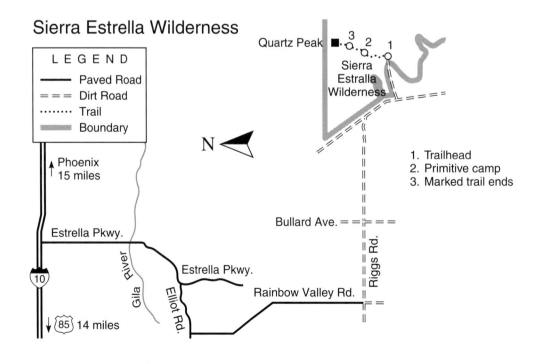

Sierra Estrella Wilderness

LEGEND
— Paved Road
=== Dirt Road
······ Trail
▬▬ Boundary

Phoenix 15 miles

Estrella Pkwy.

Gila River

Elliot Rd.

Estrella Pkwy.

10

85 14 miles

Quartz Peak

Sierra Estralla Wilderness

1. Trailhead
2. Primitive camp
3. Marked trail ends

N

Bullard Ave.

Riggs Rd.

Rainbow Valley Rd.

33. Table Top Wilderness

- Hike through a quintessential Sonoran Desert landscape.
- View fabulous panoramas of the Vekol Valley from flat-topped Table Mountain.

Area Information

Located in the southeast corner of the Sonoran Desert National Monument, the 34,400-acre Table Top Wilderness presents a quintessential Sonoran Desert landscape full of saguaro cacti forests, paloverde trees, and assorted cacti. Ironwood and mesquite trees line washes that carve across the desert floor.

This floor, called the Vekol Valley, has granite bedrock covered with sand and silt. The granite, after (geologists guess) millions of years, has decomposed to coarse sand. Lava flows, frozen in prone positions, preserve outcrops of granite.

The valley, with its loose layer of granite and open lowland, has all the makings for dust devils—or dust clouds. Here wind picks up the sandy soil and gathers it into whirlwinds or clouds that travel across the land. Usually the dust cloud only amounts to a harmless geologic tool that shifts the landscape. During the summer, when thunderstorms rip through the area, the high winds can kick up dust clouds.

But the summertime is not the best time to hike the wilderness, when triple-digit temperatures can make hikes dangerous. The best time to hike is from November through March, when temperatures moderate. During March after a wet winter, the wilderness has a delightful spread of wildflowers.

This wilderness offers an excellent chance to experience desert solitude. The area gets little use, and its primitive setting gives you a feel for what life might have been like before cities and towns grew up.

The wilderness is a wildlife and desert tortoise habitat. Desert bighorn sheep, coyote, mule deer, javelina, and sundry reptiles also inhabit the land. They may be the only beings you see on your treks in the Table Top Wilderness.

Directions: From Interstate 8 and the Vekol Road exit 144 (approximately 26 miles east of Gila Bend and 34 miles west of Casa Grande), cross to the south side of the interstate on Vekol Road and drive south to the trailhead turnoffs.

Hours Open: No restrictions.

Facilities: Three-site campground, vault toilet, and parking area.

Permits and Rules:
- No mechanized vehicles or mountain bikes are allowed.
- Pets are not allowed on the Table Top Trail, and must be leashed on the Lava Flow Trail.
- Fires are not allowed.

Further Information: Bureau of Land Management, 21605 North 7th Avenue, Phoenix, AZ 85027; 623-580-5500.

Other Areas of Interest

The Casa Grande Ruins National Monument in Coolidge features the largest Hohokam Indian structure built. Call 520-723-3172 for more information.

Table Top Trail 👢👢👢👢

Distance Round-Trip: 7 miles

Estimated Hiking Time: 4 hours

Elevation: 2,299 to 4,356 feet

Map: USGS Antelope Peak, Arizona

Caution: Warm-weather hikes should be done during the early morning hours.

Directions: From Vekol Valley exit 144 at Interstate 8, drive 15.2 miles to the trailhead.

The trail gets an easy start **[1]** as it travels effortlessly across the desert floor, dipping comfortably into shallow washes. Lava hills running horizontally to the north make an attractive sight with cobbles pouring down their dark slopes. Along the trail, you may see chunks of quartz littering the ground.

This moderate section of the trail winds through a dense saguaro forest **[2]**. These desert giants take their time reaching their 30- to 50-foot height. A saguaro grows a half-inch the first year, and may reach a foot after 10 years. The cactus doesn't bud an arm until it's 75 to 100 years old. Considering the saguaro lives 150 to 200 years, this slow growth is relative.

After the trail crosses a deep wash, it climbs up a ridge at about mile 1.5 and runs the ridgetop's rollercoaster-like length to Table Top Mountain. When the track starts its rugged climb up the mountain, vegetation dwindles to scraggly brush.

The nonstop ascent **[3]** begins at about mile 2, when the mild-mannered slope of the ridgetop meets the mountain and evolves into a series of switchbacks that start the 1,700-foot climb up 1.5 miles to the mountaintop. A loose covering of lava rocks, from pebble- to fist-sized, creates a treacherous surface in several sections.

The trail drones upward past lava avalanches and distinctive outcroppings, all the while showing off beautiful views of the Vekol Valley, named for the Pima Indian word *vekol*, meaning "silver." The last quarter-mile rounds to the top of the mountain onto a 40-acre patch of desert grassland **[4]**. At 4,373 feet, the air is cooler, the vegetation different, and the views sublime.

The highest ground for miles around, Table Top Mountain overlooks the Tohono O'odham Nation in the south. To the west, Vekol Valley reaches to the Sand Tank Mountains. Phoenix hides beyond ridgelines in the north. After you have enjoyed the view, return the way you came.

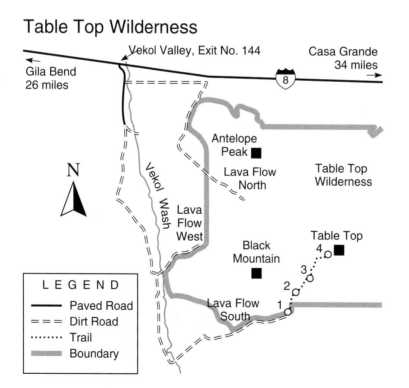

Table Top Wilderness

1. Trailhead
2. Saguaro forest
3. Steep ascent begins
4. Grassland mountain top

34. Organ Pipe Cactus National Monument

- View a pristine ecosystem in the Sonoran Desert.
- Hike up a remote canyon with stunning geology.
- See species of cacti rare to the United States.

Area Information

The sprawling 330,688-acre Organ Pipe Cactus National Monument gives visitors a feel for life in the charismatic Sonoran Desert. The Sonoran Desert has a distinctive characteristic among other deserts, inasmuch as it has two rainy seasons. Gentle rains fall in the winter, and monsoon rains come in the form of thunderstorms in the late summer. The nourishing winter rains and deluges from summer storms lure an extraordinary amount of vegetation and wildlife. The monument showcases wildlife in a desert ecosystem at its unhampered best.

The monument contains cactus exclusive to this area of the United States: the organ pipe cactus and senita cactus. Senita cacti look much like organ pipe cacti inasmuch as they grow arms from a central base on the ground. However, as the senita cactus ages, it develops twisted bristly spines that give the cactus a shaggy look. This feature gives the senita the alternate name of *old man cactus*. The senita cactus, like the organ pipe, blooms light purple flowers along the arm of the plant, but the flowers are only a quarter of the size of an organ pipe's.

The monument has 24 other species of cacti that grow in its desert environment, including the giant saguaro. If you want to view the exquisite May blossoms of the night-blooming organ pipe, senita, and saguaro cacti, you'll have to act like the animals that dwell in the monument and become nocturnal.

Other cacti show their pretty pink, yellow, and red blossoms during the day, when temperatures hit triple digits. After a wet winter, carpets of wildflowers cover the desert floor from late February through March.

Because of the high summer temperatures, the best time to hike the monument is from November through March. Dawn hikes to view night-blooming cacti work well in the warmer weather. And so do night hikes. But if you do hike at night, remember, that's when all the desert critters come out, including rattlesnakes and scorpions, as well as kangaroo rats, owls, and jackrabbits. You may catch a long-nosed bat sipping at the cup-sized blossoms of a saguaro or organ pipe cactus. Whether you hike at night or during the day, give animals and their activity the full right of way.

Directions: The monument is located 22 miles south of Why. From Tucson, follow Arizona 86 to Why, then turn south on Arizona 85. From Phoenix, take I-10 to exit 112, then drive south on Arizona 85.

Hours Open: Visitors center open daily from 8:00 A.M. to 5:00 P.M., except Christmas Day.

Facilities: Visitors center, gift shop, camping, RV camping, picnic areas, and washrooms.

Permits and Rules:
- An entrance fee of $5 per vehicle is good for 7 days. An overnight backcountry permit costs $5 and is good for up to 14 days. Primitive camping at Alamo Canyon Campground is $6 per night, and $10 per night at developed Twin Peaks Campground.
- Pack out all your litter.
- Collecting wildlife or vegetation is not allowed.
- No camping in pullouts or parking lots.
- The Archaeological Resource Protection Act and state antiquity laws protect ancient and historic ruins. Anyone found excavating, collecting, defacing, or removing an artifact can be fined $500 to $250,000 and imprisoned up to five years. If you see a relic from a historic or ancient culture, you may inspect it, but you may not take it.

Further Information: Organ Pipe Cactus National Monument, 10 Organ Pipe Drive, Ajo, AZ 85321-9626; 520-387-6849.

Other Areas of Interest

For a more remote desert experience, visit the Cabeza Prieta National Wildlife Refuge next door, to the west of the monument. Four-wheel-drive vehicles are necessary, as well as a stop in the refuge's visitors center in Ajo to register your visit. Call 520-387-6483.

Organic Pipe Cactus National Monument

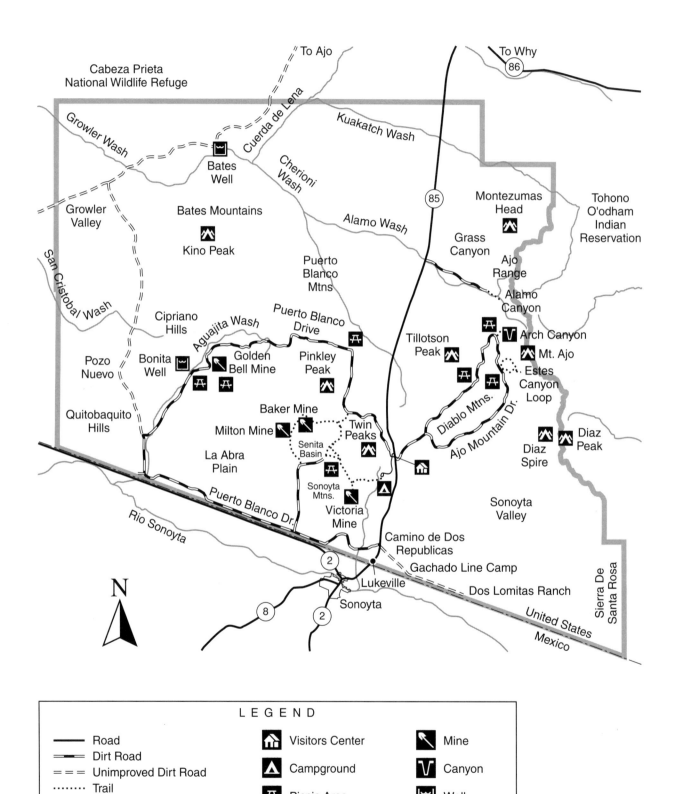

To Ajo

To Why
86

Cabeza Prieta
National Wildlife Refuge

Growler Wash

Cuerda de Lena

Kuakatch Wash

Bates
Well

Cherioni
Wash

Growler
Valley

Bates Mountains

Kino Peak

Alamo Wash

85

Montezumas
Head

Tohono
O'odham
Indian
Reservation

San Cristobal Wash

Puerto
Blanco
Mtns

Grass
Canyon

Ajo
Range

Alamo
Canyon

Cipriano
Hills

Aguajita Wash

Puerto Blanco
Drive

Pozo
Nuevo

Bonita
Well

Golden
Bell Mine

Pinkley
Peak

Tillotson
Peak

Arch Canyon

Mt. Ajo

Estes
Canyon
Loop

Quitobaquito
Hills

Baker Mine

Milton Mine

Senita
Basin

Twin
Peaks

Diablo Mtns.

Ajo Mountain Dr.

Diaz
Spire

Diaz
Peak

La Abra
Plain

Sonoyta
Mtns.

Victoria
Mine

Sonoyta
Valley

Puerto Blanco Dr.

Rio Sonoyta

Camino de Dos
Republicas

Gachado Line Camp

Dos Lomitas Ranch

Sierra De
Santa Rosa

N

2

Lukeville

Sonoyta

8

2

United States
Mexico

LEGEND

——— Road	🏠 Visitors Center	⛏ Mine
▬▬ Dirt Road	⛺ Campground	Ⅴ Canyon
= = = Unimproved Dirt Road	🏕 Picnic Area	⎵ Well
·········· Trail		
▬▬▬ Boundary	⛰ Peak	
—·—·— US Boundary		

Estes Canyon Loop 👢 👢 👢

Distance Round-Trip: 4.5 miles

Estimated Hiking Time: 3 hours

Elevation: 2,360 to 3,060 feet

Map: USGS Mount Ajo

Caution: Animal paths on the floor of Estes Canyon, as well as rocky terrain on the climb up the canyon slope, may cause confusing moments on this otherwise well-established trail.

Directions: Drive 10.3 miles east on the Ajo Mountain Scenic Drive to the signed trailhead.

This loop hike rambles in Estes Canyon, climbs to an overlook in the Ajo Mountains, then descends down an exceptionally scenic geological display of cliffs back to the parking lot.

Estes Canyon memorializes a man named Estes who homesteaded in the canyon after fighting in the Apache campaigns. His home no longer exists, nor does much memory of his stay. Now several species of desert animals call Estes' home their home. Desert bighorn sheep climb the craggy walls of the canyon, and javelina scamper on its floor. Reptiles and small mammals take to the landscape at night. Most of the animals use the washes for shade and commuting.

The trail begins **[1]** in mixed desert scrub as it wends along the canyon floor. At the junction with the Bull Pasture Trail, mile 0.1, veer left to continue on the Estes Canyon Trail.

With the western wall of the Ajo Mountains facing the trail, you can see their dramatic geological meld of textures and colors. Fins and outcroppings make curious features on the highly erodible rhyolite walls. When the trail bends south and ducks under the arm of a saguaro cactus, watch for an unusual dinosaur-shaped mound of rock to the left of the trail that has rectangular cracks like the scales of a large lizard. After the trail passes the tail, at mile 0.7, it picks through a teddy bear cholla forest **[2]**, where segments of these long-needled cacti break off and hang on the cactus arms or gather on the ground. The barbed needles of these cacti cling to anything that brushes against them, so be careful in this section.

At about mile 1.2 the trail starts its long climb up to the Bull Pasture Overlook, switchbacking up rocky terrain. At mile 1.75, the trail passes the junction with the Bull Pasture Trail **[3]**, then clambers over slickrock as it switchbacks over the rhyolite rock and enters a microclimate that is well shaded during the day.

Thick clumps of shindaggers gather along either side of the trail. In May or June, the plants will send up a stalk two to three feet long topped with a cluster of fragrant flowers. In the meantime, watch out when walking around their needle-sharp leaves. Their nickname aptly describes how the shin-high plants can hurt you.

Almost up to the top, the trail eases its strict climb momentarily and rests on a saddle crowned with ocotillo. After catching its breath, the trail continues its last heave up to the Bull Pasture Overlook **[4]**. Bull Pasture got its name from ranchers who wintered their cattle on the basin's grassy floor. Hohokam and Tohono O'odham Indians also occupied the basin in earlier centuries.

From the overlook, hike a half-mile back down the trail and veer left onto the Bull Pasture Trail. The trail continues on a downhill trek, rising briefly over a ridge and then zigzagging to a saddle on the north face of the mountains. As the trail crosses the saddle to the west side of the mountains, you get a quick glimpse of the parking area where the hike began.

At about mile 3, the trail enters a scenic spot where dark brown outcroppings poke through the mountain's slopes of jojoba bushes and juniper trees. Continuing on the downhill, the trail watches as organ pipe cacti gather in a crevice to the right, then turns its back on them to continue on its way down the mountain.

A bench **[5]** on a saddle at about mile 3.7 gives you a chance to rest if you need to. If you take a moment to scan the area, you may notice that the vegetation changes. From here, the jojoba bushes and juniper trees stay behind and get replaced by brittlebush and paloverde trees.

The trail holds onto its descent until it loops back to the Estes Canyon Trail. Turn left onto the trail and follow it 0.1 mile back to the trailhead parking area.

1. Trailhead
2. Cholla forest
3. Bull Pasture trail
4. Bull Pasture overlook
5. Bench

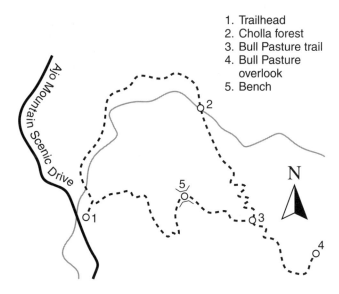

Alamo Canyon

Distance Round-Trip: 4 miles

Estimated Hiking Time: 4 hours

Elevation: 1,800 to 2,200 feet

Map: USGS Mount Ajo

Caution: Part of this hike travels an unmaintained route that requires simple canyoneering skills.

Directions: Drive north on Arizona 85 to mile marker 65.5 and turn east (left) onto unmarked Alamo Canyon Road; drive 2.9 miles to the parking area at the Alamo Canyon Campground.

This route travels up Alamo Canyon to its head in the upper reaches of the rugged Ajo Mountains. The canyon contains unique scenery, with its ruddy volcanic tuff walls fashioned into curious shapes.

An old road that follows along the canyon just above its floor starts you out on the hike **[1]**. The route passes through a bursage saguaro community where full sunshine coaxes blankets of wildflowers in the spring. At mile 0.5, the road ends at an abandoned line camp **[2]**. Cowboys used the brick and mortar building back when cattle ranching was permitted on the monument.

The route continues on a single-track path to the right of the line camp. Follow the path as it wends down to the canyon floor, crosses the drainage, and continues on the south side of the canyon to an old corral. The corral makes a good turnaround point for an easy day hike.

From here, the route continues on the gravelly canyon floor, clamoring over rocks and hopping boulders. At about mile 0.75, where floodwaters have worn the canyon floor down to bedrock, you can see tinajas. The tinajas—depressions in the rock **[3]** the size of a small puddle—fill with water during wet weather. You may also see mortar ruts worn in the stone by Hohokam Indians.

The canyon curls northward and digs farther into the mountains. Take a moment to study the canyon walls, made of pocked, stacked, and spired volcanic tuff. The soft rock easily erodes into arches and other unique shapes.

A congregation of organ pipe cacti watch from the walls and alcoves at about mile 1 as the route climbs up dryfalls that present a mild challenge to experienced hikers. Less experienced hikers should turn back if they feel uncomfortable at this point.

Once past the dryfalls, the canyon twists to the northeast and climbs up a series of terraces dimpled with tinajas. By mile 1.6, the canyon opens up and levels out, and the route reverts back to rock- and boulderhopping. At about mile 2, the route tops Alamo Canyon **[4]**. Return the way you came.

1. Trailhead
2. Abandoned camp
3. Tinajas/mortar ruts
4. Top of Alamo Canyon

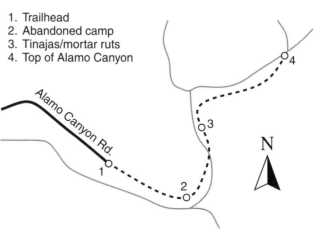

Southeast

The southeastern region of Arizona contains the sky island mountain ranges. The area spreads north from Tucson to Aravaipa Canyon Wilderness, then east to Safford and New Mexico. From there, the region extends to Mexico. This area includes parts of Pinal and Graham counties, and all of Cochise County.

Topography

The southeastern region contains a unique topographical characteristic of the state—the Madrean Archipelago. This archipelago has nothing to do with water, except if you compare the region's grasslands to seas. But it does have islands: sky island mountain ranges that rise suddenly from the desert floor just like a South Seas island would pop out of the Pacific Ocean.

The sky islands include the Santa Teresa, Galiuro, Pinaleño, Winchester, Catalina, Rincon, Santa Rita, Whetstone, Mule, Huachuca, Dragoon, Dos Cabezas, and Chiricahua mountains. These sky island mountain ranges reach upwards of 6,000 to 10,717 feet—a long, sharp ascent from an often-3,000-foot desert floor. The trails in these ranges reflect the steep terrain, often demanding several-thousand-foot ascents.

Major Rivers and Lakes

The San Pedro River, flowing north from Mexico into the Gila River, is the only major river of the southeastern region. The Southwest's longest undammed river is also one of the world's prime birding habitats. About half of the bird species seen in North America have shown up along the river. The river is second in the world only to the mountains of Costa Rica in number of animals species.

Common Plant Life

The plant life in the southeastern region encompasses just about every type of plant found in the state. And they often get jumbled up in biomes they aren't usually found in because of the sky islands' propensity for sudden elevations. Cacti can grow right next to pine and fir trees. Some ranges have species exclusive to their area.

Cactus, mesquite, and paloverde trees grow on the lowest level of most of the sky islands. The mountains then rise through the Sonoran Desert zone and into pine and oak woodlands, where a couple of sky islands top out. The tallest ranges, however, climb through transition zones full of ponderosa pine trees, and into the fir and aspens of the Canadian zone.

In autumn the canyons produce an exquisite show of color. Bigtooth maple trees produce every shade of red. Gambel oak trees turn russet. Velvet ash and Arizona walnut trees turn golden yellow. Aspen in the upper regions quiver with gold.

In the upper end of the southeastern region, Aravaipa Canyon Wilderness presents a unique situation of a perennial stream flowing through a classic Lower Sonoran Desert environment. Rhyolite cliffs brood over the creek's crystal flow of water. The riparian cover lights up in shades of gold and yellow during the area's autumn in late November.

Common Birds and Mammals

Along with such diverse vegetation comes diverse wildlife. Besides hosting common Arizona mammals such as rabbit, ground squirrel, javelina, coyotes, bear, and mountain lion, animals come in from several major areas, including the Rocky Mountains, Sierra Madre, and Chiricahuan and Sonoran deserts. Oftentimes the animals are living on the fringe of their natural environment.

Coatimundis, members of the raccoon family, appear solely in the southeastern region. The brown animals grow to about two feet long with a black-ringed tail the same length. In some parts of Mexico, they're called *mono medas*, or "little monkeys." They travel in groups of 6 to 24 and make their dens in rocky niches of wooded canyons near water. The nosy, busy creatures also have insatiable appetites for insects, lizards, fruit, eggs, and nuts.

Jaguars make their way up from Mexico along the San Pedro River. Sightings of the secretive cat are rare. Rarer than the elegant trogon, a bird which brings birders from around the world to the area to catch sight of it. The elegant trogon, along with several hundred other species, make the southeastern region one of the best for birding in the entire world. Areas in the Huachuca and Chiricahua mountains and along the San Pedro River are the top in the region.

Climate

Though the desert floor in the southeastern region has mild climate propensities, the sky islands get extreme. Weather on the sky islands can span a drastic difference between the top and bottom. While Tucson can bask in 60-degree sunshine in the winter, Mount Lemmon, an hour's drive away at the top of the Catalina Mountains, can lie several feet beneath snow. The scenario flip-flops in the summer when Tucson swelters in the 100s and Mount Lemmon relaxes in 80-degree comfort. This same thing happens with Safford and Mount Graham.

Aravaipa Canyon Wilderness, hot in the summer, stays mild throughout the rest of the year. However,

the creek water runs about 10 degrees cooler than the air temperature. Winter water temperatures can become too cold for most hikers to comfortably endure.

Best Natural Features

- Eroded granite formations in the Catalina, Dragoon, and Chiricahua mountains

- Canyons in the Chiricahua and Huachuca mountains with perennial creeks that attract lush vegetation and rich avian life

- The striking mix of desert and riparian life in Aravaipa Canyon Wilderness

- Autumn colors from bigtooth maple trees in the canyons and aspen trees on the mountaintops

- The San Pedro River, with its exceptionally rich array of wildlife in a cottonwood-willow community

35. Aravaipa Canyon Wilderness

- Wade a perennial stream that wends through a Sonoran Desert landscape.
- Explore a labyrinthic side canyon.
- Observe a rich display of avian life.

Area Information

The 19,410-acre Aravaipa Canyon Wilderness has a unique status because it has a perennial stream in a Sonoran Desert habitat. But the wilderness also encompasses one of the most rugged and biologically diverse riparian environments in the state. While you slosh through the creek's rushing waters, the desert and its prickly appointments linger just outside the creek's lush haven of a mixed broadleaf riparian plant community of willow thickets and Arizona walnut, Arizona sycamore, velvet ash, and Fremont cotton-wood trees.

You can expect a true wilderness experience when you hike the canyon. You will not find any information signs inside the wilderness. Nor will you travel on established trails—only beaten paths that wind around undergrowth and waver back and forth across the creek. And often wading the creek is the only route, so wear footgear you don't mind getting wet.

History has left a few remnants along the creek, mostly on the east end of the canyon. Historians and archaeologists have learned that the Sobaipuri Indians cultivated farms that extended into the western end of the canyon. Apaches hung out in the whole canyon, but left sparing clues. The area surrounding the canyon wilderness, however, is rich in history from several cultures.

You may get frequent chances to glimpse the wildlife in the wilderness. You will probably see javelina hoofprints or hear a group of them rooting around, if you don't actually see their scruffy gray bodies. You may see a tribe of coatimundi high-tailing it up a canyon wall, or even watch a bighorn sheep bound up an impossibly precipitous cliff. You can often see hawks soaring on thermals and colorful songbirds flitting among the trees. About 200 species of birds live in the riparian cover of the canyon.

The wilderness is best hiked from March into November. The water can get uncomfortably cold in late fall and winter.

Directions: The wilderness is located 120 miles southwest of Phoenix and 65 miles northeast of Tucson. The west entrance is located off Arizona 177 on Aravaipa Canyon Road (about 11 miles south of Winkelman). To access the east entrance, turn south from Highway 70 onto the Aravaipa/Klondyke Road and drive 32 miles to the town of Klondyke, where there is a Bureau of Land Management ranger station. From Klondyke, continue on the Aravaipa Road for 10 miles to the trailhead.

Hours Open: No restrictions.

Facilities: Campgrounds and restrooms near each trailhead.

Permits and Rules:

- Hikers must obtain a permit from the Bureau of Land Management Safford Field Office. Reservations can be made up to 13 weeks in advance. Visitation is limited to 30 people per day on the west end, and 20 on the east end. A fee of $5 per person per day is payable at the trailhead.
- Maximum stay is 3 days and 2 nights.
- Maximum group size is 10 people.
- Pets are prohibited in Aravaipa Canyon.
- Cutting or removing vegetation is not allowed.

Further Information: Bureau of Land Management, 711 14th Avenue, Safford, AZ 85546; 928-348-4400.

Other Areas of Interest

If you're entering the wilderness from the west entrance, stop at the Boyce Thompson Arboretum 13 miles east of Florence Junction to find out more about the vegetation you find in the wilderness. For more information, call 520-689-2723. If you're at the east entrance, take a hike in the neighboring Galiruo Mountains, a remote and rugged range that has scenic hikes far away from the crowd. For more information, contact the Safford Ranger District at 928-428-4150.

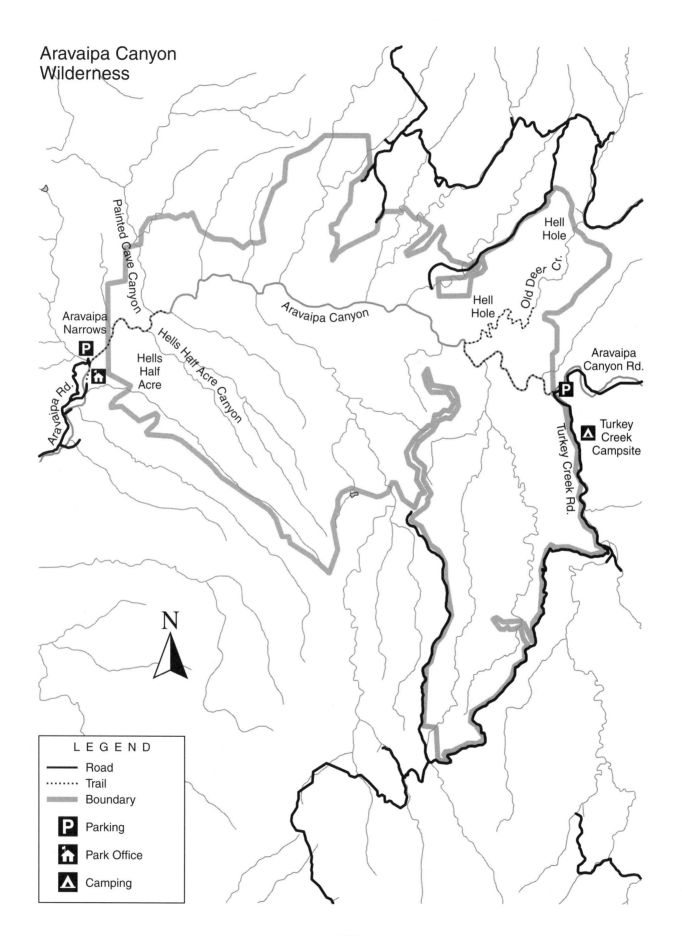

Aravaipa Canyon
Wilderness

Painted Cave Canyon

Aravaipa
Narrows

Aravaipa Canyon

Hell
Hole

Hell
Hole

Old Deer Cr.

Hells
Half
Acre

Hells Half Acre Canyon

Aravaipa
Canyon Rd.

Aravaipa Rd.

Turkey
Creek
Campsite

Turkey Creek Rd.

N

LEGEND
—— Road
.... Trail
━━ Boundary
P Parking
⌂ Park Office
⛺ Camping

Hell Hole 🥾 🥾 🥾

Distance Round-Trip: 7.5 miles

Estimated Hiking Time: 5 hours

Elevation: 3,000 to 3,060 feet

Map: USGS Broger Canyon

Cautions: This hike does not follow a maintained trail. Wear footgear you don't mind getting wet.

Directions: Start this hike from the Aravaipa Canyon's eastern trailhead.

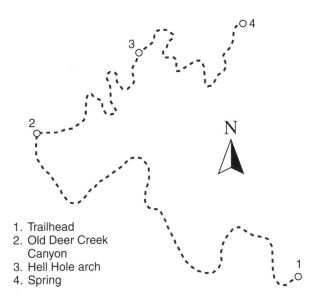

1. Trailhead
2. Old Deer Creek Canyon
3. Hell Hole arch
4. Spring

The hike to Hell Hole starts you right in the clear-flowing water of Aravaipa Creek [1], cradled between several-hundred-foot high cliffs. A riparian cover of willow, cottonwood, and Arizona sycamore trees lines the banks of the creek. Beaten paths sometimes weave back and forth alongside the creek, brushing through mesquite bosques. Up on the cliffs, saguaro cacti gaze down at the cool water.

The mouth of the Old Deer Creek side canyon [2], about mile 2, opens wide into Aravaipa Creek on the right, so you shouldn't have any trouble spotting it. When you do, turn into the side canyon.

By mile 2.25, the canyon starts to take shape as its turret-like conglomerate walls close in and cause the canyon to writhe with serpentine twists and turns. Arizona walnut, velvet ash, and Arizona sycamore trees shade the crevice where the walls don't block the sun.

By mile 3, the canyon walls become fluted and bulge with ledges. Ribbons of springwater trail along the soggy canyon floor. You may not notice the Hell Hole arch [3], at about mile 3.3, as you trek up the canyon; it is more easily seen hiking down the canyon. But you may observe how the walls become cavernous and top out with strange shapes of columns, spires, and hoodoos. This is Hell Hole.

A bit farther, a shower spring decked with bunches of crimson monkey flowers drips on the left. Then the tall walls narrow further, to about the width of a country road, forcing most of the trees out until the canyon relaxes again and benches reappear. At about mile 3.75, water gushes out of a crack in the wall on the left [4].

Beyond the spring, the canyon dries out. The walls start to melt and widen out. You may continue in the canyon, or return the way you came.

Aravaipa Narrows 🥾 🥾 🥾

Distance Round-Trip: 5 miles

Estimated Hiking Time: 4 hours

Elevation: 2,630 to 2,700 feet

Map: USGS Brandenberg Mountain

Caution: Watch for flash floods in wet weather.

Directions: Start this hike from the western trailhead.

The hike to Aravaipa Canyon's Narrows takes you into a scenic area of Aravaipa Canyon where ruddy canyon walls rise and squeeze into the creek. This moderate day hike covers several different landscapes, starting in the Sonoran Desert, passing through wooded creekbanks, traveling along sandy banks, and wading right in the creek.

The route starts **[1]** from the parking area at the western trailhead. It zigzags down a slope full of cholla, saguaro, and prickly pear cactus and drops you next to the creek **[2]** at about mile 0.25, where cottonwood, willow, and ash trees line the banks. Birds chatter all around. You might catch sight of a skittish giant blue heron taking off at the sound of your footsteps or a belted kingfisher chattering as it swoops by. Crimson-colored cardinals dart around the treetops while little warblers fidget on the limbs.

You can step right into the creek, if you want, or wait until the beaten path following along its banks crosses the water at about mile 0.35 and heads into a wooded area. While crossing back and forth over the creek, you get a look at distant canyon cliffs at about mile 0.75. At mile 1, a sign announces the start of the Aravaipa Canyon Wilderness at a gate **[3]**.

The route continues weaving across the creek and following the beaten path along the banks. At about mile 1.5, look for a foot-high foundation of a building built on a mound of conglomerate on the south bank. The masonry is one of the few historic remnants left in the canyon.

At about mile 1.8, watch for Hells Half Acre Canyon on the right **[4]**. Unless you have excellent canyoneering skills, boulder jams and pools of water will preclude any progress beyond the first 100 feet into the sliver of a side canyon. Painted Cave Canyon, however, opens wide on the left at about mile 2.

Just beyond Painted Cave Canyon **[5]**, the canyon walls rise and press into the creek. You find yourself wading the clear stream more often. But it doesn't take long for the canyon to widen again. By about mile 2.5, the immediate canyon walls retract, giving you a chance to watch the imposing surrounding cliffs come into view again.

The canyon cuts deeper into towering slopes during the next few miles as it heads to its midpoint and a more cocooned atmosphere. You may continue in the canyon if you have enough time and are a strong hiker, or return the way you came.

1. Trailhead
2. Creek
3. Wilderness boundary
4. Hells Half Acre Canyon
5. Painted Cave canyon

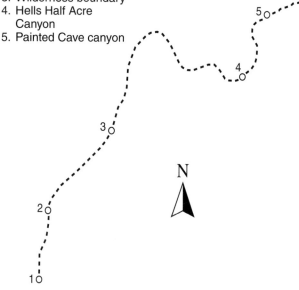

36. Pusch Ridge Wilderness

- Hike to a streamside spot in the folds of the wilderness.
- Visit a biologically diverse canyon.
- Descend the granite slopes of the Catalina Mountains past curiously carved formations.

Area Information

A trail in the 56,933-acre Pusch Ridge Wilderness can take you from the desert floor filled with saguaro cacti up the rugged slopes of the Catalina Mountains to peaks covered with pine, fir, and aspen trees. The wilderness lies on a sky island that dramatically rises over 6,000 feet above the desert.

A large variety of vegetation and wildlife lies in the elevation difference. The area supports plant communities as biologically diverse as those encountered on a trip from Mexico to Canada. You may see bighorn sheep traversing a ridgeline. A black bear might lumber along the path. Mule deer and coatimundi may dart in the woods. Stellar's jays will squawk among the pines, while cactus wren will grind out their gravelly cry in the desert where javelina, rattlesnakes, and Gila monsters dwell.

The mountains' unique characteristics—curious rock formations of stacked granite boulders, jagged ridgelines, soaring precipitous cliffs, and plunging canyons—make the scenery in this wilderness exquisite. However, hiking this land of extremes is not an easy process.

The trails often make long, steep climbs. The drastic elevation differences between start and finish sometimes require hiking uncomfortable temperatures. For instance, the high end of a trail in the pines will have a refreshing start in the summer, but get uncomfortably hot as it enters the intense heat in the desert region. In the winter, you may encounter snow at the higher trailheads while desert regions hover in the 60s. Temperatures between trailheads can differ as much as 20 degrees. Base

your hiking decisions on the elevation the trail spans and current weather conditions.

Water is generally scarce in most of the wilderness, except for canyon streams. You must filter all water before drinking.

Directions: The wilderness is located about 25 miles north of Tucson off the Catalina Highway.

Hours Open: Some lower-elevation trailhead parking areas are open from 5 A.M. to 10 P.M.; others have no restrictions.

Facilities: Developed campgrounds, picnic areas, and washrooms.

Permits and Rules:

- The Forest Service charges a $5-per-day fee to use national forest facilities.
- Motorized and mechanized vehicles and equipment and mountain bikes are not permitted in the wilderness.
- Maximum stay is 14 days.
- Maximum group size is 15 people for day use; 6 people for overnight use.
- Fireworks are not permitted.
- Pets must be leashed, but no pets are allowed in the Bighorn Sheep Management Area.
- Keep wildlife wild—don't leave food scraps around.

Further Information: Santa Catalina Ranger District, 5700 North Sabino Canyon Road, Tucson, AZ 85750; 520-749-8700.

Other Areas of Interest

The Sabino Canyon Recreation Area, located on Sabino Canyon Road near the base of the Catalina Mountains, takes you into an oasis-like habitat in the Sonoran Desert. You may hike, take a tram, swim, or learn about the area in the visitors center. Call 520-749-8700 for more information.

Pusch Ridge Wilderness

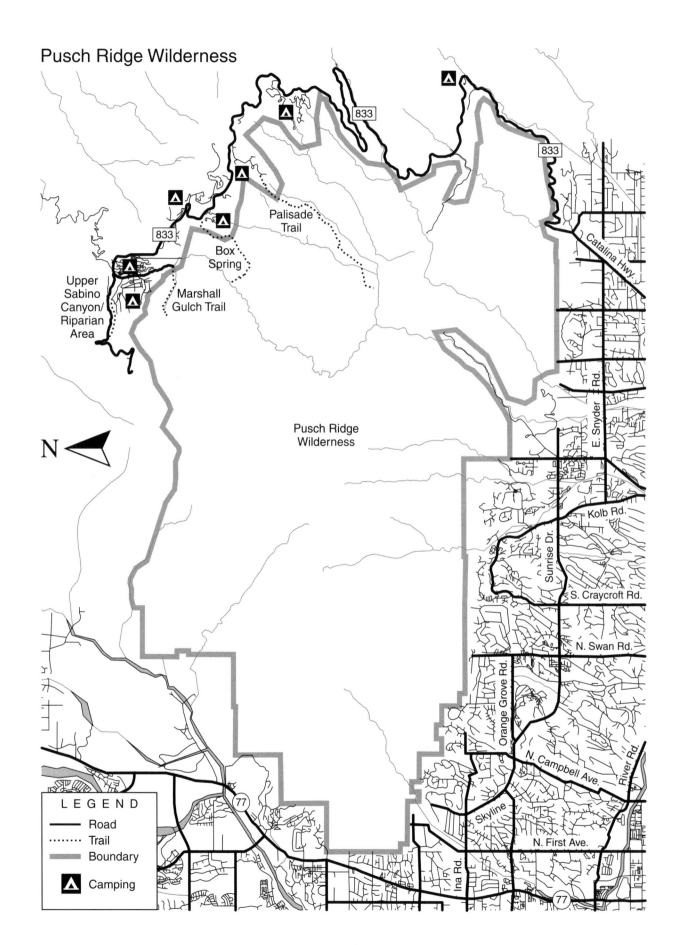

Palisade Trail

833

Box Spring

Upper Sabino Canyon/ Riparian Area

Marshall Gulch Trail

833

N

Pusch Ridge Wilderness

Catalina Hwy.

E. Snyder Rd.

Kolb Rd.

Sunrise Dr.

S. Craycroft Rd.

N. Swan Rd.

Orange Grove Rd.

N. Campbell Ave.

River Rd.

Skyline

N. First Ave.

Ina Rd.

77

77

L E G E N D
— Road
····· Trail
━━ Boundary
▲ Camping

Palisade Trail 🥾🥾🥾🥾

Distance Round-Trip: 14 miles

Estimated Hiking Time: 7 hours

Elevation: 4,100 to 7,800 feet

Maps: Coronado National Forest, USGS Mt. Lemmon

Caution: Only well-conditioned hikers should attempt to hike the whole trail. All others should turn back at Mud Springs for a moderate day hike.

Directions: Drive about 20 miles on the Catalina Highway, then turn west (left) onto Organization Ridge Road; drive a half-mile to the trailhead.

The Palisade Trail starts **[1]** in an old-growth pine forest on the upper reaches of the Catalina Mountains and heads toward Sabino Canyon, traveling on a downhill route along Pine Canyon. The trail provides tremendous views of Tucson, surrounding mountain ridges, and the strange sculpted granite landscape of the Catalina Mountains.

The steepest grades occur within the trail's first two miles, which travel under the cover of pine and oak trees. Along the way, the path demurely offers quick glimpses of Tucson and attractive granite outcroppings. But by mile 3, at Mud Springs **[2]**, the trail flaunts some of the most exquisite views it has to offer.

Hikers can drop into the springs' golden bedrock chasm, where water slithers from one pool to another, and see an incredible meld of wilderness and urban sprawl in a panorama of Tucson framed by lower Pine Canyon's wild landscape of peaked, spired, and stacked rocks. This makes a good turnaround point for a shorter day hike.

By mile 4, the trail leaves the shady forest behind and hugs a rim overlooking Pine Canyon **[3]** and its curious rock formations, then crosses a rocky ridge to look into Palisade Canyon and its massive wall of mountains to the north. During the last two miles, the trail indulges itself and switchbacks lackadaisically into the craggy terrain. The trail experiences some confusing moments when it crosses patches of bedrock and wends through rocky jumbles. Simply watch for cairns that guide you through these dicey areas.

Near the trail's end and intersection with the East Fork Trail, a small gathering of saguaro cacti show up, reminding you of how far you've descended. At the East Fork Trail, you may continue your hike into Sabino Canyon, or return the way you came.

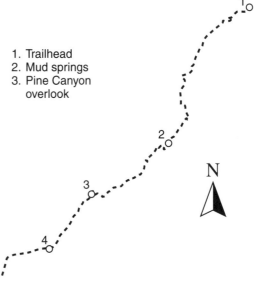

1. Trailhead
2. Mud springs
3. Pine Canyon overlook

Box Spring 👢 👢 👢 👢

Distance Round-Trip: 5.8 miles

Estimated Hiking Time: 3 hours

Elevation: 6,650 to 8,050 feet

Maps: Coronado National Forest, USGS Mt. Lemmon

Caution: The last mile of this trail travels down an especially steep path.

Directions: Drive about 22 miles on the Catalina Highway just past the Spencer Canyon turnoff to the trailhead.

In the 1870s and 1880s, the Box Camp Trail was the quickest route to Soldier Camp from Tucson. Soldiers tracking Geronimo and his warriors stayed at Soldier Camp. Geronimo, a Bedonkohe Apache Indian, had southeast Arizona on edge for about 15 years. He finally surrendered in 1886.

This hike follows the Box Camp Trail 1.3 miles to the Box Spring Trail, then follows the Box Spring Trail 0.9 miles to a secluded area along Sabino Creek.

The trail begins **[1]** on a short climb up a ridge, then levels out on a stretch of bedrock **[2]** with a collection of weather-smoothed granite boulders. At about mile 0.3, the trail ducks under the cover of mixed conifers and winds back and forth a couple times across the wilderness boundary before it finally settles inside the wilderness. During this waver, the path makes a gradual descent to a drainage that adds rocky features to the trailside terrain.

A brief zigzag of switchbacks drops you into a ravine **[3]**. During wet weather, the floor of the ravine will have a carpet of grass dotted with wildflowers. The gentle scene evokes a soothing atmosphere. Also during wet weather, a stream will fill the shallow drainage running along the path.

The trail alternates back and forth across the streambed, dropping with the drainage down a slope. Look for a cascade that falls over a ledge in the stream near the bottom of a handful of switchbacks. The trail quickly pulls away from the stream and finishes its descent to a signed trail junction where you turn right onto the Box Spring Trail **[4]**.

The trail starts its manic 1,000-foot descent in just under a mile through a forest of pines and firs. About three-quarters of the way down, the path turns to decomposed granite, and you start to see the granite rock formations on Mount Lemmon across Sabino Canyon. Just before the trail drops into the drainage, look for a rock arch **[5]** carved in the granite wall to the left (you will probably notice it more easily on your way out).

Once on the canyon bottom, the trail ends at a lush streambed that hosts a number of wildflowers, such as agrimonia, horsetail, Virginia creeper, cow parsnip, false Solomon seal, hop vine, and New Mexican raspberry. Enjoy the rollicking stream that cascades down its rocky bed, but don't drink the water without proper filtration. Return the way you came.

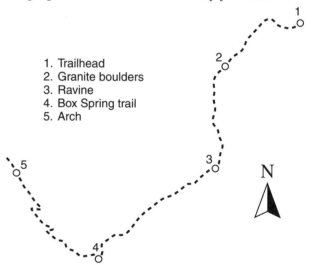

1. Trailhead
2. Granite boulders
3. Ravine
4. Box Spring trail
5. Arch

Upper Sabino Canyon Riparian Area 🥾🥾

Distance Round-Trip: 2 miles

Estimated Hiking Time: 1 hour

Elevation: 8,000 to 8,300 feet

Maps: Coronado National Forest, USGS Mt. Lemmon

Caution: Parking is limited at the trail's southern access.

Directions: Drive north on the Catalina Highway to Ski Run Road (to Mount Lemmon Ski Valley) and turn right; follow the road to the ski area and park. Cross the road to the guardrail across from the Iron Door Restaurant and follow the path to the Upper Sabino Canyon Riparian Area.

Opposite the wide-open desert terrain of Lower Sabino Canyon, the upper end, where the canyon gets its start at the top of the Catalina Mountains, has a narrow corridor cloistered by trees. In the summer, the trailsides pack with wildflowers. The fall brings spectacular colors from hardwood and aspen trees.

The hike starts [1] at the Mount Lemmon Ski Valley on the Aspen Draw Trail. The trail makes a short, sunny descent into Sabino Canyon. The ski lift to the country's southernmost ski area strings up a slope to the west. When the path enters a mixed conifer forest, follow along the orange fencing. At a fork in the trail [2], about mile 0.2, veer left.

The trail follows alongside the banks of Sabino Creek, cloistered by tall trees and vegetation attracted to the constant water supply. In the summer, you may recognize the parsley family's cow parsnip in the streambed right away by its massive, many-pointed leaves. Brown-eyed Susan displays tall yellow daisy flowers with brown centers. Golden columbine grow all along the trail from its start to its finish.

At about mile 0.3, the trail passes a sign identifying the northern access [3] to the Upper Sabino Canyon Riparian Area. Veer right at an upcoming fork in the trail.

The trail enters a moist area [4] where seeps ooze from the aspen-covered slope into the creek running alongside the trail below. Lichens mottle the forest floor and drip from conifer branches. In August, berries cluster on plants tips. The false Solomon's seal may have edible, but bitter, white or purple berries. Baneberry bushes have shiny red berries that are poisonous.

The trail drops a bit to join a road at about mile 0.7. Watch for a particularly attractive section of the stream below just past two large tanks.

The hike ends at a sign identifying the Upper Sabino Canyon Riparian Area at a small parking area ringed by agrimonia and red raspberry bushes. You may follow the paved road a mile into the town of Summerhaven, or return the way you came.

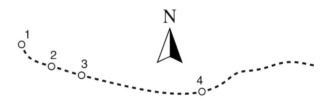

1. Trailhead
2. Veer off Aspen Draw trail
3. Upper Sabino Canyon Riparian Area boundary sign
4. Seeps

Marshall Gulch Trail 👢 👢 👢

Distance Round-Trip: 2.4 miles

Estimated Hiking Time: 1.5 hours

Elevation: 7,360 to 8,115 feet

Maps: Coronado National Forest, USGS Mt. Lemmon

Caution: Watch for poison ivy along the trail.

Directions: Take the Catalina Highway to the town of Summerhaven; drive through the town to the signed trailhead.

Treading through a forested canyon with a perennial stream, the Marshall Gulch Trail has a particularly rich array of ferns, wildflowers, berry bushes, and giant firs and pines. As you enter the woodland [1], stay on the path right next to the drainage. You may spot over a dozen different wildflowers during the summer within the first 100 yards.

The path brushes next to giant gray boulders topped with moss and picks through tangles of tree roots crossing the trail to draw moisture from the creek. These features give a gothic look to the forest. During October, leaves from bigtooth maple trees along the trail turn fiery, and velvet ash leaves turn golden.

The trail follows the gulch, crossing its stream often. Agrimonia, a flower from the rose family, crowds around stream crossings. Deeper in the gulch, about mile 0.6, the trail hints of rainforest characteristics. Pewter walls [2] drip with seeps, and thick mats of moss cover giant boulders. Red-osier dogwood forms thickets in the gulch. Alum-root likes to hang out on the weeping rockwalls.

At about mile 0.8, the trail starts to climb briefly, moving from a maple forest into a Gambel oak grove, then entering another maple forest as the trail levels out. In the summertime, a handful of mountain ash trees along this stretch display orange clusters of berries after a show of white flower clusters in June.

By about mile 1, the trail climbs away from the stream, leaving wildflowers and showy hardwoods behind. Ponderosa pine trees, interspersed with occasional bursts of boulders, cover the landscape. The trail ends at the intersection with several other trails on Marshall Saddle [3]. You may return the way you came, or continue on one of the trails.

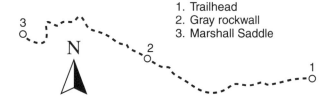

1. Trailhead
2. Gray rockwall
3. Marshall Saddle

N

37. Catalina State Park

- Visit Hohokam Indian ruins.
- Picnic beside pools of cold mountain water.
- See dozens of species of wildflowers after a wet winter.

Area Information

Catalina State Park has several washes that slice through its 5,493 acres of high desert terrain. As if tracing an open-ended box, the Canada del Oro runs along the west end of the park; Sutherland Wash runs along the east end, then bends along a ridge above the southern portion; and Montrose Wash branches off the Sutherland Wash. The Hohokam Indians built a village along the southern end of Sutherland Wash. Archaeologists call the village the Romero Ruins.

More than 1,500 years old, the 15-acre Romero Ruins is one of the larger sites on the Tucson Basin. Over 30 other sites have been found around the park.

The Hohokam lived in the Romero Ruins village for about a thousand years before abandoning it. They etched petroglyphs in canyons, grew crops, and even played ball games.

In the 1800s, Francisco and Victoriana Romero used the Romero site to build their ranch home in the canyon. The land stayed in the Romero family's hands until Arizona State Parks purchased it in 1983.

The best time to hike in the park is November through March. After a wet winter, the trails in Catalina State Park color with wildflowers in Febru-ary and March. Over 300 different species of wildflowers have been identified in the park. In late April and into May, the desert colors with flowers from cacti and trees.

You may see jackrabbits, cottontails, javelina, mule deer, and any of over 150 species of birds while on the trail. Watch out for rattlesnakes and Gila monsters, too.

Directions: The park is located 20 miles north of Tucson off Arizona 77.

Hours Open: Visitors center open from 7 A.M. to 5 P.M.

Facilities: Campground, restrooms, showers, picnic areas, equestrian center, visitors center.

Permits and Rules:

- Arizona State Parks charges a $5-per-car admission fee (up to 4 people).
- Maximum stay is 15 days.
- Pets must be kept on a leash no longer than 6 feet.

Further Information: Catalina State Park, 520-628-5798.

Other Areas of Interest

Learn more about the Sonoran Desert and the plants and animals within it at the Arizona–Sonora Desert Museum, located 12 miles west. Call 520-883-1380 for more information.

Romero Canyon Trail 👢 👢 👢

Distance Round-Trip: 14.4 miles

Estimated Hiking Time: 8 hours

Elevation: 2,800 to 6,300 feet

Maps: Coronado National Forest, USGS Mt. Lemmon

Caution: Trail surfaces can get crumbly and compromise footing.

Directions: Drive 1.9 miles to the end of the main park road to the signed trailhead.

The Romero Canyon Trail, named for rancher Francisco Romero, offers an interesting variety of terrain and special features such as several dozen different species of wildflowers along the trail after a wet winter.

The trail immediately heads down [1] into the Sutherland Wash and picks across the wide streambed. During wet weather, you'll have to rockhop across it. The short but steep climb out of the wash rises to a hilltop that overlooks the wash and the landscape to the north.

The trail enters a mesquite flat, an easy stretch of level hiking. Veer right at a signpost at mile 0.6. The path pulls closer to Montrose Canyon [2] to the south. At mile 1.1, the trail takes a look at a cluster of deep pools in Montrose Canyon from a signed overlook.

The Romero Canyon Trail veers left, then starts an austere climb up the ridge with a panorama of the town of Oro Valley at its back. The trail often gets to peer into Montrose Canyon as it struggles up to the Montrose-Romero Divide.

By about mile 1.8, the trail contours the ridge and enters a saguaro cactus forest interspersed with Engelmann's prickly pear and staghorn cholla cacti. Ocotillo may show flames of red flower clusters at their tips.

Once the trail drops over the divide, about mile 2.6, the town of Oro Valley disappears and a remoteness takes over. The trail wends through a rock-ribbed landscape next to oaks and cacti. You can hear the cascades of water pouring into Romero Pools as the trail starts to drop into Romero Canyon. In the canyon, social paths take off from the trail to explore the pools in the chasm, a particularly pretty oasis.

The Romero Pools [3], mile 3, make a good turn-around point for a short day hike. To continue on this hike, cross the stream at the pools and follow the trail eastward.

The trail clatters along a stretch of bedrock bordered by a stream that strings together more pools and pouroffs. By mile 3.6, the canyon walls start to tower around the trailside landscape covered with piñon pines and oaks.

Romero Springs [4], about mile 5, draws a shady riparian cover of hardwoods and pines to the trail that continues as the path weaves back and forth along the drainage. At about mile 6.4, the trail starts a dramatic heave out of Romero Canyon under the cover of mixed conifers that drop a sweet scent into the air. The intensely steep climb, and the trail, finally end at Romero Pass, where several trails meet. The open-aired overlook gives you a view of Cathedral Rock to the south and the Sabino Canyon system in the east. Return the way you came.

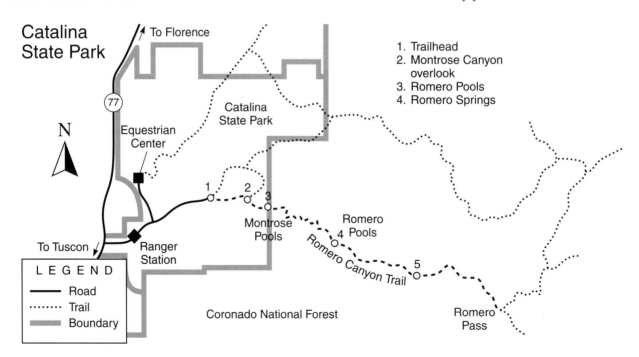

38. Mount Wrightson Wilderness

- Hike in one of the top birding areas of the world.
- Discover remnants from mining days.
- Get 360-degree views of southeast Arizona from the highest peak in the Santa Rita Mountains.

Area Information

The 9,452-foot-high Mount Wrightson stands with some of the highest peaks in Arizona. Topping off the sky island Santa Rita mountain range, the peak inspired the name of the 25,260-acre wilderness that spreads right in the middle of the granite mountains.

After the Planchas de Plata silver strike in 1736, a wave of miners headed to the Santa Rita Mountains to plumb precious minerals from the mountains' golden granite depths. First came the Spanish, then the Jesuits via Indian workmen. The Apache Indians, however, forced all of them out.

In the mid-1850s, a handful of savvy Anglo prospectors tried to reopen the abandoned mines. But the Apache Indians cleared them out, too.

When the Apaches were relegated to reservations by the 1880s, mining boomed for the next two decades. Many of the deep canyons of the mountains show scars from gold mines dug into their sides.

With Indian wars and mining the mountain passé, the lovely mountain range has recouped its peaceful demeanor. Now natural features and wildlife, rather than precious metals and bloodshed, draw attention to the mountains.

The mountains' landscape starts in semiarid grassland foothills and climbs through a zone of oaks and pines up to ponderosa pines and douglas firs. Mexican plants nestle in water-fed canyons where wildlife such as bear, coatimundi, and deer drink. Birds draw birders from all over the world to the mountains.

One of the Santa Rita Mountains' more idyllic spots, Madera Canyon, has become a top birding area in the world. About 240 species of birds live in the canyon. The canyon has become a popular starting point to access trails in the Mount Wrightson Wilderness.

The best time to hike the wilderness is March through November. Winter snows can linger in the higher elevations and make trails inaccessible.

Directions: The wilderness is located about 30 miles south of Tucson. Take Interstate 19 to Green Valley's Continental Road exit 63; drive 1.1 miles east on Continental Road to House Canyon Road, then turn south (right); drive 12.8 miles to the developed recreation area.

Hours Open: No restrictions.

Facilities: Campgrounds, picnic areas, and toilets in recreation sites near the wilderness.

Permits and Rules:

- The Forest Service charges a $3 user fee to enter the wilderness.
- No mechanized vehicles or mountain bikes are allowed.
- In developed recreation sites, pets must be restrained on a leash no longer than 6 feet.
- Fireworks are prohibited.
- Fires must be attended at all times.
- Maximum stay is 14 days.
- Maximum group size is 10 people.

Further Information: Nogales Ranger District, 303 Old Tucson Road, Nogales, AZ 85621; 520-281-2296.

Other Areas of Interest

See where the Jesuits lived at the San Xavier del Bac Mission, just north of the wilderness off Interstate 19. For more information, call 520-294-2624.

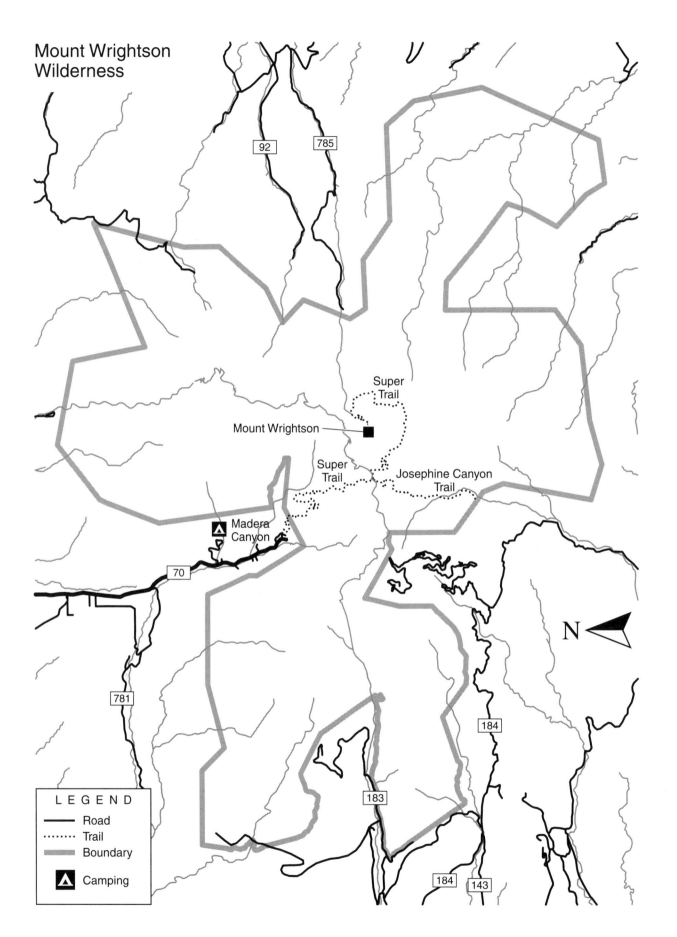

Mount Wrightson
Wilderness

92 785

Super
Trail

Mount Wrightson ■

Super
Trail

Josephine Canyon
Trail

Madera
Canyon

70

N

781

184

183

LEGEND
——— Road
········ Trail
▬▬▬ Boundary
▲ Camping

184 143

Super Trail 👢 👢 👢

Distance Round-Trip: 16.4 miles

Estimated Hiking Time: 9 hours

Elevation: 5,240 to 9,453 feet

Maps: Coronado National Forest, Nogales and Sierra Vista, USGS Mt. Wrightson

Cautions: Take plenty of water for this long hike. If you plan to get water from springs along the trail, be sure to filter it.

Directions: Drive 12.8 miles to the Roundup Trailhead.

The climb up the Super Trail to the top of Mount Wrightson might be long, but it's a manageable trek for a day hike. The trail starts creekside **[1]**, under a cool riparian cover of oak, Arizona sycamore, and juniper trees. Big boulders in the drainage create gentle cascades and clear pools of water. Moisture in side drainages may attract wildflowers such as bouvardia, windmills, or golden-beard penstemon.

By about mile 0.5, the trail leaves the creek. Switchbacks become common as the south-facing trail plods upward on a golden granite tread in a high desert terrain.

Sprung Spring **[2]**, a metal tank with a pipe pouring water into it, appears at mile 2.8. Purify this water before you drink it. The trail climbs a bit farther to reach Josephine Saddle **[3]**, where it touches base with several other trails. One is the Old Baldy Trail, a shorter, steeper route that also goes to the top of Mount Wrightson. The trail is named after the nearly treeless peak of Mount Wrightson, nicknamed Old Baldy.

Continue on the Super Trail, following signs to Mount Wrightson at each trail intersection. Also, watch for the rocky citadel through windows in the trees.

The trail continues its upward climb on long, casual switchbacks as it contours the south side of the mountain. As the trail travels along the more

exposed south face, it sees the trees dwindling in size. After climbing up and over Riley Saddle **[4]**, about mile 5.5, the path heads to the eastern side of the mountain, where pine trees start to gather. Right after dipping in and out of a drainage, the trail passes the Gardner Canyon Trail, about mile 6.4.

Now the path has risen into a cool forest of mixed conifers. On an afternoon hike in the summer, after the monsoon rains have started, this section can take on an exceptionally sullen demeanor as thunderclouds gather around the mountain.

Harsh weather has stunted and flagged the trees on Baldy Saddle **[5]**, mile 7.2. Fallen logs lie pell-mell among a scattering of conifers on the grassy saddle. The trail meets with the Old Baldy Trail here and continues another mile up to the top of the mountain.

The climb up Old Baldy is steep, rocky, and full of tight switchbacks. Once on the summit **[6]**, where an old lookout tower once stood, swifts slice through the air, ravens hover on thermals, and pines splay across rocky outcroppings. When you have enjoyed the 360-degree view of southeastern Arizona, return the way you came.

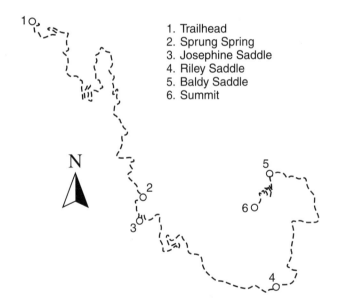

1. Trailhead
2. Sprung Spring
3. Josephine Saddle
4. Riley Saddle
5. Baldy Saddle
6. Summit

Josephine Canyon Trail

👢 👢 👢

Distance Round-Trip: 13.6 miles

Estimated Hiking Time: 3 to 7 hours

Elevation: 5,720 to 7,200 feet

Maps: Coronado National Forest, Nogales and Sierra Vista, USGS Mt. Wrightson

Cautions: This hike may be accessed at its southern trailhead off backroads that require a four-wheel-drive vehicle. You must purchase a permit from the Arizona State Lands Department to cross certain sections. Portions of the roads travel across private land, and passage is not guaranteed. Because of difficult road conditions, it is recommended that you start this hike on the Super Trail to Josephine Saddle.

Directions: Drive 12.8 miles to the Roundup Trailhead.

Access to this trail [1] demands the extra effort of a 4-mile hike up the 8-mile-long Super Trail to Josephine Saddle (see page 145), but the sweet atmosphere of Josephine Canyon is worth the inconvenience. Once you reach Josephine Saddle, turn right onto the Josephine Canyon Trail.

The trail starts a steep zigzag descent into the canyon on a narrow path that travels under the cover of ponderosa pine and oak trees. The path often has a cover of oak leaves that may create slippery conditions.

By about mile 0.7, the trail assumes a tamer demeanor. Though it continues downhill, it does so on a more comfortable grade. The path saddles up to a streambed, often picking across it or rambling alongside it. The water coaxes wildflowers in the warmer months. Canyon grape drapes from the limbs of streamside trees.

The trail rises and falls as it continues to dig deeper into the canyon. A remote atmosphere starts to contain the path. By about mile 1.3, remnants of civilization appear along the trail [2]. The old stone cabin right along the path, and one across the stream, were used by prospectors in the 1800s looking for veins of gold and silver.

The trail continues on a mild downhill. The large juniper trees with the fissured bark are alligator juniper trees. The older trees have one- to two-inch chinks in their bark that resemble the hide of an alligator. Watch for stunning profiles of Mount Wrightson through the treetops.

At about mile 2.3, you may hear a cascade coming from the creek [3] before you see it. If you look below the trail into the drainage, you can see the beautiful waterfall creating the sound. It's an easy drop down into the drainage on a beaten path and a short walk across a grassy bank to take a closer look. You can see a series of delicate waterfalls cascade into emerald pools. Yellow columbine arch their complicated flower heads over the falls, and coral Indian paintbrush contrast boldly with the delicate grasses along the streambank.

Back on the trial, the hike continues above the drainage to its end at FR 143. Return the way you came.

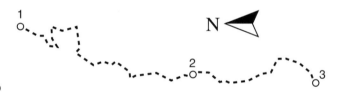

1. Trailhead/Josephine Saddle
2. Cabin
3. Waterfall

39. Saguaro National Park East

- Learn about the saguaro cactus and its environment.

- Hike through a cactus forest.

- See fabulous views from the tallest peak in the Rincon Mountains.

Area Information

Saguaro National Park is dedicated not only to the saguaro cactus, as the name suggests, but to the collection of vegetative and animal life in the Sonoran Desert. The park has two sections: its west end sweeps across the Tucson Mountains, and the eastern section covers the Rincon Mountains.

The Tohono O'odham Indians lived in the Rincon Mountains; then, later, the Apaches. The Tohono O'odham Indians used the saguaro cactus for food, shelter, and fences. The saguaro fruit harvest signified the beginning of their year. The Indians would knock the red fruit off the tall cacti with long poles, then make syrup, jam, and wine.

Ranching in the foothills of the mountains started in the late 1800s. Overgrazing ravaged the foothill slopes until Homer Shantz, president of the University of Arizona, came on the scene. Ecologically minded Shantz worked toward having the land preserved, and today it is a stunning example of a desert ecosystem.

If you hike during the day in the lower elevations, you won't see many animals, save for maybe a jackrabbit. A hike near twilight might see javelina, Gambel's quail, roadrunners, desert tortoise, and Gila monsters. If you hike at night, watch for cactus mice and beware of rattlesnakes.

Also, look to the saguaro cacti to catch a glimpse of wildlife. Many different birds, like the Gila woodpecker and gilded flicker, live in the towers. These birds peck fist-sized holes into the saguaros in which to nest. But unless the cavity, which runs about 20 degrees cooler in the insulated walls of the cactus, is just right, they leave it to create another cavity. Other birds, like warblers, wrens, owls, and kestrels, move in; and sometimes bees do, too. Hawks like to stuff bulky nests in the arms of the cacti.

In the highcountry of the park, you enter a completely different world. Grasslands rise to a pine-oak zone and top off in ponderosa pines laced with douglas fir and aspen. Jays squawk from treetops, hawks screech in the sky, and bears and deer roam the slopes. The weather is considerably cooler, too. The best time to hike highcountry trails is March through November, while the desert biome works best from November through March.

After a wet winter, wildflowers will cover the desert floor in March. Cacti and desert trees bloom from April through June. To enjoy the later blooms, be sure to start your hike as close to dawn as possible.

Directions: The park is located just east of Tucson. Drive east on Broadway Boulevard to Old Spanish Trail; turn south (right) and drive to the national park entrance. To access the eastern section of the park, drive east of Tucson on Interstate 10 to Mescal exit 297; turn north (left) onto Mescal Road (FR 35).

Hours Open: Park roads are open daily from 7 A.M. to sunset. The visitors center is open from 8:30 A.M. to 5 P.M.

Facilities: Visitors center, restrooms, picnic areas at the park entrance; no facilities on the eastern end.

Permits and Rules:

- The National Park Service charges a $6 entry fee good for one week from the day of purchase.

- Backcountry camping is permitted; a free permit must be obtained at the visitors center.

- Leave all plants, animals, rocks, wood, and other natural features undisturbed.

- Off-trail hiking is prohibited in the Cactus Forest Trail System.

- Firearms and other weapons are prohibited.

- Pets are allowed on paved roads only and must be leashed.

- Camping and fires are permitted in designated areas only.

- Trash must be packed out or placed in litter containers.

- Horses are allowed on designated trails and in washes.

- Bicycles are permitted only on the 8-mile paved loop road and in the picnic areas.

Further Information: Saguaro National Park, 3693 Old Spanish Trail, Tucson, AZ 85730-5601; 520-733-5100.

Other Areas of Interest

After you've driven the desert landscape of the park on Cactus Drive, head north and take a drive up to the highcountry at the top of Mount Lemmon in the Catalina Mountains on the Catalina Highway.

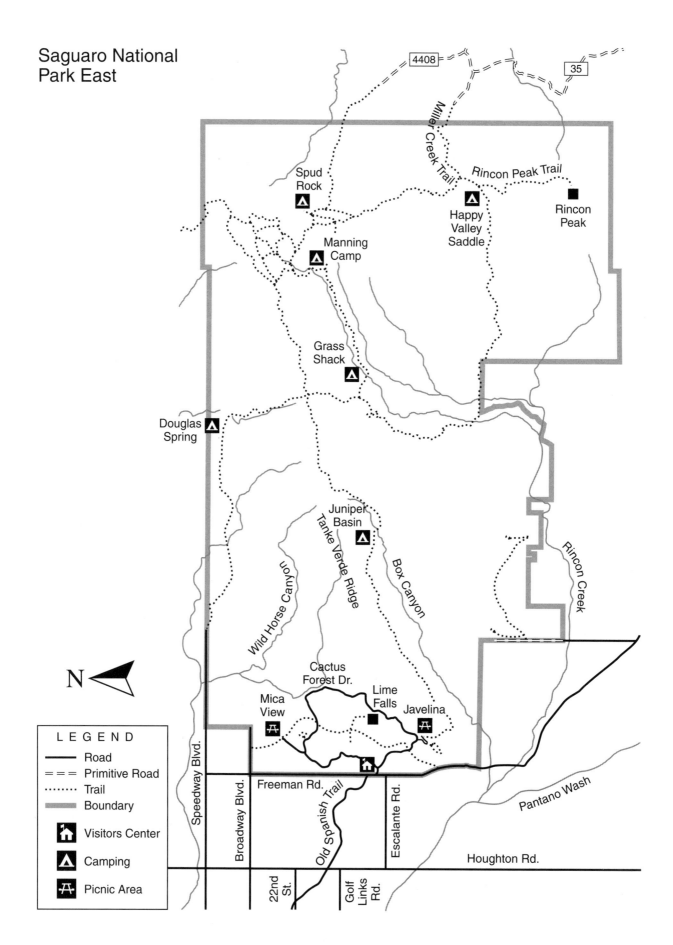

Saguaro National
Park East

Spud
Rock

Manning
Camp

Happy
Valley
Saddle

Rincon Peak Trail

Rincon
Peak

Miller Creek Trail

4408

35

Grass
Shack

Douglas
Spring

Juniper
Basin

Tanke Verde Ridge

Box Canyon

Wild Horse Canyon

Rincon Creek

Cactus
Forest Dr.

Lime
Falls

Mica
View

Javelina

N

Speedway Blvd.

Broadway Blvd.

Freeman Rd.

Old Spanish Trail

Escalante Rd.

Pantano Wash

Houghton Rd.

22nd
St.

Golf
Links
Rd.

LEGEND
——— Road
= = = Primitive Road
.... Trail
▬▬▬ Boundary
Visitors Center
Camping
Picnic Area

Lime Falls 👢 👢

Distance Round-Trip: 2.6 miles

Estimated Hiking Time: 1.5 hours

Elevation: 2,900 to 2,920 feet

Maps: Coronado National Forest, Safford and Santa Catalina Ranger District, Tanque Verde Peak

Caution: Hike in the early morning hours to avoid extreme temperatures if you plan to view cactus flowers.

Directions: Take the Cactus Forest Drive approximately 3 miles to the north trail access onto the Cactus Forest Trail.

Maintaining a relatively flat tread in the Rincon Mountain foothills, this hike makes it easy to view the Sonoran Desert environment. The route, which starts out on the Cactus Forest Trail [1] and ends at Lime Falls on the Dead End Trail, is one of the best to view an assortment of cacti and desert trees.

Even if the herbaceous flowers don't bloom because of a lack of precipitation, the cactus flowers and trees remain faithful. Mature saguaro cacti, a few species of prickly pear cacti, several species of cholla cacti, paloverde trees, and a few species of woody bushes splash the spiny landscape with their colorful flowers in April and May. The most prolific of the cacti, Engelmann's prickly pear, makes a stunning show of yellow flowers that turn light orange as they age.

The trail, wide and flat, heads south, paralleling the Rincon Mountains in the east. The trail travels in the thick of a large assortment of cacti [2] until about mile 0.25, when it passes a concrete foundation marking where the park's first ranger station stood. Cacti crowd around the trail again once past the foundation.

The path bends toward the Rincon Mountains around mile 0.75, giving you a good look at the drainages carved into slopes that rise up to 8,500 feet. Some shine from the sun hitting bedrock polished by the elements.

A sign at mile 0.9 identifies lime kilns [3] located on the east side of the trail inside a drainage. Constructed in 1880, the kilns fired the area's limestone caliche to produce lime. Ranchers put a stop to the firing to protect the browse for their cattle. The cattle grazing stopped when the last of the cattle grazing permits expired in 1979.

The lime kilns have become a favored hangout for Africanized honeybees. If you stop and inspect the kilns, keep your distance from bee activity.

At mile 1, the trail intersects with the Dead End Trail [4]. Veer left onto the Dead End Trail and follow it as it takes its time descending into a wash that eventually leads to Lime Falls.

When the trail reaches the wash, about mile 1.2, it veers south. Follow the wash until a trail forms on the west bank at mile 1.3. After a short distance the trail walks across a scenic section of bedrock [5] in the wash that may have remnants of recent rains pooled in pockets in the rock called tinajas.

As the trail exits the wash, it climbs up a low ridge and then quickly heads to its end at Lime Falls [6], a dryfall gouged by wet-weather runoff. You can see the path the water takes once it pours down the toast- and gray-toned rockwall and bounces down a jumble of ledges and boulders into the wash. A cascade of water may prevail after enough wet weather. Return the way you came.

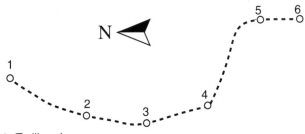

1. Trailhead
2. Ranger station foundation
3. Lime kilns
4. Dead End trail
5. Bedrock wash
6. Lime Falls

Rincon Peak Trail 👢 👢 👢 👢

Distance Round-Trip: 16.2 miles

Estimated Hiking Time: 8.5 hours

Elevation: 4,250 to 8,482 feet

Maps: Coronado National Forest, Safford and Santa Catalina Ranger Districts, USGS Mica Mountain

Caution: The last mile of this trail is steep and difficult to travel, and does not allow horse travel.

Directions: From Tucson, drive east on Interstate 10 to Mescal exit 297; turn north (left) onto Mescal Road (FR 35), then drive 16.3 miles to FR 4407; turn west (left) and drive 0.2 miles to the trailhead. The road can accommodate passenger cars.

The route begins [1] on the Miller Creek Trail, right along the Miller Creek drainage, as it heads west across Happy Valley toward the Rincon Mountains. The valley's name comes from the Happy Valley Ranch operated in the later 1800s by Charley Page. The trail travels through grassy oak groves, back and forth across the sandy drainage, sometimes lingering long enough in the rocky wash for you to have to keep a watchful eye for cairns to lead your steps in and out of the drainage.

At about mile 1.25, the trail passes through a gate to enter the Saguaro National Park [2] and begins climbing a steep, steady zigzagging path through jumbles of weather-worn boulders on its start up the Rincon Mountains. Bunches of grasses form a matrix between the boulders strewn on the rocky slope, making the trail hard to follow at times. Watch for cairns to lead you through sketchy stretches, then take a moment to enjoy the views behind you that show off Happy Valley and the surrounding mountains.

The trail escapes the sun-drenched slope and dips into an exceptionally pretty ravine [3] at the boulder-filled head of Miller Creek. Canyon grape, which prefers moist environments, dangles from tree limbs. Wildflowers decorate the trailsides in the summer.

After a short twist through the drainage, the trail starts climbing steeply again. The path enters a ponderosa pine forest on its climb up to Happy Valley Saddle. When the trail meets the Heartbreak Ridge Trail [4] at about mile 4.4, veer left to continue on the Miller Creek Trail. The trail plods across the grassy Happy Valley Saddle with its distinctively serene atmosphere and meets up with the Rincon Peak Trail [5] at mile 4.7. Turn left to continue on the Rincon Peak Trail.

Now heading south toward Rincon Peak, the trail crosses some scenic sections as it climbs ridges, drops into ravines, and crosses rocky outcroppings. The views along this stretch reach to the Catalina Mountains, the eastern Rincon Mountains, and (at times) into Tucson.

At mile 7.1, where a sign reads "Foot Trail Only, No Stock," [6] the hardest climb of the trail begins. Unreasonably steep and damply cloistered in the shadows of aspen and pines, this last stretch of trail makes a hard grind. Pick your way through a jumble of boulders that appear just before the trail's end at a giant stack of rocks. Enjoy the view of southeastern Arizona, then return the way you came.

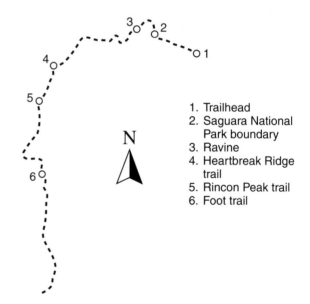

1. Trailhead
2. Saguara National Park boundary
3. Ravine
4. Heartbreak Ridge trail
5. Rincon Peak trail
6. Foot trail

N

40. Dragoon Mountains

- Hike through the wildly eroded landscape that Cochise and his band of Indians hid in.
- Catch a glimpse of a peregrine falcon.
- Watch rockclimbers scale granite cliffs.

Area Information

Lying like a scaly, lazy dragon stretched across the high desert grasslands floor, the Dragoon Mountains create an aura of fantasy with their strangely sculpted peaks and outcroppings. The Dragoons' unique granite landscape of towering pinnacles, boulders precariously balanced atop one another, and spiny peaks that look like fingers pointing every which way makes a perfect hideaway.

The Dragoons' confusing jumble of rocks became the last stronghold of Cochise and his relentless band of Apache Indians. With a mind-set that "a hundred white men should die for every Apache killed," Cochise precipitated hundreds of deaths and thousands of dollars in damage to property as he tenaciously held on to the land with which his ancestors were well acquainted.

Cochise always retreated to his stronghold in the Dragoon Mountains. Like an impenetrable rocky cocoon, the Dragoons never failed to protect Cochise as he turned southeast Arizona on end. The Dragoons still keep watch over Cochise, never telling which chasm or mountaintop his fellow Indians buried his body in.

The tiny sky island, which abruptly rises 3,000 feet above a sea of grasslands punctuated by oaks and agave, still remains an attractive year-round destination. Its terrain, quintessential southeast Arizona, makes a scenic base for camping, hiking, mountain biking, and rockclimbing.

An eight-mile road that wends along the Dragoons' western flanks is the gateway to explore the Dragoons' less-visited western slope. The gravelly road passes the Dragoons' exquisite scenery as it slices through wavering grasslands and ducks under groves of oaks. The gently rolling route has some spots that require a high-clearance vehicle, and it is perfect for mountain bikes. Several ancillary forest routes lead to cozy, primitive camp sites nestled next to rockwalls or under oaks.

You may find rock art, metates, and smoke smudges from campfires that blazed thousands of years ago if you take the time to rummage through the tumble of smooth granite rocks piled atop one another. Cochise chose Council Rocks, a field of boulders near the mouth of Stronghold Canyon, in which to hold treaty meetings. Naturally formed chambers hide inside the jumble of rocks, and towering pinnacles provide excellent vantage points.

The Dragoon Mountains provide a number of technical climbing routes ranging from 5-10a to 5-12a (the hardest ascent in the United States is rated 5-14b). You can often see a climber scaling the smooth golden granite walls on weekends.

Directions: The mountains are located about 25 miles south of Benson. Drive about 25 miles south on Arizona 80 to Middlemarch Road, then turn east (left); drive 9.4 miles to FR 345 (Cochise Stronghold Road) and turn north to access trails on the west side. To access the east side of the mountains, drive south of Interstate 10 on U.S. 191 about 17 miles and turn west (left) at a signed turnoff for Cochise Stronghold. Drive about 8 miles to the trailhead.

Hours Open: No restrictions.

Facilities: Campground, picnic areas, and restrooms at the east trailhead. No facilities on the western side.

Permits and Rules:
- In developed recreation sites, pets must be restrained on a leash no longer than 6 feet.
- Fireworks are prohibited.
- Fires must be attended at all times.
- Maximum stay is 14 days.
- Maximum group size is 10 people.

Further Information: Douglas Ranger District, 3081 North Leslie Canyon Road, Douglas, AZ 85607; 520-364-3468.

Other Areas of Interest

Visit the historic mining town of Tombstone, coined "the town too rough to die," located about a mile south of Middlemarch Road on Arizona 80. The Tombstone Courthouse State Historic Park will give you a good idea of what it was like to live when the town was in its heyday. Call 520-457-3311 for more information.

Dragoon Mountains

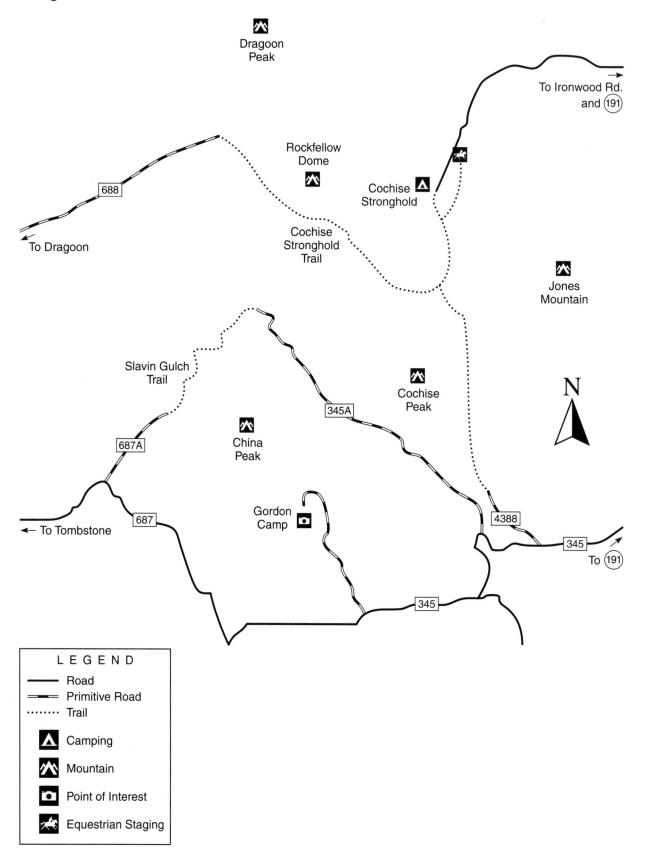

Dragoon Peak

Rockfellow Dome

Cochise Stronghold

To Ironwood Rd. and (191)

688

To Dragoon

Cochise Stronghold Trail

Jones Mountain

Slavin Gulch Trail

Cochise Peak

345A

N

687A

China Peak

687

← To Tombstone

Gordon Camp

4388

345

To (191)

345

LEGEND
— Road
Primitive Road
...... Trail
🏕 Camping
⛰ Mountain
📷 Point of Interest
🏇 Equestrian Staging

Cochise Stronghold Trail

👢 👢 👢

Distance Round-Trip: 10 miles

Estimated Hiking Time: 5 hours

Elevation: 5,000 to 6,000 feet

Maps: Coronado National Forest, Chiricahua, Peloncillo, and Dragoon Mountain Ranges, USGS Cochise Stronghold

Caution: The decomposed granite trail surface can provoke skids on the downhill.

Directions: This hike starts at the eastern trailhead.

This trail explores one of the canyons in the Dragoon Mountains where Cochise and his band of Apaches traveled during their last years of conflict. The complicated and confusing rock formations, now pleasing to view, provided the perfect environment for the Apaches to evade their adversaries.

At the campground trailhead **[1]**, make your way toward the bridge that crosses the wash in Stronghold Canyon East. Veer left onto the nature trail, which takes you to the Cochise Indian Trail.

The trail follows a shady course along Stronghold Canyon East in a landscape filled with agave, oaks, and grasses. At about mile 0.8, the trail approaches a patch of bedrock **[2]** where it climbs up, and squeezes between, the weather-smoothed boulders. Cairns can help you through the minor maze of rock that drops a hint of how the upcoming terrain looks.

Bouldery sections along the trail require you pay attention in order not to stray from the path, especially around stream courses. At about mile 1.8, the trail enters the trademark terrain of the Dragoons where columns of rock stand solo, fluted section of rock stand on end, and boulders teeter on pedestals.

The trail spends the next 0.6 mile climbing to Half Moon Tank **[3]**. The dammed pond supports a handful of cottonwood and willow trees, a scenario that attracts a variety of avian life.

The trail resumes its climb, offering a scenic stopping point on an overlook at mile 2.4 that looks at the meticulously eroded ridges of the mountains. The trail peaks at the Stronghold Divide **[4]**, mile 3, then starts an almost nonstop descent to its western trailhead in Stronghold Canyon West.

The downhill starts out on an easy grade, but as the path heads back into Stronghold Canyon the pitch steepens. Footing may become dicey on these steep sections where decomposed bits of granite provoke skids.

The landscape becomes more enchanting the deeper the path descends into the canyon. Watch for Rockfellow Dome **[5]** at mile 4. The citadel rises directly across the canyon. This favorite haunt of rockclimbers also attracts peregrine falcons.

You may see a peregrine falcon soaring overhead. You can identify it by its flattened wings, outspread tail, and short, powerful wing beats. The falcon hunts via a vertical dive. With wings tucked tight against its body, it can reach 200 miles per hour during the dive and capture its prey in flight. The Forest Service closes Rockfellow Dome from February through June to avoid any disturbance during the falcons' nesting period.

As the trail approaches the canyon floor, it passes through a thick cover of manzanita. Once on the floor, grasses take over and spread under oaks, juniper, and piñon pine trees. The trail ends at the wash in Stronghold Canyon West.

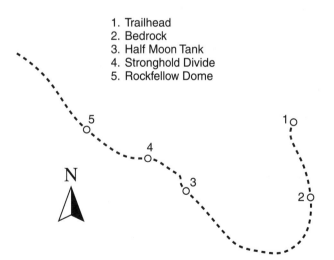

1. Trailhead
2. Bedrock
3. Half Moon Tank
4. Stronghold Divide
5. Rockfellow Dome

Slavin Gulch Trail 🥾 🥾 🥾

Distance Round-Trip: 7.4 miles

Estimated Hiking Time: 3.5 hours

Elevation: 5,000 to 6,800 feet

Maps: Coronado National Forest, Chiricahua, Peloncillo and Dragoon Mountain Ranges, USGS Cochise Stronghold; Knob Hill

Caution: Relics of an old copper mine at the end of the trail have unstable paraphernalia. The mine is honeycombed with tunnels and is unsafe for exploration.

Directions: Drive 2.6 miles on FR 345 (Cochise Stronghold Road) to a road marked "closed" where the road bends west sharply, then park. The trail starts on the east side of the road on the closed road.

Unmarked and inconspicuous, you couldn't tell the Slavin Gulch Trail even existed. But once you get on the path, you step into the Dragoon Mountains' wild landscape filled with trademark granite rock formations and intriguing history.

The trail starts **[1]** on FR 687A, now closed to vehicular traffic, and makes its way on a relatively level grade to the mountains' distinctive granite ridges eroded into choppy spires and peaks. Oak and piñon trees climb in between eroded boulders, forming a matrix of green in the buff-colored rock. You can see how the Apaches turned the melange of rock into a decade-long stronghold during their last years of freedom (see page 151).

A barbed wire gate **[2]** at mile 1.1 separates the trail's level beginning from its climb up the canyon into the Dragoons' labyrinth of rock. This makes a good turnaround point for an easy day hike. If you continue, latch the gate behind you.

The path climbs with Slavin Gulch past a wall several hundred feet high, above cascades of water splattering into pools **[3]** gathered around huge boulders in the gulch, and through jumbles of rocks. By about mile 2.25 the trail touches base with the drainage and sticks with it, crisscrossing the stream a few times.

A large cairn on the west side of the streambed at about mile 2.4 may catch your attention and divert you several yards off the trail to a modern ceremonial site full of prayer wheels, prayer rocks, and sundry offerings. A juniper tree on the site often has bundles of offerings wrapped in colored material hanging from its boughs.

Beyond the modern-day ceremonial site, the trail climbs harder and requires simple route-finding skills in some areas. With that in mind, the site makes a good turnaround point for inexperienced or less conditioned hikers.

The trail continues in the streambed a short distance, then resumes its climb. It hops rocks, crosses bedrock, and teeters along eroded ruts following the streambed up a ridge next to curious rock formations. The path finally settles down and contours a slope.

At about mile 3.6, the trail gives you fabulous views **[4]** of the Huachuca Mountains and the town of Tombstone. The Dragoons' dramatic terrain stacks all around.

The path continues a short distance to a mangled mine flume **[5]**. You can see how a landslide damaged the flume when it washed out a section of the mountain it braces on. The last 100 feet of trail that climbed up to its alternate trailhead near the mine at the end of FR 345A disappeared in the washout, too. The mine was originally constructed for copper but was kept alive by selenium.

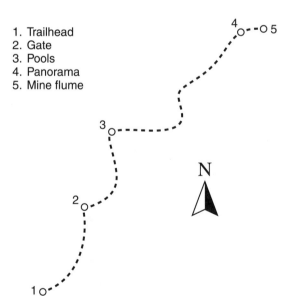

1. Trailhead
2. Gate
3. Pools
4. Panorama
5. Mine flume

41. Santa Teresa Wilderness

- Explore one of the wildest and most remote wildernesses in the state.
- Get a panoramic look at where outlaws used to hide out.

Area Information

Unsigned, secluded, and many miles and hours from help, the 26,780-acre Santa Teresa Wilderness can make you feel like a timid guest in a wilderness with a spirit much bigger than your own. Its unkempt geology shows a hodgepodge of spired ridgelines, precipitously gouged canyons, and slabs of rock slanting down slopes. Hiking the wilderness is not for inexperienced hikers.

For all their remoteness, the mountains exude an intriguing warmth. Their personality lags decades behind the 21st century, as if the mountains reside in a time warp where nature still rules and the men who frequent its slopes often look the same as the cowboys who tried to tame it.

The wilderness' secluded outback presented a natural haven for people who wanted to disappear, such as outlaws and draft dodgers. Holdout Canyon was the area of choice for men on the lam. The epitome of the Santa Teresa Wilderness, Holdout Canyon has an incredibly untamed and remote landscape full of caves, alcoves, and stacks of granite boulders that can disorient even the most seasoned of hikers.

You can pretty much count on not seeing another human when you hike in this wilderness, but you should prepare yourself for wildlife encounters. The Santa Teresas have the highest concentration of mountain lions in the state. You may find cat tracks almost as big as a hand along the trail, as well as bear signs and deer prints. Coatimundi like to scamper around the boulders. Watch for peregrine falcons along the mountains' precipitous cliffs.

The best time to hike the wilderness is from October through April, when the days cool down from their summer sizzle. Water is at a premium, so pack in all you will need—especially during the dry years, when the wildlife will need all the water they can find in meager pools left in Holdout Creek.

Directions: The wilderness is located about 30 miles west of Safford. Access the wilderness by turning south from U.S. 70 onto the Aravaipa-Klondyke Road.

Hours Open: No restrictions.

Facilities: None.

Permits and Rules:

- No mechanized vehicles or mountain bikes are allowed.
- In developed recreation sites, pets must be restrained on a leash no longer than 6 feet.
- Fireworks are prohibited.
- Fires must be attended at all times. During May, June, and early July, the forests may have campfire and smoking restrictions.
- Maximum stay is 14 days.
- Maximum group size is 10 people.

Further Information: Safford Ranger District, P.O. Box 709, Safford, AZ 85548-0709; 928-428-4150.

Other Areas of Interest

Take a hike in the neighboring Galiruo Mountains, a remote and rugged range that has scenic hikes far away from the crowd. For more information, contact the Safford Ranger District at 928-428-4150.

Holdout Overlook 🥾🥾🥾🥾

Distance Round-Trip: 6.5 miles

Estimated Hiking Time: 4 hours

Elevation: 4,200 to 5,000 feet

Maps: Coronado National Forest, Safford and Santa Catalina Ranger Districts, USGS Cobra Grande Mountain; Jackson Mountain

Caution: This trail gets little use and even less maintenance. Hikers need to have experience hiking in remote areas as well as excellent route-finding skills. Take a USGS topological map of the area.

Directions: From the town of Klondyke, drive about 2.5 miles to an unmarked dirt road and turn north (right); drive 3.1 miles on the four-wheel-drive track to a hilltop and park.

The hike to the Holdout Overlook starts [1] at a hilltop on the lonely Reef Basin Trail. Heading north, the gnarly trail travels an easy downhill grade, ducking under mesquite tree branches and sidestepping prickly pear cacti. The trail lands in a gravelly drainage at about mile 0.3, where an ephemeral spring [2] coaxes a thicker growth of catclaw and mesquite.

The trail stays in the drainage for a while before climbing out around mile 0.5, then rises high above it. The path climbs above the rugged and raspy walls of the drainage into a different biome, about mile 0.75, where juniper trees and manzanita bushes replace mesquite and acacia trees.

The trail continues heading northward, but you have to watch for it. Rock-ribbed and faint, the path fades in spots and you can easily find yourself on a

cattle track or erosion gully if you don't pay attention. Occasional cairns help keep you on track.

Let the cottonwood trees that come into view at about mile 1.25 help guide you to Reef Tank [3] at mile 1.5. Stay on the right side of the tank and look for cairns to signal where the Holdout Trail comes in east of the tank.

The trail, heading into an eastern canyon, starts on a mild uphill that tops out on a ridge at about mile 1.75. You can see formations carved into buff-colored granite deep in Holdout Canyon in the distance. The path continues in the hilly contours of the landscape, dipping inside folds and climbing over rises.

After a gradual drop, the trail lands in a drainage [4] at about mile 2 and follows along it, crisscrossing it several times. It's not unusual to find animals traces, such as mountain lion tracks and bear signs, along this stretch.

By about mile 3, the trail starts climbing up a ridge with golden granite outcroppings, giant boulders, and slabs of tilted granite along the trailsides. Piñon pine trees and agave stuff themselves in cracks and crevices along the path.

The trail clamors over a stretch of bald rock at the top of the ridge, then comes to a magnificent overlook of Holdout Canyon [5] located deep in the mountain range's belly. The landscape looks like a granite wonderland where giant boulders loll around and columns of rock teeter precariously on one another.

This hike ends at the overlook, but the Holdout Canyon Trail continues down the ridge and into the confusing landscape of Holdout Canyon. The trail gets faint and is difficult to follow without extraordinary route-finding skills. Return the way you came.

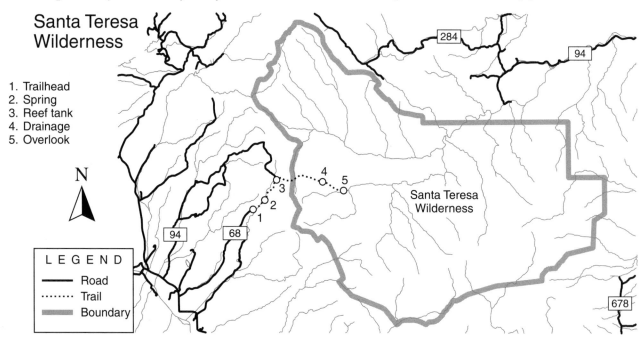

Santa Teresa
Wilderness

1. Trailhead
2. Spring
3. Reef tank
4. Drainage
5. Overlook

N

Santa Teresa
Wilderness

LEGEND
——— Road
········· Trail
━━━ Boundary

42. Whetstone Mountains

- Picnic by remote pools.
- Explore old ranch routes.
- View unusual geological formations.

Area Information

Of the handful of sky islands located in the Coronado National Forest, the Whetstone Mountains have remained one of the least accessible. Even when the heyday of Tombstone and the Indian wars of Cochise started to color southeast Arizona's history pages, the mountains skulked in the shadows and earned a reputation of having, as one writer penned, "about the roughest country you could get a horse through." This remoteness gave the tiny mountain range a mystique that encouraged some tall tales.

A tongue-in-cheek article from the Tombstone *Prospector* reported "strange phenomena occurring in the Whetstones" where oaks reportedly dripped globules of honey from the tips of their acorns. This caused bees to "abandon the more laborious process of extraction from flowers and fall for this mellifluous get-rich-quick scheme."

The article admits that honey-producing oaks paled in comparison to the gold-producing cattle found in the Whetstones. The cattle, the *Prospector* explained, had a propensity to lick a ledge of stone that contained gold. When "[the cattle] sweat, the gold which had thus been subjected to a sort of bovine smelter, or reduction works, was precipitated upon the hair."

Aside from fanciful reports of honey dripping from the tips of acorns and gold dust oozing from cows, the secluded mountain range contains some truly phenomenal points of interest: springwater sliding down travertine ledges to the slow drip of a subterranean flow off Kartchner Caverns' colorful limestone formations; intricate canyons where Indians hid in ambush and secret ceremonial caves where they worshiped; unusual geological formations in French Joe Canyon; the scrubby grasslands of the foothills that drone into the horizon.

However, getting to know these mountains takes some blood, sweat, and tears. With just one maintained trail (the Guindoni Loop accessed in Kartchner Caverns State Park) and only a handful of difficult roads not gated by private land, the Whetstone Mountains do not make the most user-friendly destination. Explorers should accept scrapes from prickly vegetation, strenuous cross-country hiking, and scratched vehicles as part of the territory.

Because of the area's remoteness, wildlife sightings are common. You may see coatimundi, rattlesnakes, bats, spotted owls, warblers, and deer. If you do see wildlife, give each creature a wide berth and the right-of-way.

Hiking the mountains will be comfortable from October through April. Summers get too hot, and the landscape offers little shade.

Directions: Located about 10 miles south of Benson, just west of Arizona 90.

Hours Open: No restrictions.

Facilities: Campground, picnic areas, washrooms in Kartchner Caverns State Park.

Permits and Rules:
- A $10 entrance fee is charged to enter Kartchner Caverns State Park.
- In developed recreation sites, pets must be restrained on a leash no longer than 6 feet.
- Fireworks are prohibited.
- Fires must be attended at all times.
- Maximum stay limit is 14 days.
- Maximum group size is 10 people.

Further Information: Sierra Vista Ranger District, 5990 S. Highway 92, Hereford, AZ 85615; 520-378-0311.

Other Areas of Interest

A tour through the colorful subterranean caverns of Kartchner Caverns, located 9 miles south of Benson on Arizona 90, will give you a look at the inside of the Whetstone Mountains. For more information call 520-586-4100.

French Joe Canyon 🥾🥾🥾🥾

Distance Round-Trip: 4 miles

Estimated Hiking Time: 2.5 hours

Elevation: 4,275 to 4,500 feet

Maps: Coronado National Forest, Nogales and Sierra Vista Ranger Districts, USGS Apache Peak

Cautions: The trail in French Joe Canyon is not maintained; some route-finding skills are necessary. Hikers must have a permit to cross a section of state land on the unmarked road leading to the canyon.

Directions: Drive south on Arizona 90 from Benson about 9.7 miles to an unmarked turnoff near mile marker 302; turn right and drive 0.8 miles to a National Forest sign, then veer left; drive another 2 miles and park. The road requires a high-clearance vehicle.

Having one of the few water sources in the Whetstone Mountains, French Joe Canyon begins and ends in oak groves fed by springs.

The route, which begins on a beaten path **[1]**, starts at the mouth of the canyon about 20 feet away from a four-foot pouroff near a concrete trough. The pools of water in this area attract a variety of wildlife. Birds commonly create a chatter in the bankside trees. Birders come from all over the world to catch sight of the rufous-capped warbler found in the canyon.

A colony of coatimundi like to hang out in this scenic area, too. Members of the raccoon family, the coatimundis grow to about two feet long with a black-ringed tail that matches their body length. In some parts of Mexico, they're called *mono medas*, or "little monkeys." The females and youngsters travel in groups of 6 to 24 and make their dens in rocky niches of wooded canyons near water.

You may also encounter night creatures, such as rattlesnakes or bats. When you enter this riparian area, be careful for yourself and the animals that depend on its waters.

The path crosses a large meadow, then heads toward a drainage. In wet seasons, tall grasses may envelop the path, while drier months expose tangles of catclaw. Near the drainage, the trail enters a gate, then continues on the path as it joins the drainage.

In the first half of the route, the drainage walls are low enough for you to notice the odd geology of the area: a massive wall of slickrock **[2]** slants into the drainage, dramatic uplifting tilts neighboring peaks, and limestone strata appear in northern ridges. You can diverge from the trail here and hike up the slickrock slab to a cloistered area full of a string of pools.

Back on the trail, the walls eventually rise enough to block out the countryside by about mile 1. Continue to follow the sinewy drainage along its gravelly floor to a fork in the canyon, then veer right. Here the route requires easy scrambles up or around small pouroffs. The drainage, often gurgling with water, attracts oak trees to the route. You may see spotted owls along this wooded section.

The trail ends at a natural feature called the Cape **[3]**. This unique wall of limestone drips with travertine deposits. The tunnel that burrows a short distance into the limestone was probably made by a rancher to access water. Return the way you came.

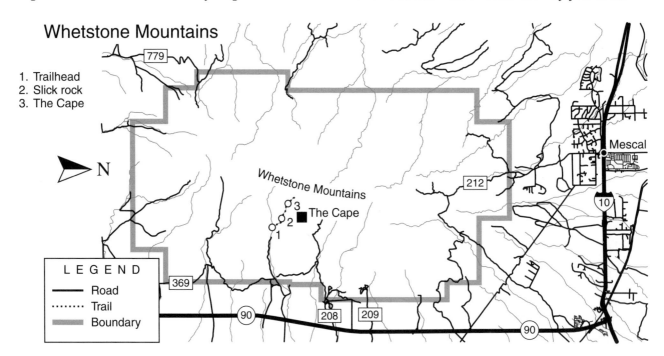

Whetstone Mountains

1. Trailhead
2. Slick rock
3. The Cape

LEGEND
—— Road
······ Trail
━━ Boundary

43. Huachuca Mountains

- Experience one of the most ecologically diverse areas in Arizona.

- Spot rare birds.

- Hike canyons and mountain peaks filled with color in autumn and mountain slopes colored with wildflowers in the summer.

Area Information

Like a chain of islands surrounded by the sea, the name of the sky island mountains of southeastern Arizona, separated by grasslands instead of water, has an island connotation. Called the Madrean Archipelago, the sky islands rise in a swatch of lowland that separates the Rocky Mountains in the north and Sierra Madre in Mexico. This archipelago is labeled as one of three megadiversity centers of the world.

The sky island range of the Huachuca Mountains, part of the Madrean Archipelago, has a rich mélange of activity from birds, insects, butterflies, and animals. The mountains draw plants and animals that seem to thrive there while they struggle in other locations.

Rare birds, such as the elegant trogon, whiskered screech-owl, blue-throated and white-eared hummingbirds, and red-faced warbler, visit the mountains' Edenic canyons that provide avian life with all the comforts of home—water, plenty of trees for nesting, and insects to eat.

On the mountaintops, often crowned with stands of aspen, you get panoramas that articulate the sky island concept with a full-page look at neighboring sky islands, as well as a look into Mexico. Miller Peak, the highest, southernmost peak in the United States, lies in the center of the Miller Peak Wilderness that sprawls across the southern end of the mountains.

You may see animals wherever you hike in the mountains. You might catch a mother bear and her cub scuttling down a ponderosa pine tree, or see a lone male coatimundi traipsing across an oak limb. Deer may spring through the woods.

You can hike all but the mountains' uppermost trails, which get snow in the winter, throughout most of the year. But certain seasons draw different attractions—birds migrate in the spring and fall, butterflies and hummingbirds proliferate in the summer when wildflowers peak, and late autumn brings exquisite fall color to the canyons and mountaintops.

Directions: The mountains are located about 6 miles west of Sierra Vista in southeastern Arizona. From Interstate 10, drive about 25 miles south.

Hours Open: No restrictions.

Facilities: Campgrounds, picnic areas, and washrooms at recreation sites.

Permits and Rules:
- No mechanized vehicles or mountain bikes are allowed in Miller Peak Wilderness.

- In developed recreation sites, pets must be restrained on a leash no longer than 6 feet.

- Fireworks are prohibited.

- Fires must be attended at all times.

- Maximum stay is 14 days.

- Maximum group size is 10 people.

Further Information: Sierra Vista Ranger District, 5990 S. Highway 92, Hereford, AZ 85615; 520-378-0311.

Other Areas of Interest

You can visit the San Pedro River, often part of the fabulous panoramas you see from Huachuca mountaintops, if you stop at the San Pedro House located 6 miles east of Arizona 92, on Arizona 90 in the San Pedro Riparian National Conservation Area. The area is one of the best in the nation for birdwatching, as well. For more information, call 520-458-3559.

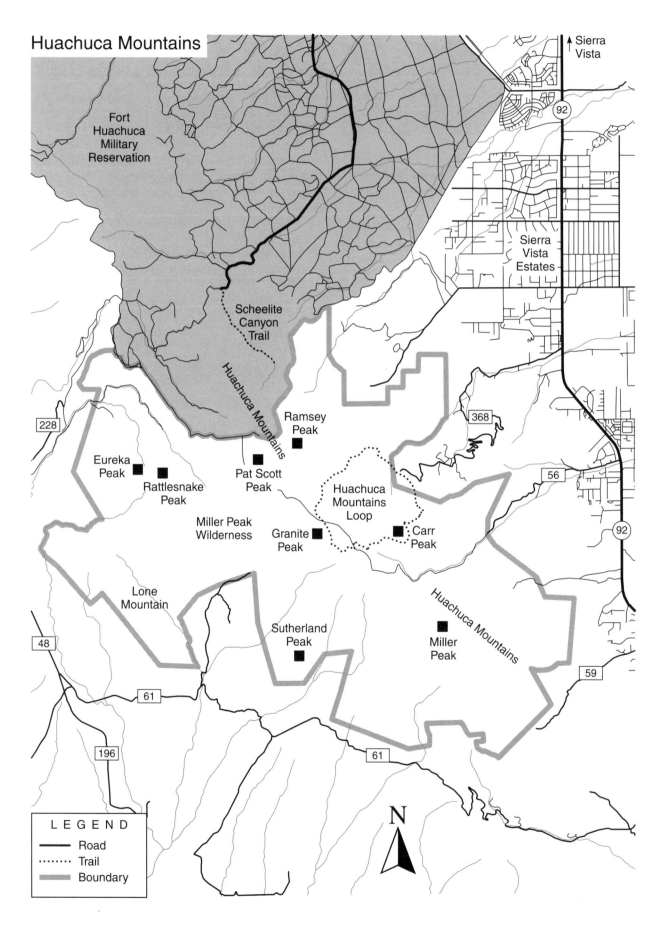

Huachuca Mountains

Fort Huachuca Military Reservation

Scheelite Canyon Trail

Huachuca Mountains

Sierra Vista

92

Sierra Vista Estates

Ramsey Peak

368

56

92

228

Eureka Peak

Rattlesnake Peak

Pat Scott Peak

Miller Peak Wilderness

Granite Peak

Huachuca Mountains Loop

Carr Peak

Lone Mountain

Huachuca Mountains

48

Sutherland Peak

Miller Peak

59

61

61

196

LEGEND
Road
Trail
Boundary

N

Scheelite Canyon Trail

🥾 🥾 🥾 🥾

Distance Round-Trip: 8 miles

Estimated Hiking Time: 4 hours

Elevation: 5,525 to 8,350 feet

Maps: Coronado National Forest, Nogales and Sierra Vista Ranger Districts, USGS Miller Peak

Cautions: Fort Huachuca may be closed to civilians for indefinite periods of time for reasons of national security, and parts of the post, including the road into Garden Canyon, are often closed for short periods for military exercises. Visitors must sign in at the Public Affairs Office before approaching this hike. For more information on access and visitor regulations, call 520-533-7083.

Directions: From Sierra Vista, enter the main gate of Fort Huachuca, and stay on the main road for 9.5 miles following the signs to Garden Canyon at all intersections; the trailhead starts 0.7 mile from where the pavement ends.

Hiking the Scheelite Canyon Trail can turn into an exciting experience if you have a chance meeting with the wildlife that frequent the steep gorge. Mexican spotted owls, protected by the Endangered Species Act, frequent the canyon; elegant trogons make rare appearances. If you do spot any wildlife, watch with respect and caution.

Cocooned in a wooded canyon, the trail starts **[1]** its almost nonstop climb along a drainage that eventually ends on Scheelite Ridge. The moist environment nurtures continuous stands of Gambel oak, bigtooth maple, and velvet ash trees that create one of the best displays of fall color in southeast Arizona.

Almost a mile into the trail, the canyon walls grow, and the trail brushes past a smooth perpendicular wall to the right of the drainage. The riparian cover of hardwoods stretch their limbs to reach the sunlight, forming a ceiling over the drainage. On the opposite side of the drainage, the trail passes a huge honeycombed limestone boulder as gnarly as the Gambel oak trees that surround it. The canyon's steel gray walls and the old logs strewn in the drainage give the canyon an untamed feel.

The trail crosses a section of bedrock, then bends to the left and takes a rocky route up the canyon wall on a stretch of rocky steps **[2]**. Next, the trail squeezes between boulders, then continues on a slight uphill until the canyon floor meets up with it again.

For the next quarter-mile, the trail settles down to a near-level course. Then it's up and climbing again to the top of the west wall, where it waits for the drainage to catch up so it can make another stream crossing.

At about mile 1.5, the canyon narrows enough to force the trail into the drainage. Watch out for poison ivy in this section. The plant can cause an irritating rash even when it has turned scarlet in the fall.

The trail continues in the drainage for a while, clamoring over dryfalls. As the canyon opens up momentarily, the trail walks over a slab of bedrock **[3]** through which a stream has cut a trough. In the summertime, this exposed section sees a rich gathering of wildflowers. The trail drops back into the drainage when the canyon closes up again. After another section of bedrock, watch for cairns on the left that will lead you around a dryfall.

Finally, the canyon widens enough for the trail to separate from the drainage and continue its climb along the streambed.

The trail separates from the streambed **[4]** at about mile 2.5 and starts a relentlessly steep slog up to the Huachuca Crest Trail. Once on the ridge, you are privy to incredible views of the surrounding mountainsides and the city of Sierra Vista. Return the way you came.

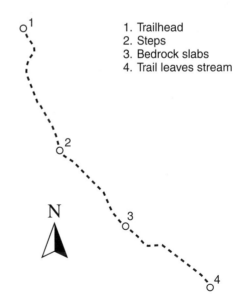

1. Trailhead
2. Steps
3. Bedrock slabs
4. Trail leaves stream

Huachuca Mountains Loop

🥾 🥾 🥾

Distance Round-Trip: 10.4 miles

Estimated Hiking Time: 5 hours

Elevation: 6,700 to 9,200 feet

Maps: Coronado National Forest, Nogales and Sierra Vista Ranger Districts, USGS Miller Peak

Cautions: Summer monsoon storms frequent the mountains. Bring rain gear and a lightweight jacket in case of rain. Stay off high ground during lightning storms.

Directions: Drive 7.8 miles on Carr Canyon Road [FR 368] to the trailhead at the Ramsey Vista Campground (past the Old Sawmill Spring Trailhead). A high-clearance vehicle is best for this road.

This loop links several trails that present different aspects of the Huachuca Mountains. Traveling clockwise, the route starts out **[1]** on the Carr Peak Trail. This trail shows scars from two fires in 1977 and 1991. The trail quickly enters one of the burn areas at the Miller Peak Wilderness boundary. A swatch of ghostly gray pine skeletons curls around Carr Peak, allowing only occasional patches of green.

Right after passing the intersection with the Comfort Springs Trail, about mile 0.6, views of the San Pedro Valley open up to the east. The city of Sierra Vista splays across the valley. Behind it, the Mule and Dragoon mountains rise in the east.

At about mile 1.5, after passing through a mix of conifers, the trail pushes through a thicket of snowberry and New Mexico locust bushes, then crosses a slab of bedrock.

After a fire in a conifer forest, aspen seeds or suckers from existing root systems will sprout in the land cleared by the flames. In a decade or two, the aspens' shade creates a cool and moist environment for conifers to spring up. By the time the aspens have lived a century, the conifers have grown to the same height and the trees compete for sunshine. In another 50 years, however, the conifers usually win, growing taller than the aspens. The aspens die out, leaving decayed trunks that make temporary homes for fungus and insects before they dissolve and return nutrients to the soil. When another fire levels the conifer forest, the aspen life cycle begins again.

The trail leaves the aspens behind and travels through ridgetop meadows that become a riot of color in the summer from blankets of wildflowers. At mile 2.6, the trail junctions with the Carr Peak Spur Trail **[2]**.

You can hike to the top of Carr Peak by veering right onto the spur trail. Enjoy views of the San Pedro Valley and Mexico atop Carr Peak, then return to the route and continue on the Carr Peak Trail, which contours the southern slope of Carr Peak. At mile 4.1, the path junctions with the Crest Trail **[3]**. Turn right onto the Crest Trail, which contours the western slopes of Carr Peak. At mile 5.6, turn right onto the Hamburg Trail **[4]**.

The route follows along Wisconsin Canyon as it heads for the inner crevices of the Huachuca Mountains. The trail parallels a creek as it drops toward Ramsey Canyon under the cover of a cool pine forest. The trail continuously crosses the creek and the pretty cascades that flow after wet weather.

When the route connects with the Comfort Springs Trail **[5]** at mile 7.9, it climbs out of Ramsey Canyon. The route climbs right across from the canyon's distinctive rocky outcroppings that poke through a dense carpet of pines. Climbing over the ridgeline and dropping into a scenic niche in a neighboring canyon, the route passes Comfort Springs **[6]** at mile 9.4.

Comfort Springs got its name from a logging camp built near it in the early 1900s named Camp Comfort. Almost all the remnants of the camp, including a reportedly haunted cabin, were burned in the 1977 fire.

During a severe winter in the early 1930s, several woodcutters died of pneumonia. The cabin was said to be haunted by their returning spirits. The cabin's incineration in the 1977 fire, however, remedied any further ghost stories.

The trail climbs over a swell, drops in and out of a drainage, then makes its final ascent back to the trailhead.

1. Trailhead
2. Spur trail
3. Crest trail
4. Hamburg trail
5. Comfort Springs trail
6. Comfort Springs

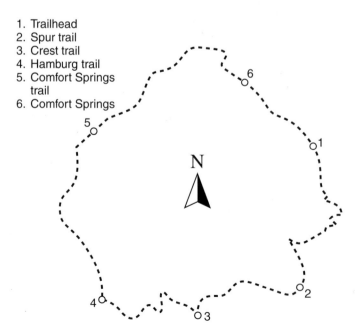

44. Chiricahua Wilderness

- Visit one of the world's top birding centers.
- Hike trails located on a biodiverse sky island.
- View extraordinary autumn color.

Area Information

The 87,700-acre Chiricahua Wilderness has some of the most attractive but impenetrable mountainscapes in the southwest. With dense thickets of brush and timber growth, maniacally steep elevations, precipitous canyon walls, and uncertain water sources, the wilderness' 13 established trails don't see much activity. But when you make the effort to hike one of these trails, you always get a reward.

Panoramas of the mountains' distinctive volcanic geology make a consistent compensation for your efforts. In a cataclysmic act of volcanism, the lava that formed the mountains was catapulted from the bowels of the Earth, scientists say, some 25 million years ago as incandescent ash and molten pellets of pumice. As the thick layer of tuff cooled, erosion had its artistic way, forming the spires, hoodoos, and bridges.

As if this spectacular geological history weren't enough, the flora and fauna are askew with weird placements and appearances. The mountains are a crossroads for plants and animals; a mixed-up area, not only because of the sky island (a name given to high-altitude mountains that rise abruptly in a sea of desert; the mountains have a wide spectrum of plants and animals concentrated in a relatively small area); but because it has Rocky Mountain, Sierra Madre, and Chiricahuan and Sonoran Desert plants and animals living on the fringe of their natural environment.

A trail, too, may reward you with an animal sighting, especially deer, black bear, and coatimundi. Avian sightings are legend. Birders come from all over the world to get glimpses of rare species, from the hummingbird to the elegant trogon.

The best time to hike the Chiricahua Mountains is from March through November, with summer absolutely delightful. The mountains, however, lie in an oasis zone that quickly responds to the warm, moist Gulf of Mexico air that rises to meet its mountain-cool temperatures with precipitation. Occasionally, the Gulf of California throws in a low-pressure system that creates a *chubasco*. These storms have hurricane characteristics and last several days. Consequently, the mountains can get outright balmy. Bring your rain gear if you plan on a summer hike. Fall hikes produces stunning autumn colors from bigtooth maple trees.

Directions: The wilderness is located about 120 miles southeast of Tucson. Drive east on Interstate 10 to the U.S. 80 exit (7 miles into New Mexico), drive south about 28 miles to the turnoff for the town of Portal and the Chiricahua Wilderness, and turn west (right); drive 7 miles to Portal.

Hours Open: No restrictions.

Facilities: Campgrounds, washrooms, and picnic areas at recreation sites.

Permits and Rules:

- A $3 user fee is required at some trailheads.
- No mechanized vehicles or mountain bikes are allowed.
- In developed recreation sites, pets must be restrained on a leash no longer than 6 feet.
- Fireworks are prohibited.
- Fires must be attended at all times.
- Maximum stay is 14 days.
- Maximum group size is 10 people.

Further Information: Douglas Ranger District, 3081 North Leslie Canyon Road, Douglas, AZ 85607; 520-364-3468.

Other Areas of Interest

The Chiricahua National Monument in the northeast corner of the Chiricahua Mountains has an extraordinary array of strangely stacked columns of rock. For more information call 520-824-3560.

Chiricahua Wilderness

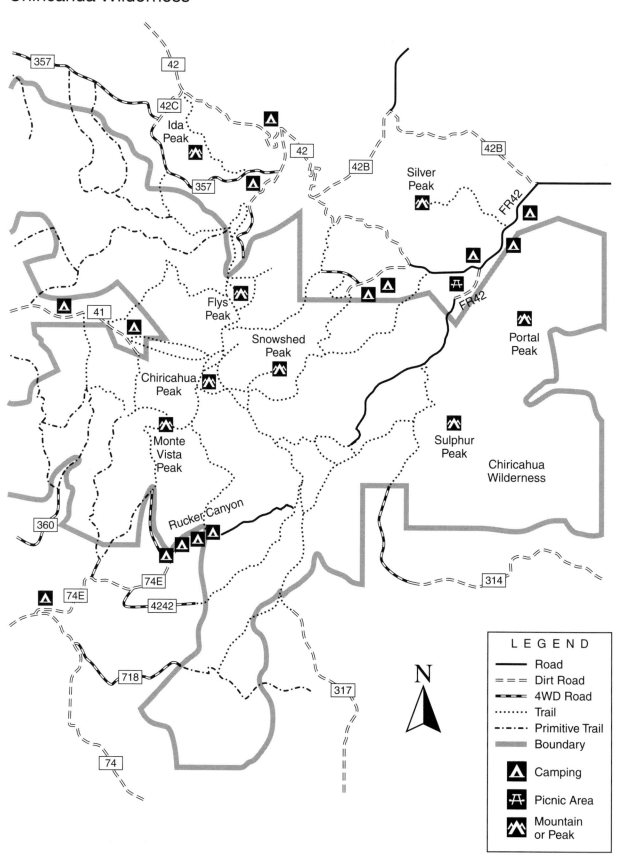

South Fork Trail 👢 👢 👢

Distance Round-Trip: 10 miles

Estimated Hiking Time: 5 hours

Elevation: 6,800 to 8,400 feet

Maps: Coronado National Forest, Chiricahua, Peloncillo, and Dragoon Mountain Ranges, USGS Portal Peak

Caution: The last 1.5 miles of the trail (not included in this hike) are extremely difficult to follow because of a 1994 forest fire.

Directions: Drive south on FR 42 about 2 miles; at a fork, veer left onto FR 42E and drive 1 mile to the trailhead.

The South Fork Trail showcases all of the chief characteristics of the Chiricahua Mountains, from diverse vegetation to stunning geology. In autumn, the trail has incredible fall color from stands of bigtooth maple trees that gather along the South Fork of Cave Creek.

The trail starts **[1]** in a cozy corridor of mixed oaks growing between the raspy rhyolite walls of the cavernous Cave Creek canyon system. Following the stream course of the South Fork of Cave Creek, the trail travels a lush area where poison ivy likes to hang out. Be careful of the three-leaved plant when it encroaches into the path.

At about mile 0.5, the canyon cliffs start to rise and squeeze in on the trail. This moist environment draws Arizona sycamore trees and the first show of bigtooth maple trees along the trail. The trees, fittingly called canyon maple, turn fiery colors in autumn. The maple trees inspired a crew of Forest Service workers to name a nearby area in which they camped after them. The trail passes the spot, Maple Camp **[2]**, at mile 1.5.

The water, nesting opportunities, and food make the Chiricahua Mountains, especially the South Fork Trail, a world-class birding area. You may get glimpses of some unusual birds while hiking the trail. One of the more sought-after is the elegant trogon. With its red breast, long tail, and arf-like cry, the elegant trogon makes an unusual sight, as well as an unusual sighting. Favorite nesting spots are Arizona sycamore trees. Consider yourself lucky if you see one along the trail.

Beyond Maple Camp, the trail sticks close to the creek, crossing back and forth over its rocky bed. At mile 1.8, the trail junctions with the Horseshoe Pass Trail. Continue straight on the South Fork Trail.

After mile 2.5, the trail starts a noticeable upward trek as it climbs up the canyon walls above the creek. It continues a nonstop climb to its end at the Crest Trail. In the meantime, curious spires and columns of rock jut out from background ridges. A panoramic view of the whole canyon and its unique formations eroded in the canyon walls comes in view at about mile 3.5. A bit farther, the trail separates from the main creekbed **[3]** and follows its tributary heading southwest. This makes a good turnaround point for a shorter day hike that does not require any route-finding skills.

After this point, the trail runs up and down the canyon walls, flirting with the stream as it crosses back and forth over it. This area shows the aftermath of a 1994 fire with fallen logs, burned stumps, and eroded areas. Several areas of downfall require adroit maneuvers. Some areas require simple route-finding skills.

By mile 5, the turnaround point for this hike **[4]**, the trail gets dicey with fallen logs and washouts. You'll need a dose of adventure to continue, as good route-finding skills will become more in demand from this point to the end of the trail. When you decide to end the hike, return the way you came.

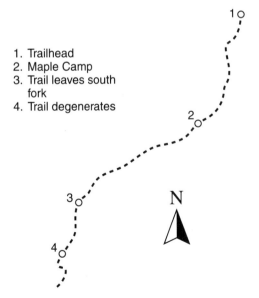

1. Trailhead
2. Maple Camp
3. Trail leaves south fork
4. Trail degenerates

Rucker Canyon Trail 🥾 🥾 🥾

Distance Round-Trip: 9.2 miles

Estimated Hiking Time: 5 hours

Elevation: 6,800 to 8,260 feet

Maps: Coronado National Forest, Chiricahua, Peloncillo, and Dragoon Mountain Ranges, USGS Chiricahua Peak

Cautions: The second half of the trail climbs steeply. Loose stones may make footing unstable.

Directions: Drive to the Rucker Canyon Recreation Area and the signed trailhead near the campground.

The trail begins **[1]** right at the Rucker Canyon campground. Before you start, take a moment to peruse the campground's streamside habitat. You may spot painted redstarts flitting around Arizona sycamore and Arizona cypress trees, hear Stellar's jays squawking in the pines, and catch hummingbirds sipping nectar from flowers.

The trail stays on the outskirts of the campground, curving to the left. It passes the turnoff for the Raspberry Ridge Trail at about mile 0.2, and continues through an S gate up an old road that saddles next to a stream.

The trail winds back and forth across the creek several times on a generally level course interrupted a couple of times when the path climbs briefly above the creek onto the canyon wall and then back down again. Yellow columbine like to gather around the path at stream crossings. Prairie smoke and lupine fill sunny sections.

At about mile 2, the canyon starts to take definition when its cliffs rise high above the canyon floor. The north wall takes an attractive turn when it shows fiery orange tinges. Boulders that tumbled from the colorful walls lodge along the trail at about mile 2.2.

If you look up at the north wall through the trees you can see columns of rock **[2]**.

From here, the path becomes labor intensive and starts climbing a series of switchbacks up the south wall. An opening in the trees at about mile 2.5 shows you a stunning view **[3]** of Rucker Canyon. Look for a window rock in an outcropping in the south wall. The path calms down a bit at about mile 2.75 when it levels out and contours the folds in the canyon walls. The trail latches onto an ancillary drainage and follows it up the canyon wall until it takes off on its own on another series of tight switchbacks.

At about mile 3.6, the trail meets the Sage Peak Trail **[4]**. Veer left to continue on the Rucker Canyon Trail and finish its switchbacks that take you up to the top of the raspy ridge. Now on the sun-drenched ridgetop, the trail steps onto the other side of the ridge and twists through a cover of manzanita. At about mile 3.8, you get a look at the crowd of ridges neighboring the trail. The trail continues in this exposed environment, glancing at panoramas, until its end at a powerful overlook of the area at the Price Canyon Trail. You may continue on the Price Canyon Trail, or return the way you came.

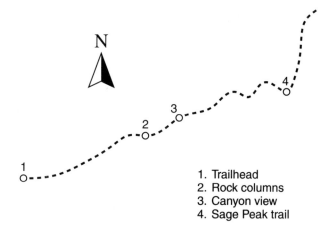

1. Trailhead
2. Rock columns
3. Canyon view
4. Sage Peak trail

45. Pinaleño Mountains

- Hike a trail with some of the best views in America.

- Spot animals and vegetation exclusive to the Pinaleño Mountains.

- Experience a mixture of vegetation that ranges from cacti to fir-aspen forests.

Area Information

The Pinaleño Mountains once went by the apropos name of Sierra Bonita, Spanish for "beautiful mountain." The name applies not only to the mountains' appearance, but to the rich cache of wildlife and biological diversity they hold. Scientists call the mountains a biologically unique area because 18 species and subspecies of plants and animals found in the mountains exist nowhere else on the planet.

The diversity comes from the sky island principle; the range rises almost 8,000 feet above the desert floor. Its highest peak (and the highest in southern Arizona), 10,720-foot Mount Graham, contains more life zones than any other single mountain in North America.

The mountains' old-growth spruce-fir forests drew loggers in the late 1800s and early 1900s, and several mills once ran in different spots around the range. You may see mill remnants as you hike some of the mountains' trails. Despite the area logging, old-growth forests still prevail. A Douglas fir tree in the mountains that dates to A.D. 1257 is listed on a database of the world's most ancient trees.

These old-growth forests shelter numerous indigenous plant and animal species. One species, the Mount Graham red squirrel, has made the Pinaleño Mountains infamous, as telescopes built on the mountain peaks have interfered with the squirrels' habitat to the point of endangering the species. Other threatened or vulnerable species (the Mexican spotted owl and Apache trout) share this fragile environment with the Mount Graham red squirrel, making the mountain range an intense point of interest for environmentalists.

Old-growth forests only grow on the mountains' tops. Cacti cover the base of the mountains, and pine-oak forests the midsection. Ponderosa pine trees blanket the upper realms. Because of this vegetative variance, a hike on some trails can start in the desert and end in a fir-aspen forest. When you plan a hike in the Pinaleño Mountains, stay in the lowlands in the winter and head for the peaks in the summer. The aspen forests and Rocky Mountain maple trees in the high country produce a beautiful display of autumn color in early October.

The Apache Indians considered the mountain range sacred, and the San Carlos Apache still consider Mount Graham spiritually significant. The San Carlos call the mountains' high point, Mount Graham, *Dzil nchaa si an*. They gather on *Dzil nchaa si an* where the *Ga'an* (mountain spirits) reside and perform ceremonies.

Sacred. Controversial. Beautiful. The Pinaleño Mountains fit every name.

Directions: The mountains are located 10 miles south of Safford. Drive south on U.S. 191 to Arizona 366, then turn west (right).

Hours Open: No restrictions.

Facilities: Campgrounds, picnic areas, and restrooms at recreation sites.

Permits and Rules:
- No mechanized vehicles or mountain bikes are allowed in wilderness areas.

- In developed recreation sites, pets must be restrained on a leash no longer than 6 feet.

- Fireworks are prohibited.

- Fires must be attended at all times.

- Maximum stay is 14 days.

- Maximum group size is 10 people.

Further Information: Safford Ranger District, P.O. Box 709, Safford, AZ 85548-0709; 928-428-4150.

Other Areas of Interest

Visit Discovery Park, southeastern Arizona's space, science, and cultural center, located south of Safford on Discovery Park Avenue. For more information, call 928-428-6260.

Arcadia Trail 👢👢👢

Distance Round-Trip: 10.2 to 12.2 miles

Estimated Hiking Time: 5 to 6 hours

Elevation: 6,700 to 10,022 feet

Maps: Coronado National Forest, Safford and Santa Catalina Ranger Districts, USGS Mt. Graham

Caution: Afternoon rainstorms occur in July and August. Take rain gear and a light jacket in case of rain.

Directions: Drive 10.8 miles on Arizona 366 to the trailhead in the Upper Arcadia Campground.

The trail gets a flourishing start [1] as it switchbacks up the stream-fed crevice of Wet Canyon. Box elder, aspen, and bigtooth maple trees create a shady environment for the trail as it climbs up the canyon near its streambed.

By mile 1, the trail dries out as it climbs through a ponderosa pine forest with intermittent views of southeast Arizona [2]. You might see the Peloncillo Mountains rise along the New Mexican border in the east, or the Cabezas Mountains run into the Chiricahua Mountains in the southeast, at occasional outcroppings that jut through the forest and open up to panoramic views.

The trail enters a beautiful forest at about mile 3 filled with exceptionally tall Douglas fir and Engel-mann spruce trees [3]. These conifers, shaggy with lichen, perfume the air. Aspen trees make a regular appearance and provide a pretty golden sheen in the fall. At the intersection with the Noon Creek Ridge Trail, mile 3.2, continue on the Arcadia Trail.

Bold gray outcroppings push their way through thickets of New Mexican locust trees that infringe on the trail. When you pass them, watch out for their inch-long thorns. Watch, too, for more views to appear. Because of the trail's exceptional views, it has been designated as a National Recreation Trail, distinguishing it among the best trails in the nation.

At the trail's intersection with the Heliograph Trail [4] at mile 4, you can continue on the Arcadia Trail. Or, you can take a side hike up the mile-long trail that climbs 800 feet to Heliograph Peak. Named for the signal mirrors called heliographs used during an 1880 campaign against Geronimo and his band of Apaches, the peak is now a lookout tower that signals fires from May 1 through July 31.

While on the peak, you might see the Mount Graham red squirrel. The small squirrel has made the Arizona Game and Fish Department's list of threatened native wildlife in Arizona and is classified as endangered by the federal government.

Back at the Arcadia Trail, you may continue another mile at it descends to its end at the Shannon Campground, or return the way you came.

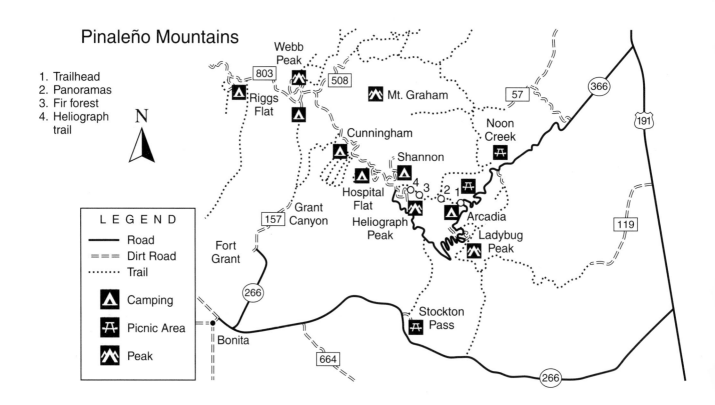

Pinaleño Mountains

1. Trailhead
2. Panoramas
3. Fir forest
4. Heliograph trail

N

LEGEND
— Road
=== Dirt Road
····· Trail
▲ Camping
🏕 Picnic Area
⛰ Peak

East

The eastern region of Arizona covers the area south of Arizona 260 from the Fort Apache Indian Reservation to the Gila River. The area contains all or parts of Navajo, Gila, Apache, Greenlee, and Graham counties.

Topography

The White Mountains are the central feature of the eastern region. Climbing from a desert elevation to a subalpine vegetation zone, the mountains contain some of the state's tallest peaks.

If you take a ride on the scenic route from Clifton to Alpine on U.S. 191, you get a good idea of the physical composition of the area. Starting in an Upper Sonoran life zone at Clifton, the highway soon winds through the mining town of Morenci. The geology of the area produced some of the richest copper caches in the state. A closer exploration along trails and the San Francisco River would find teal patinas on rockwalls, geodes, and chalcedony.

Continuing northward, the road engages in hairpin turns for a couple dozen miles to reach the start of the ponderosa pines. A couple dozen more miles of tight switchbacks that demand you abide by the 15-M.P.H. speed limit on the highway take you to lookout points that allow you to see right into New Mexico. On a clear day, you can see all the way to the San Francisco Peaks at Flagstaff from some trails.

When the highway nears Hannagan Meadow, you enter a subalpine environment of pine, fir, and spruce interrupted by grassy meadows. The next 20 miles to Alpine travel past luscious meadows in the highcountry.

If you were to take a side road, such as the eastbound Red Hill Road just north of Hannagan Meadow or the southward Blue River Road from Alpine, you would see how the lower altitudes of the White Mountains look. You would get a look at the stunning geology of the mountains, with sections of sandstone bluff and purple conglomerate—an altogether beautiful sight.

Major Rivers and Lakes

The eastern region has the water in the state of Arizona: lakes, streams, rivers, and creeks. Even cienegas, where groundwater pools during wet weather. Several of the state's major rivers flow through the region. The Black, Little Colorado, and San Francisco rivers get their start in this region. Dozens of lakes, reservoirs, and streams lure fishermen to their sides. Some waterways, such as the West Fork of the Black River, are classified as blue-ribbon trout streams.

Common Plant Life

With such a great spread in elevation, the eastern region has a diverse variety of vegetation. The lower elevations have a high desert look—prickly pear cactus, yucca plants, and juniper and piñon pine trees. Low-elevation canyons contain cottonwood and willow trees.

Ponderosa pine forests and Gambel oak groves show at about 5,000 feet and dominate the landscape until spruce and fir arrive over 7,000 feet. Canyons in the mountains' midrange have bigtooth maple and sycamore trees. Aspen arrive on the scene in the highest elevations.

The cool, moist meadows of the higher elevations, and high-elevation creeks and streams, draw dozens of species of wildflowers. Dark aspen-spruce forests coax dozens of different kinds of mushrooms, too.

Common Birds and Mammals

Over 400 species of wildlife inhabit the eastern region. While coyote, mountain lion, rabbit, antelope, deer, and bighorn sheep roam the lower levels of the eastern region, big game animals, including some unusual ones, appear in the higher elevations. In the early morning, you may see elk or deer browsing in the meadows. Canyon trails may reveal bear, mountain lion, or turkey signs. You might hear the bark-like cries of the endangered spotted owl, and you may get a lucky glimpse of a Mexican gray wolf. Hundreds of different birds—game birds, songbirds, raptors—fly in the region.

Climate

The climate in the eastern region ranges from mild to freezing, depending on elevation and season. The lower elevations usually keep mild-mannered temperatures. Up in the highcountry, however, you can experience some interesting weather.

Springtime comes late in the highcountry, usually in May. Sometimes you have to wait until June. And it's not unusual to see snow during a monsoon storm in the depths of summer. Hail is a common occurrence during these storms when winds push the temperatures down 20 to 40 degrees. The highest elevations of the eastern region take the look of a coastal rainforest when daily monsoons produce enough moisture for creeks to overflow, springs to appear, cienegas to flood, and lichen to drip from the evergreens' boughs like sage-colored tinsel.

Fall, which starts in September, brings cool days and frosty nights. Fall color is at its best from late September to early October. Winter sees several feet of snow.

Best Natural Features

- Fabulous views from mountain peaks and viewpoints
- Sprawling stands of aspens producing some of the state's best autumn color
- Wildflowers in alpine meadows and along high-elevation creeks
- Sacred Mount Baldy on the Fort Apache Indian Reservation
- Blue-ribbon trout streams
- The spectacular geology along the Blue River

46. Lower Coronado Trail

- Visit old homesteads in remote canyons.
- Find chalcedony and geodes.
- Hike a wild and remote canyon.

Area Information

The Coronado Trail, a Scenic Byway that winds between Springerville and Clifton (U.S. 191), does not exactly follow the historic route of its namesake, Francisco Vásquez de Coronado, during his 16-day pass through the White Mountains. But the road gets close.

Looking for the gold-gilded city of Cibola, the Spanish Coronado led a flamboyant entourage of 225 *caballeros* (horsemen), 60 infantry, a thousand native helpers, a handful of black slaves, and a couple of white women over a precipitous route just west of the highway in 1540 A.D. The route left them bedraggled and starving.

Though Coronado never found the legendary cities of gold, the area he traveled through did have a rich cache of precious metals. In the 1870s, prospectors dug some of the richest copper mines in the Southwest around the town of Clifton. Prospectors eked out a living mining for minerals in the mountains around Clifton.

Later, cattlemen came. They settled along the Blue River, just over a dozen miles from the Coronado Trail. Fred Fritz, Sr., had a home just north of Clifton. His Triple X brand became one of the most famous in Arizona. German-born Fritz could neither read nor write English, and signed his name as an "X" when registering his brand. His cowpunch witnesses, neither of whom could read or write, each signed their names as an "X." When Fritz was told to draw his brand for the federal files, Fritz looked at the three "X" signatures and drew three Xs as his brand.

A visit to the country along the Lower Coronado Trail will find remnants from these ranching and mining days, as well as signs of Indian cultures.

The prehistoric Mogollon culture lived in the area from around 1200 A.D. to 1600 A.D. and left behind petroglyphs and pueblo ruins. The Apaches lived in the area in the 1800s.

The landscape presents mineral-rich craggy ridges divided by dramatic canyons. Springs and streams nourish rich riparian covers along canyon floors. In these lower mountain elevations, a high desert vegetation dominates. Cacti hold hands with juniper and piñon trees on exposed slopes. Ruddy bluffs and outcroppings cut through pine forests stuffed in canyons or crowning the upper reaches. Fall and spring make the best seasonal use here.

Directions: Located about 15 miles north of Clifton along U.S. 191.

Hours Open: No restrictions.

Facilities: Campgrounds, picnic areas, and restrooms at recreation sites.

Permits and Rules:

- In developed recreation sites, pets must be restrained on a leash no longer than 6 feet.
- Fireworks are prohibited.
- Fires must be attended at all times. During May, June, and early July, the forests may have campfire and smoking restrictions.
- Maximum stay is 14 days.
- Maximum group size is 10 people.

Further Information: Clifton Ranger District, HC 1, Box 733, Duncan, AZ 85534; 928-687-1301.

Other Areas of Interest

Drive the full Coronado Trail. Its most scenic section, the 97 miles between Clifton and Alpine, will take almost four hours. Along the way, visit the Fritz Cabin, 3 miles north of Juan Miller Road along the Blue River. For more information, call the Clifton Ranger District, 928-687-1301.

Lower Coronado Trail

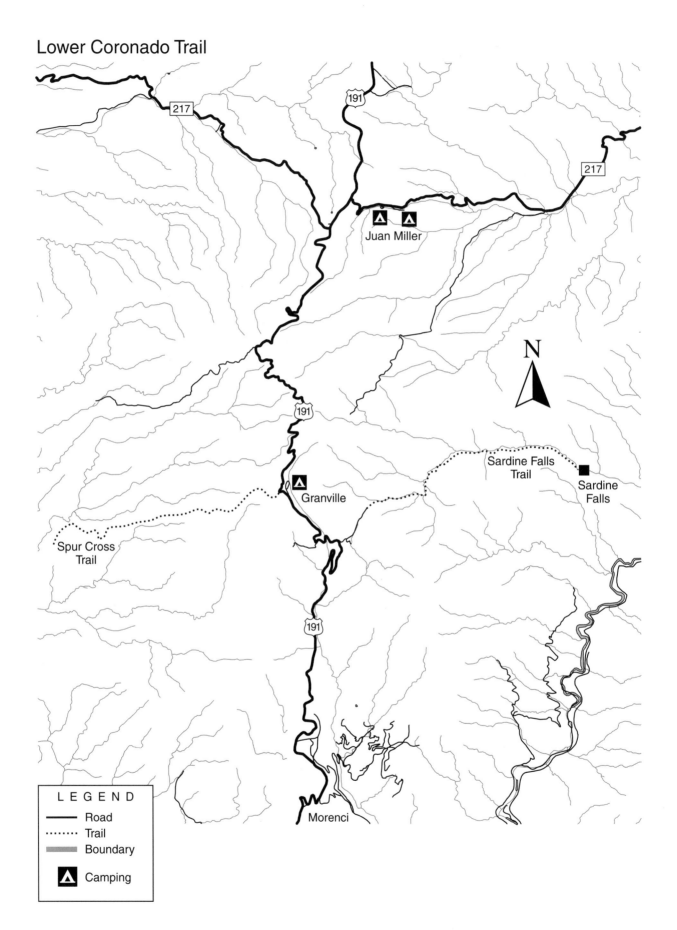

LEGEND
— Road
...... Trail
▨▨▨ Boundary
⛺ Camping

Sardine Canyon Trail

Distance Round-Trip: 3.6 to 7.2 miles

Estimated Hiking Time: 2 to 8 hours

Elevation: 4,800 to 6,120 feet

Maps: Apache-Sitgreaves National Forest, USGS Mitchell Peak

Caution: The first half of this route follows a trail; the last half does not and requires canyon experience and physical fitness.

Directions: From Clifton, drive about 25 miles north on Highway 191 to an unmarked road east of the highway and make a hairpin right turn onto it. From here, a high-clearance vehicle is required. Drive 0.8 mile and veer right; then drive 0.6 mile to the trailhead.

Long and thin like the sliver of a fish from which it gets its name, Sardine Canyon wriggles through remote and rugged country to 50-foot Sardine Falls. The trail that travels to the falls is being reengineered by the Forest Service and is only partially done at the time of this book's printing. You can still enjoy the exquisite scenery the gorge offers on the completed segment of trail.

Everyone can enjoy the Sardine Trail's first couple of miles. The trail drops into the canyon **[1]** on an old road that a man named Alfred Noah used when driving in and out of the canyon. The road ends at mile 0.5 at a corral **[2]** on the canyon floor where a single-track trail takes off.

Noah lived on a private piece of land in the palm of the canyon handed down to him from his brother, Herman. He and his brother had built themselves a comfortable little ranch where peach and apple orchards covered benches, cows lolled around wooded creek banks, and a stone house kept the Noahs safe from the elements.

After Herman Noah died, Alfred Noah remained in Sardine Canyon. He would pack his fruit harvest on the back of a burro, transport it on the trail from his ranch to his truck, sell the fruit in town, buy his supplies, then mosey back to his canyon home. The corral on the canyon floor replaced the garage where Noah kept his truck.

From the corral, the path follows the drainage along erosion-chewed creekbanks. The trail rockhops across icy mountain water that starts its flow at about mile 1, admires colonies of yellow monkey flowers clustered along slabs of red-tinged bedrock, and ducks under yellow columbines and coral Indian paintbrush clinging to mossy walls oozing with seeps.

Relatively flat and easy to follow, this section of the trail makes an ideal day hike. By mile 1.8, when the canyon makes a sharp bend north **[3]** and a side canyon branches to the south, the original trail all but disappears. At this point, the options to continue to Sardine Falls aren't for everyone.

You can hike a bit farther on the partially reengineered trail. The path leaves the canyon floor just past an alcove on the north side of the canyon and follows a ridgeline in a pine-juniper forest. But if you want go to the falls or at least see where old Alfred Noah lived, you can continue in the canyon and take the route Noah did.

The route, which even experienced hikers will find challenging, clamors over ruddy bedrock pocked with pools and then barges through thickets. It squeezes through a section of narrows with stormy-gray walls hardly a dozen feet apart that magnify a cascade to a thunder. It edges along curls of rock crowned with spires and pinnacles, then charms its way into wooded sections where bears leave brawny pawprints.

A long day will take you to Noah's ranch **[4]**, mile 3.6, and back. If the terrain is too uncomfortable to travel, you should turn back, as getting help may turn into a difficult procedure. You can expect to travel about a mile an hour on the canyon floor, and a hike to the falls requires an overnight backpack.

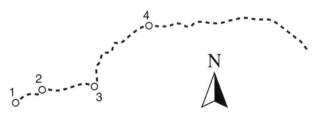

1. Trailhead
2. Corral Canyon
3. Canyon bends north
4. Noah Ranch

Spur Cross Trail 🥾 🥾 🥾 🥾

Distance Round-Trip: 11.8 miles

Estimated Hiking Time: 6 hours

Elevation: 4,800 to 6,900 feet

Maps: Apache-Sitgreaves National Forest, USGS Clifton

Caution: Some sections require route-finding skills.

Directions: From Clifton, drive north on U.S. 191 about 27.6 miles to the trailhead on the west side of the highway, just north of milepost 170.

The Spur Cross Trail never gives a clue about its wild side when it first starts out on its 1,800-foot descent to the Spur Cross Ranch in Dark Canyon. The trail makes an uneventful climb **[1]** up a ridge through a pine-oak forest to mile 0.5. Then at the ridgetop the trail politely shows off rows of mountains in the distant north and south.

The trail doesn't reveal its true personality, however, until it bottoms out on its first descent at mile 1. Here you'll observe an instant character change. The path breaks free from its evergreen cocoon and lands in a bald rock basin **[2]** where dwarfed juniper trees and needle-tipped Parry's agave appear as if they were a vegetative afterthought. Flamboyant landscape shifts like this become a habit with the Spur Cross Trail.

Rock cairns guide you across the peculiar basin, then hold your hand as the route scrambles across a terraced downslope. After a quarter-mile, the path makes another quick change, this time slogging the next three-quarters of a mile up a steep slope and contouring the mountain just below its peaks at a vista full of erosion-carved bluffs.

You get to look at the showy panorama **[3]** between the semisized boulders the trail passes on the way to its next surprise when the trail suddenly drops into a series of bluffs. In keeping with its untamed nature, the trail steps down the bluffs' smooth ledges, then starts a mile-long skid down a south-facing slope to a saddle. If you hike in the spring after a wet winter, you may see a nice display of wildflowers, including western wallflower, verbena, Indian paintbrush, banana yucca, phacelia, and desert onion. Another saddle and a brief uphill around a cone-shaped mountain bring the trail back to a downhill.

At about mile 4, the trail levels out under a series of bluffs and stares right into an attractive canyon to the south the locals have dubbed Cottonwood Canyon **[4]**. The gorge's conglomeration of ruddy spires and pinnacles make a dramatic presentation.

By mile 5.4, the trail makes its final descent into Dark Canyon **[5]**, where the Spur Cross Ranch sits. Route-finding skills help you connect the cairns stacked atop the sprawling section of bedrock that slopes toward the canyon. The trail then slides down the last quarter-mile along the southern canyon wall while eyeing the northern wall, held up by large hoodoos, all the way down to the canyon floor.

The Spur Cross Ranch lies just beyond a stream on the canyon floor. If you have enough time (and energy to make the climb out), you may explore the red rock cliffs up the canyon, too.

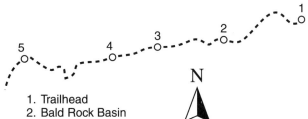

1. Trailhead
2. Bald Rock Basin
3. Panorama
4. Cottonwood Canyon
   Overlook
5. Descent into Dark
   Canyon

47. White Mountains

- Fish lakes and miles of cold-water streams.
- Find dozens of species of wildflowers in sub-alpine meadows.
- Spot black bear, mountain lion, elk, deer, turkey, and Mexican gray wolves.

Area Information

Spreading around the east-central edge of Arizona, the White Mountains have dozens of lakes and reservoirs and several hundred miles of rivers and streams. The national forest in which the mountains lie, the Apache-Sitgreaves, has more waterways than any other Southwestern national forest. Several Arizona rivers start in the White Mountains, including the Black, the Little Colorado, and the San Francisco.

The mountains' sub-alpine ridgelines have mixed conifer forests swaddled in a sweet pine redolence and dripping with moss. Stands of aspen form a matrix through the dark green timberland. In summertime, these concentrated woodlands harbor mushrooms of all shapes, sizes, and colors. Unusual moisture-loving wildflowers grow on the forest floors.

Meadows separate forests of aspen, pine, and fir trees. During August, the lush green parks become dotted with colorful wildflowers. In the early mornings and evenings, elk and deer browse on the sweet blossoms. At night, you can hear the clumsy elk knock their hooves on downfall. In autumn, the elks' loud screech, called a *bugle*, signals their mating season.

Also at night, you may hear the eerie howl of the Mexican gray wolf. If you bring your dog, the highly territorial wolf may come and check out its fellow canine-family intruder. Wolves have been known to attack dogs, and the Forest Service recommends leaving your dog at home if you want to travel in wolf country.

A hike in the White Mountains can mean a mild-mannered stroll along a rollicking streambed that meanders in a mountain meadow, or it could entail a tough slog up one of the mountains' miles-high peaks where panoramas peer into New Mexico. It might include hearing deer crash in trailside thickets, following the arrow-like prints from a turkey, or watching a black bear grub along the path. It may even allow a chance meeting with a mountain lion.

Because of the high elevations, weather goes to extremes in the White Mountains. During the summertime, monsoon storms can make temperatures

reel with 30-degree drops in minutes, and hailstorms can leave several inches of ice pellets on the ground, looking like a fresh cover of snow.

Nevertheless, summer is one of the best times to visit the mountains. Springtime can come late in the mountains; May snowstorms are not unusual. But by June, the mountains become user friendly. While the desert swelters in summer monsoon season heat and humidity, the mountains relax with 80-degree days and nights visiting the 40s. The cool days and frosty nights of autumn bring some of the best color in the state. In late September and early October, miles of aspen forests covering the mountainsides glimmer gold.

Directions: Located about 250 miles northeast of Phoenix in east central Arizona. Drive east on Arizona 260 to Show Low.

Hours Open: No restrictions.

Facilities: Campgrounds, picnic areas, and restrooms at recreation sites; visitors centers, fishing and boating stations, horse staging areas.

Permits and Rules:

- No mechanized vehicles or mountain bikes are allowed in wilderness areas.
- In developed recreation sites, pets must be restrained on a leash no longer than 6 feet.
- Fireworks are prohibited.
- Fires must be attended at all times. During May, June, and early July, the forests may have campfire and smoking restrictions.
- Maximum stay is 14 days.
- Maximum group size is 8 people per developed campsite and should not exceed 10 people in wilderness areas or in the primitive area.

Further Information: Alpine Ranger District, P.O. Box 469, Alpine, AZ 85920; 928-339-4384.

Other Areas of Interest

Visit the mountain town of Greer, located on Arizona 261, while traveling the White Mountains. The one-mile Butler Canyon Nature Trail, on the north side of town, takes you through several different environments you may experience while hiking in the White Mountains, such as a moist mixed conifer forest, sunny meadows, fertile stream crossings, and a pine forest.

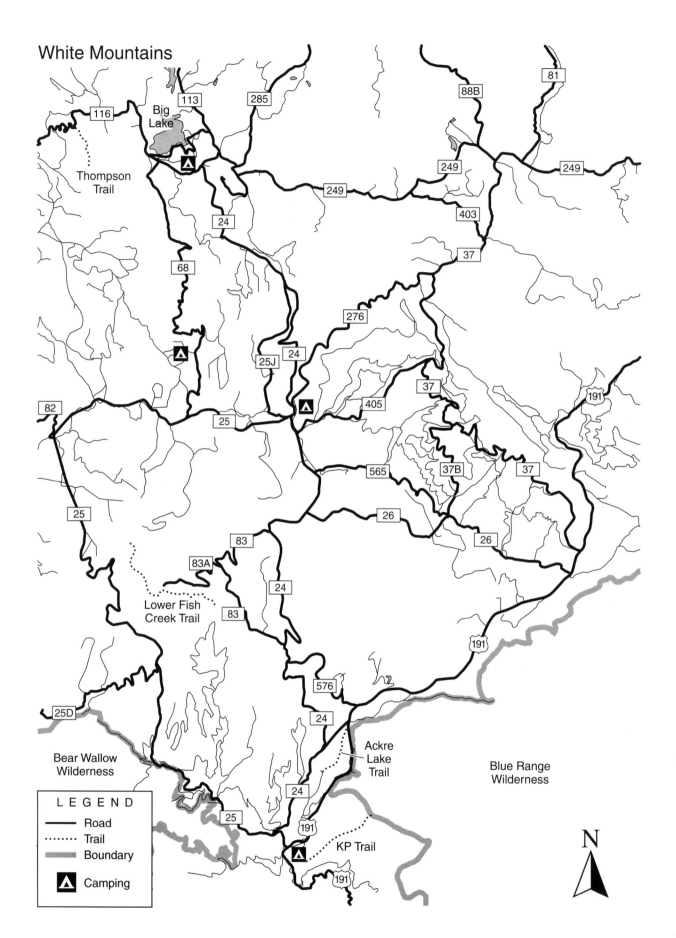

White Mountains

Big Lake

Thompson Trail

Lower Fish Creek Trail

Ackre Lake Trail

KP Trail

Bear Wallow Wilderness

Blue Range Wilderness

LEGEND
— Road
····· Trail
— Boundary
⛺ Camping

N

Thompson Trail 🥾 🥾 🥾

Distance Round-Trip: 5 miles

Estimated Hiking Time: 2.5 hours

Elevation: 8,600 to 8,840 feet

Maps: Apache Sitgreaves National Forest, USGS Big Lake North

Caution: The trail is open to foot travel only. Mountain bikes and horses are not allowed.

Directions: From Eager, drive 3 miles west on Arizona 260 and turn left onto Arizona 261; drive 17 miles and turn right onto FR 113; drive about 3 miles to FR 116 and turn left; drive about 4 miles to the trailhead.

The trail begins [1] near the Thompson Ranch at the confluence of Thompson Creek and the West Fork of the Black River. The path follows right along the West Fork of the Black River, passing through meadows, alongside aspen forests, and under ponderosa pine stands in a wide canyon bottom.

From its start, colorful wildflowers spread along the trail if you hike mid-July through August. Fall brings out the golds in aspens intermixed with pines and firs climbing the canyon's sloped walls.

Traveling on an old road, the trail drops a dozen feet into the canyon. You can see the steep beaten path fishermen like to use that stays right by the stream. The West Fork of the Black River is a nationally recognized blue-ribbon fishery. To get a blue-ribbon designation, a trout stream must have excellent water quality, diverse insect life and fly hatches to support high-quality stocks of wild native trout, contain the physical characteristics to accommodate fly-casting but be shallow enough to wade, and have a reputation for providing a quality trout fishing experience.

The road passes along several avalanches of gray boulders that tumble down the canyon walls and into the river. The soggy meadow along the river usually has western bistort, towering polemonium, and sneezeweed growing in it during July and August. You may get a whiff of onion from Geyer's onions' grasslike leaves.

At mile 0.5, the trail passes a fish barrier [2] installed to allow fish to swim downstream but keep non-native rainbow trout from spawning up the creek. An old railroad bed located just up the slope from the trail provides a path for mountain bikes and horses, which cannot use the trail (to sustain water and soil quality). Several paths lead up to it during the course of the trail. To stay on the Thompson Trail, veer left toward the creek.

The trail whittles down to a single track after passing through a gate and into a wooded section. At a second dam, the trail might get its feet wet in a bog where Rocky Mountain iris thrives. Stepping-stones help you navigate through this spongy area and other boggy stretches that appear during wet weather on the trail.

At about mile 1 the trail leaves the boggy area [3], dries off in another meadow, then squishes through another bog before climbing out of the lowlands up a rise scattered with jagged boulders. Once past the rocky section, the trail crosses a hillside, then heads back down to the creek as the waterway bends to the east.

Watch for the squat stalks of yellow Mogollon Indian paintbrush—its only appearance along the trail—as the path crosses a wide meadow [4]. The path heads for the meadow's edge at about mile 2, weaving around spruce trees. The trail ends in a meadow at the intersection with the West Fork Trail. You may continue on the West Fork Trail, which travels 3 miles one way through an old-growth forest, or return the way you came.

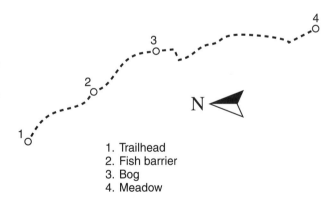

1. Trailhead
2. Fish barrier
3. Bog
4. Meadow

Ackre Lake Trail 🥾 🥾 🥾

Distance Round-trip: 7 miles

Estimated Hiking Time: 3.5 hours

Elevation: 9,100 to 8,700 feet

Maps: Apache Sitgreaves National Forest, Hannagan Meadow

Cautions: Give wildlife enough space should you encounter any.

Directions: From Alpine, drive south on US 191about 22 miles (0.25 mile past Hannagan Meadow) to the trailhead on the west (right) side of the road.

This trail explores the fascinating environment of an aspen-fir forest. The trail keeps a moderate grade as it makes its way from Hannagan Meadow to pond-sized Ackre Lake.

The loose-knit forest in which the trail starts [1] shows several species of wildflowers during different months. In the springtime, you may see calypso orchid, Rocky Mountain iris, and elkslip along the path; summertime brings violet, thimble-berry, sneezeweed, and lupine. In the fall, leaves on the aspen trees turn golden. Downfall scattered densely on the forest floor shows how nature thins out the forest naturally during harsh winters and summer storms.

At about mile 0.8, [2] the trail bends around a meadow, then twists deeper into the forest. At first blush, the forest floor looks like a cover of decay with old aspen leaves, tree branches, downfall, and bits of boughs from the evergreens matted upon it. However, if you take a moment and scrutinize the trailsides, you may find several species of wild-flowers—shadow lovers such as orchids, death camas, and violets. Also, you will find different sizes, shapes, and colors of mushrooms that take to the decayed logs.

Small meadows pool along the trail, breaking up the shadowy sections of forest with islands of green grasses, ferns, and flowers. The meadows pull in lupine, thermopsis, sneezeweed, and bracken fern.

At mile 2, the forest parts for Butterfly Cienega [3], a long meadow where groundwater gathers in its low lands. In wet weather, the path squishes across the meadow, guided by marked posts, then continues traveling the forest-and-meadow land-scape. The forest gets denser as the trail nears Ackre Lake. Trees get shaggy with lichen that hangs like tinsel.

Ackre Lake [4] fills the lowland of a large meadow at the trail's end. The two-acre lake draws wildlife, and you might get lucky and site some. The reintroduced Mexican gray wolves often hang out in the area; elk and deer browse the meadow. Fly fisherman can throw in a lure to catch one of the stocked trout in the lake. After you have taken in the scenery surrounding Ackre Lake, return the way you came.

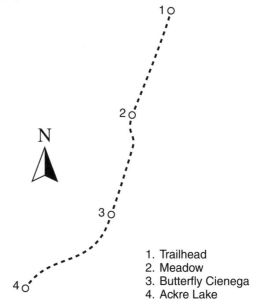

N

1. Trailhead
2. Meadow
3. Butterfly Cienega
4. Ackre Lake

Lower Fish Creek Trail

🥾 🥾 🥾

Distance Round-Trip: 11 miles

Estimated Hiking Time: 6 hours

Elevation: 6,800 to 8,400 feet

Maps: Apache Sitgreaves National Forest, USGS Hoodoo

Caution: Watch for patches of poison ivy at the lower elevations of the trail.

Directions: From Hannagan Meadow, drive 0.1 mile north on U.S. 191 to FR 576 and turn left; drive about 4 miles to FR 24, then turn right; drive 1 mile to FR 83, and turn left; drive about 5 miles and turn left onto FR 83A; drive 1.3 miles and turn left on the signed road to the trailhead; drive 0.4 miles to the trailhead. A high-clearance vehicle is necessary. (The 1977 Forest Service map shows a different alignment for FR 24 than is actually on the ground. Follow this narrative description and not the 1977 Forest Service map; the map is currently being revised.)

The lower half of Fish Creek travels through a particularly remote part of the White Mountains. Cradled in a cozy wooded canyon that opens up several times to accommodate meadows of wild-flowers, the path follows a historic route used by cattlemen and forest rangers between Hannagan Meadow and the Black River.

Fish Creek, named for its good fishing, maintains a pure population of Arizona's state fish, the Apache trout, because of a barrier installed by the Arizona Game and Fish Department and the Forest Service across the creek to keep the Black River's rainbow trout from hybridizing with the threatened natives. The native trout run about eight inches.

Fish Creek Canyon's steel-gray walls, with their strange spires and hoodoos chiseled by the elements, set the scene with an untamed feeling. Don't be surprised if you encounter wildlife such as bear, deer, turkey, or elk instead of people.

The trail starts out **[1]** on a steep downhill path on an access trail to Fish Creek. The access trail travels down a sunny section of the canyon slope as it picks around cobbles. The trail turns a bend past a line of currant bushes into a ponderosa pine forest. The trail arrives at the creek at mile 0.6 into a mélange of wildflowers and red-osier dogwood bushes. Poison ivy likes the creekside, too, so watch carefully for the three-leaved plant throughout the hike. This makes a good turnaround point for a short day hike. To continue on this hike, turn right.

The trail makes its way through a forest of firs, pines, and aspens. Small clearings attract spreads of wildflowers. At about mile 2, the canyon walls narrow briefly, becoming hanging gardens. The canyon opens back up quickly, however, and the trail alternates between stands of oaks and pines and grassy meadows.

The trail climbs up a sunny rise around mile 3 and stays above the creek for a while before it drops into the drainage again. You may smell a colony of the lily family's nodding onion as the trail enters an area splintered by a tornado years ago **[2]** at mile 3.6. Trees, yanked from the ground or snapped at their trunks, lie all over the canyon slopes.

The trail gradually transitions from sun-drenched meadows back to the cover of mixed conifers and intermittent clearings. At a large clearing surrounded by ponderosa pine trees, mile 4.4, the trail passes through the remnants of an old cowboy camp **[3]**. Watch out for barbed wire around the camp.

The trail heads back into the conifers. Be careful at about mile 5, when the path brushes against several patches of poison ivy that encroach on the trail. Trailsides are particularly alluring to this irritating plant that favors disturbed areas. The Black River **[4]**, and trail's end, lies just beyond a primitive camp and gate. When you reach the river, return the way you came.

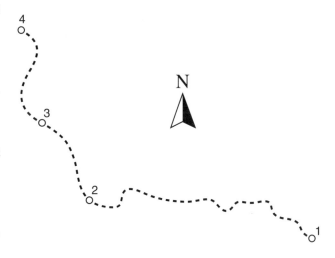

1. Trailhead
2. Tornado damage
3. Cowboy camp
4. Black River

KP Trail 🥾 🥾 🥾

Distance Round-Trip: 5.8 miles

Estimated Hiking Time: 3 hours

Elevation: 7,800 to 8,960 feet

Maps: Apache Sitgreaves National Forest, Strayhorse; Bear Mountain

Caution: Part of this trail is located in the Mexican gray wolf recovery area and may be closed because of denning. Check with the Forest Service for trail status.

Directions: From Alpine, drive south on U.S. 191 about 28 miles to the signed turnoff to the KP Campground and turn left; drive 1.2 miles to the trailhead.

The KP Trail follows the South Fork of KP Creek as it tumbles 2.9 miles and 1,160 feet to its confluence with the North Fork of KP Creek. The two creeks combine at this point to form KP Creek. The trail continues another 6.5 miles, following KP Creek much of the way, to the Steeple Trail.

For a comfortable day hike, this hike follows the trail down to the confluence. The path travels through a wooded canyon of mixed conifers and aspen trees—prime spotted owl habitat—as it follows the South Fork of KP Creek. You may see one of the brown and white raptors flapping below the treetops, or you may hear its doglike barks and cries. You may also get a glimpse of a Mexican gray wolf.

The trail gets its start **[1]** in a sunny meadow called a cienega, a name for a wetland fed by groundwater. The patches of Rocky Mountain iris that dwell in the soggy lowlands of the meadow bloom in June.

Just before the trail enters the woods, about mile 0.1, it squishes through a stream stuffed with water-loving plants. Once in the forest's shade, the trail starts heading downhill, deeper into the forest. During the fall, red tones show on Rocky Mountain maple trees, and an aspen stand at about mile 0.6 turns gold. The south wall across the canyon will have a cover of gold from aspen stands.

The trail follows two tight switchbacks and lands on the canyon bottom **[2]** at mile 0.9. Once streamside, the trail enters a wet world where cascades flow, moss-covered rocks scatter on the canyon slopes, and tree trunks drip with lichen.

The trail begins to parallel the stream as it continues its downhill destination to KP Creek, crisscrossing the south fork several times along the way. Sidestep a giant deadfall at about mile 1.7 by detouring to the left of it, then watch out for the poison ivy that appears at about mile 2.

At about mile 2.7, as the trail heads for another stream crossing, it brushes up against a rockwall on the right **[3]**. If you're hiking during July or August, look for white shooting star flowers growing on the rockwall.

The trail climbs out of the south fork drainage and crosses a slope, then bends to the west. After a few switchbacks bring the trail back into the drainage, rather than crossing the creek to continue on the KP Trail take a hairpin right and follow a path down to a waterfall **[4]** and the confluence of the north and south forks where they form KP Creek. You may continue on the KP Trail, or return the way you came.

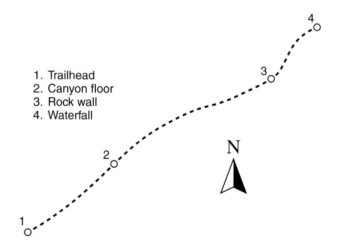

1. Trailhead
2. Canyon floor
3. Rock wall
4. Waterfall

N

48. Bear Wallow Wilderness

- Picnic along a perennial stream.
- Fish for native Apache trout.
- Watch for wildlife along remote trails.

Area Information

The Bear Wallow Wilderness, located on the western edge of the Apache-Sitgreaves National Forest's midsection, takes a tucked-away stance in location and atmosphere. Though small, only 11,080 acres, the wilderness has a big variety of trees, wildlife, plants, and moods.

The wilderness encases the Bear Wallow Creek and its tributaries. Bear Wallow Creek, which flows year-round, supports Apache trout and draws a rich riparian cover to its banks. During the summer, dozens of species of wildflowers crowd around the creekbanks. Poison ivy makes a big show along the creek, too, so be careful.

The ecosystem along the creek takes on a coastal rainforest environment during the monsoon rains in the summer, creating a moody feeling when you walk the trail along the canyon floor.

The wilderness also has one of the largest stretches of virgin ponderosa pine in the Southwest. Ponderosa pines, tall trees with orange-tinged trunks easily measuring four feet around, mingle with aspen, spruce, and fir trees. You may even see a maple tree lodged right next to the creek in some spots. Gambel oaks gather in the lower elevations in the canyon.

With a rich tree cover, a reliable water supply, and abundant plants for browse, the wilderness provides a home for several big game animals. As its name suggests, bears roam around the wilderness. If you don't catch sight of one, chances are you may follow fresh footsteps or signs along the trail. The same goes for elk, turkey, and deer. Chances are smaller that

you'll see Mexican gray wolves and mountain lions, but they do lurk in the canyon.

The best time to hike the wilderness is from May through October. August produces the most vibrant wildflower displays, and early October has fall color.

Directions: The wilderness is located about 28 miles south of Alpine. Drive south on U.S. 191 to Hannagan Meadow, and turn right onto FR 24; drive about 5 miles and turn west (right) onto FR 25; drive about 3 miles to the signed Bear Wallow Trailhead on the left.

Hours Open: No restrictions.

Facilities: None in the wilderness, but campgrounds and restrooms are located nearby (see White Mountains on page 175).

Permits and Rules:

- No mechanized vehicles or mountain bikes are allowed.
- In developed recreation sites, pets must be restrained on a leash no longer than 6 feet.
- Fireworks are prohibited.
- Fires must be attended at all times. During May, June, and early July, the forests may have campfire and smoking restrictions.
- Maximum stay is 14 days.
- Maximum group size is 10 people.

Further Information: Alpine Ranger District, P.O. Box 469, Alpine, AZ 85920; 928-339-4384.

Other Areas of Interest

If you like to fish, take a scenic drive following FR 25 as it wends northward, joining FR 24, toward Big Lake. The lake has boating and developed campgrounds.

Bear Wallow Wilderness

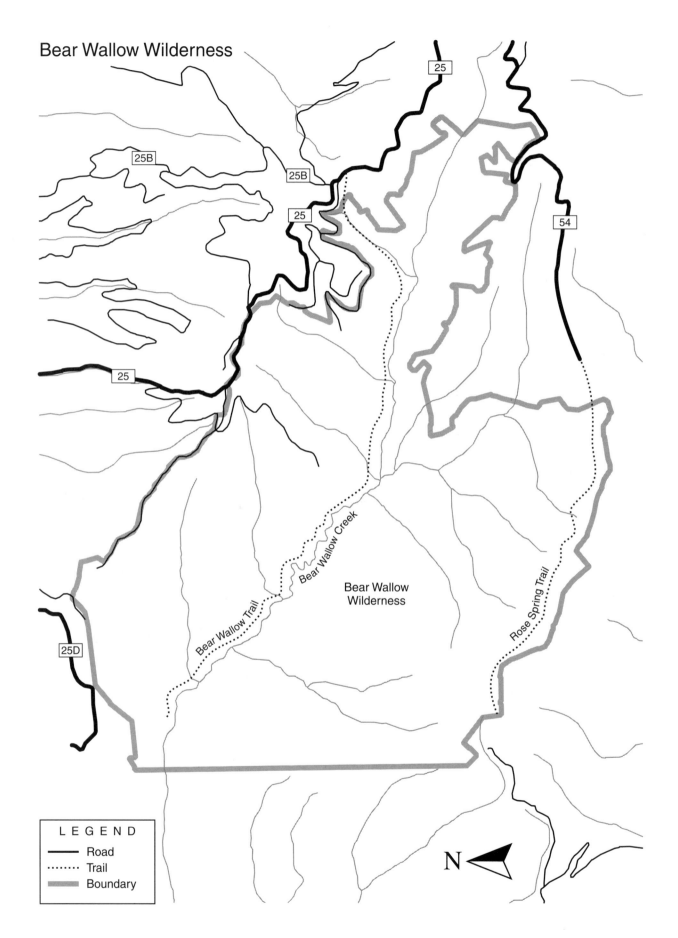

Bear Wallow Creek

Bear Wallow Wilderness

Bear Wallow Trail

Rose Spring Trail

LEGEND
— Road
····· Trail
━ Boundary

N

Bear Wallow Trail 👢 👢 👢

Distance Round-trip: 15.2 miles (shuttle 10.8 miles one-way)

Estimated Hiking Time: 8 hours

Elevation: 8,700 to 6,700 feet

Maps: Apache Sitgreaves National Forest, Baldy Bill; Hoodoo Knoll

Cautions: Purify all trailside water. Stream crossings may be dangerous during wet weather. A permit is necessary to enter the San Carlos Apache Indian Reservation.

Directions: From Alpine, drive about 22 miles to Hannagan Meadow, and turn west (right) onto FR 24, drive about 5 miles, and turn west (right) onto FR 25; drive about 3 miles to the signed trailhead on the left. To set up a shuttle, drive a second vehicle to the Gobbler Point Trailhead by continuing on FR 25 to Gobbler Point Road (FR 8154), and turn left; drive 3 miles to the trailhead.

The Bear Wallow Trail follows a perennial stream in a remote canyon. The setting makes an attractive habitat for wildlife. Bear wallows were a common occurrence in this canyon when rancher Pete Slaughter drove cattle through it in the late 1800s. The bears liked to laze in the wallows in the summertime to get relief from biting flies. They still like to hang out in Bear Wallow Canyon. A glimpse of one of them—as well as an elk, mountain lion, or even a Mexican gray wolf—or at least seeing their signs is not unusual.

After the trail crosses an unmarked road **[1]** (look for cairns if there is no sign indicating where the trail picks up on the other side of the road), the path enters a mixed conifer forest laced with meadows. The trail tumbles down the canyon slope, often flowing with water during wet weather, down to the canyon floor. During the summer, the trailsides fill with wildflowers.

At mile 1.5, the trail lands in Bear Wallow Canyon **[2]** next to the North Fork of Bear Wallow Creek. The path heads west to the North Fork's confluence with Bear Wallow Creek, passing

through stands of mixed conifers and aspen separated by meadows. The trail meets with Bear Wallow Creek just after it intersects with the Reno Trail at mile 2.6 **[3]**. In the summertime, this area gets particularly rich with wildflowers.

From here, the trail rockhops or wades across the creek often as it keeps its westerly direction alongside the creek. At mile 3.5, the path passes the Schell Canyon Trail **[4]**. At this point, the canyon narrows dramatically. The walls become higher, and stands of trees huddle along the stream. The sliver of trail gets pinched between the canyon's north wall and the creek, until creekside thickets finally force it partway up the canyon wall.

At about mile 6, the canyon widens, and the trail returns back to the canyon floor and takes to crisscrossing the creek again. Watch for a fish barrier at mile 6.6 **[5]** that protects the native Apache trout in Bear Wallow Creek from hybridization. Also watch for poison ivy along this stretch of trail.

The trail passes the Gobbler Point Trail at mile 7.1 **[6]**, then heads to its end at a fenceline on the San Carlos Apache Reservation. You may return the way you came, or take the Gobbler Point Trail out of the canyon if you have set up a shuttle.

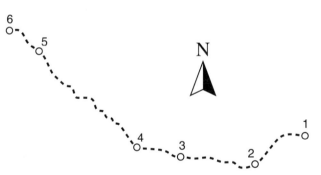

1. Trailhead
2. Bear Wallow Canyon
3. Reno Trail junction
4. Schell Canyon Trail junction
5. Fish barrier
6. Gobbler Point Trail junction

Rose Spring Trail 👢 👢 👢

Distance Round-trip: 10.8 miles

Estimated Hiking Time: 5.5 hours

Elevation: 8,700 to 6,700 feet

Maps: Apache Sitgreaves National Forest, USGS Baldy Bill

Cautions: Give wildlife enough space should you encounter any. A permit is necessary to enter the San Carlos Apache Indian Reservation.

Directions: From U.S. 191 and FR 25, drive south on US 191 about 0.3 miles, and turn west (right) onto FR 54; drive about 6.6 miles to the trailhead at the end of the road.

This trail, also called the Rim Trail, travels a remote route along Arizona's eastern end of the Mogollon Rim to the San Carlos Apache Indian Reservation. The 2,000-foot-high escarpment brings exquisite views to the path, and remoteness presents opportunities to encounter wildlife. You may see elk, deer, mountain lion, or bear as you hike the forested path.

Snapshot panoramas appear from the trail's start [1]; but better views wait. A carpet of ponderosa pine needles softens the rock-strewn path as it heads westward, often less than 100 feet from the Rim. To the north, the steep-walled Bear Wallow drainage digs deep into the Bear Wallow Wilderness. Fir, aspen, and pine trees cover the slopes.

The trail climbs up and down rounded ridges in a forest of pine and oak trees, leaving you far enough from the Rim to keep the views just out of sight, but close enough to emanate the brightness that hints of an overlook. You can veer off trail at any time to take a look at the extended views. The views reappear at the trail when it crosses a saddle at mile 0.9; [2] but better views wait.

Dropping from the saddle down a ridge, the trail pulls away from the Rim into a forest of firs and aspen then returns to the Rim by mile 2.7. At mile 3.4, [3] the trail passes the Schell Canyon Trail, marked by an unobtrusive sign nailed to a pine tree. The Schell Canyon Trail lands you in the heart of the Bear Wallow Wilderness.

Just beyond Schell Canyon, the Rose Spring Trail draws so close to the Rim, it teeters at its edge, showing you the escarpment's dramatic drop off. When it bends to the northwest, Gambel oak and juniper trees replace the pines and firs; and the views are at their best. During the summer, wildflowers like to congregate in this exposed area.

At mile 4.2, the trail pulls away from the Rim and heads back into a pine forest environment. A waist-high cairn at mile 5.2 [4] signals the San Carlos Apache Indian Reservation, and the trail veers to the right onto an old road to Rose Spring. Return the way you came.

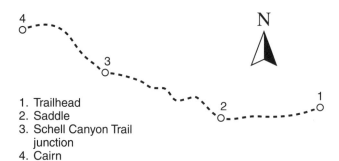

1. Trailhead
2. Saddle
3. Schell Canyon Trail junction
4. Cairn

49. Blue Range Primitive Area

- Visit the last designated primitive area in the United States.
- Hike trails where you may not see anyone for days, even weeks.

Area Information

When mountain man James O. Pattie trapped beaver in the Blue Range Primitive Area in 1825, he marveled at the area's clear-running streams, lush canyon vegetation, and abundant wildlife. Some things never change. The 173,762 acres of wild and remote land that make up the Blue Range Primitive Area, designated as such in 1933, continue to have clear-running streams (still, you should purify all water before drinking), lush canyon vegetation, and abundant wildlife.

The Blue, as locals affectionately call it, remains one of Arizona's unaltered areas of backcountry. The landscape has rugged mountains, steep canyons, and stark ridges. Geological quirks create the Breaks, a section of red conglomerate rock formations along the Grant Creek Trail; the Red Rock Pillars, more colorful conglomerate; and the strange peaks and hoodoos of the Bluffs along the Blue River.

As remote and lonely as the land remains, it has an extensive trail system that makes it highly accessible. Most of the trails have their roots as Indian paths. Later, ranchers developed the paths to run their cattle between the highcountry and the Blue River. Consequently, most trails run in long, diagonal routes between the river and highcountry.

Hiking these long trails requires a backpack in several vegetative zones that range from high desert near the Blue River, where piñon pines and juniper trees mix with cacti, and a subalpine habitat full of spruce, fir, and aspen trees. The higher, and wetter, aspen-fir forests rise in the western end of the Blue; ponderosa pines cover the Blue's midsection and eastern flank; and the region's southern flanks tend toward high desert country. Trails that follow creeks draw wildflowers in July and August, and their riparian covers produce exquisite autumn color in early October.

Because the Blue gets little visitation, the chances of spotting wildlife or signs of wildlife

during a hike are good. Bears roam around in the Blue, along with turkey, mountain lion, Mexican gray wolf, elk, and deer. Reports say the last grizzly in the state lived in the Blue. The bear was killed in 1930 near Strayhorse Campground in the southern portion of the Blue.

Whether you do a day hike or several-day backpack in the Blue, its trails will take you into remote and lonely country far from help. Go equipped and prepared for emergencies, and savor the feeling of being in a land much bigger than you.

Directions: The Blue is located on top of and below the Mogollon Rim, east of U.S. 191, and about 10 miles north of the San Francisco River. From Alpine, drive south on U.S. 191.

Hours Open: No restrictions.

Facilities: None in the wilderness, but campgrounds and restrooms are located nearby [see White Mountains, page 175].

Permits and Rules:

- No mechanized vehicles or mountain bikes are allowed.
- In developed recreation sites, pets must be restrained on a leash no longer than 6 feet.
- Fireworks are prohibited.
- Fires must be attended at all times. During May, June, and early July, the forests may have campfire and smoking restrictions.
- Maximum stay is 14 days.
- Maximum group size is 10 people.

Further Information: Alpine Ranger District, P.O. Box 469, Alpine, AZ 85920; 928-339-4384. Also, you may contact the Clifton Ranger District, HC 1 BOX 733, Duncan, AZ 85534; 928-687-1301.

Other Areas of Interest

Picnic or camp at Hannagan Meadow, just west of the Blue on U.S. 191. The beautiful meadow is a favorite with visitors to the area. For more information contact the Alpine Ranger District.

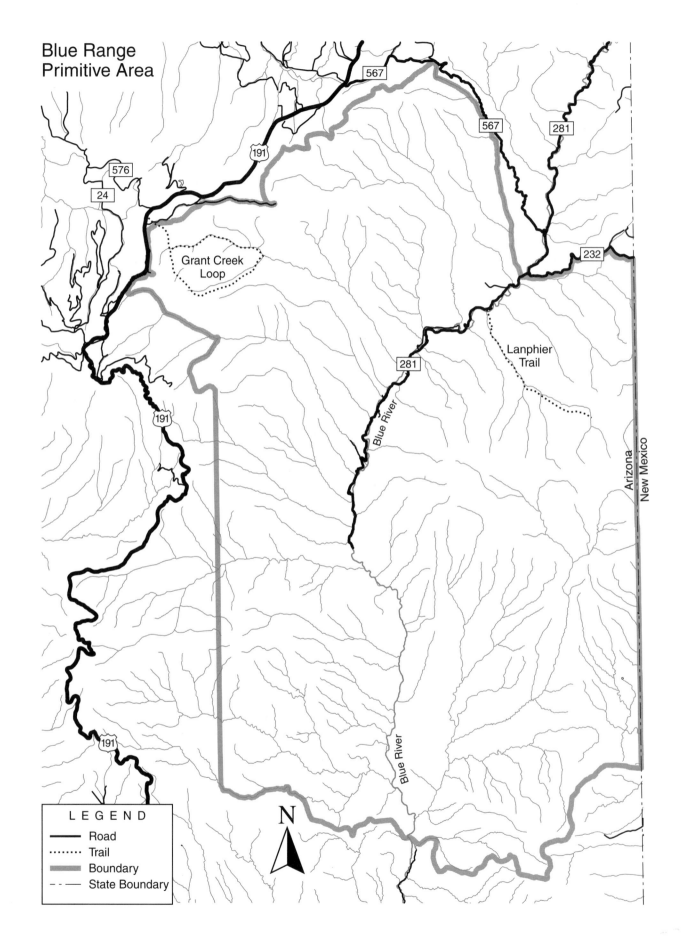

Blue Range
Primitive Area

567

567   281

191

576

24

232

Grant Creek
Loop

281

Lanphier
Trail

Blue River

Arizona

New Mexico

191

Blue River

191

LEGEND
—— Road
······ Trail
━━ Boundary
—·— State Boundary

N

Lanphier Trail 👢 👢 👢

Distance Round-Trip: 11.2 miles

Estimated Hiking Time: 6 hours

Elevation: 5,600 to 7,360 feet

Maps: Apache Sitgreaves National Forest, USGS Bear Mountain; Blue

Caution: Watch for poison ivy along the trail.

Directions: From Alpine, drive about 3 miles east on Highway 180, then turn right (south) onto FR 281 (Blue River Road); drive about 25 miles to the Blue Administration Site and a trailhead marked "Largo and Foote Creek Trailhead." Walk to the right of the trailhead posterboard through two gates to the Blue River. Cross the river and head to a corral, which marks the beginning of the trail.

Tucked in the folds of the Blue Range Primitive Area, Lanphier Canyon makes a wild and remote environment for a hike. A corral marks the beginning of the hike **[1]**, which starts on the Largo Canyon Trail and makes its climb up to the top of a ridge about a half-mile away.

As the trail drops over the ridgetop **[2]**, veer left onto the Lanphier Trail. The trail parallels Lanphier Creek for the next 2.6 miles. Gambel oak trees sprawl across the path, creating a cavern-like effect. Velvet ash and Arizona walnut trees crowd around the creek. Canyon grape twines everywhere, and patches of poison ivy prevail along the path. During the fall, this section becomes a tapestry of color

At the Red Rock Pillars **[3]**, mile 1.5, purple conglomerate bluffs squeeze into the canyon. The trail sticks close to the creek, giving you a good opportunity for a chance meeting with wildlife. You may catch a deer lapping from the stream, or run into a partridge protecting her brood of chicks.

The trail runs up and down the canyon walls as it continuously crisscrosses the stream. At Indian Creek Canyon **[4]**, mile 3.2, watch for trout in the pools that form when Indian and Lanphier creeks merge. This watery conjunction makes a pretty scene; tree branches, emerald from summer foliage or colored with autumn reds, reflect on the shimmery surface of limpid pools.

At about mile 3.7, the trail starts to climb sharply up the canyon slope. As the trail tops out, it lingers long enough to catch its breath and enjoy views of Bear Mountain, Lamphere Peak, and Lanphier Canyon, then heads for the inner folds of the slopes. For the next mile, the trail rambles in and out of secluded basins filled with groves of Gambel oak, then once again drops all the way into Lanphier Canyon.

You may not notice unassuming Whoa Canyon **[5]** emptying into the creek on the right. But you will notice when the trail arrives at Cashier Spring **[6]** at mile 5. The spring's lush environment attracts bigtooth maple trees.

From Cashier Spring, it's 0.6 mile to the trail's end at its intersection with the Cow Flat Trail just northeast of Campbell Flat. A handful of aspen trees in a crook may surprise you as you start the climb out of the spring into a ponderosa pine forest on Campbell Flat. The microclimate created at this low elevation allows them to thrive. At trail's end, you may continue on one of a network of trails meeting atop Cow Flat, or return the way you came.

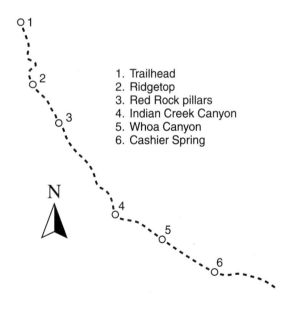

1. Trailhead
2. Ridgetop
3. Red Rock pillars
4. Indian Creek Canyon
5. Whoa Canyon
6. Cashier Spring

N

Grant Creek Loop 🥾 🥾 🥾 🥾

Distance Round-Trip: 11.4 miles

Estimated Hiking Time: 12.5 hours

Elevation: 7,120 to 9,040 feet

Maps: Apache Sitgreaves National Forest, USGS Hannagan Meadow; Strayhorse

Cautions: The Long Cienega Trail gets little use and may require route-finding skills to follow in some parts. Parts of the Steeple and Upper Grant Creek trails, and all of the Long Cienega Trail, are located in the Mexican gray wolf recovery area and may be closed because of denning. Check with the Forest Service for trail status.

Directions: From Alpine, drive south on U.S. 191 about 23 miles to the signed turnoff for the Steeple Trail; (across from Hannagan Meadow), then turn east (left); drive 0.4 mile to the trailhead parking area.

This loop hike takes you through a remote section of the Blue Range Primitive Area where cowboys worked and moonshiners hid decades ago. Today, bears grub around downfall and Mexican gray wolves roam the forests.

The trail begins **[1]** on the Steeple Trail on a downhill course in an aspen-fir forest carpeted with bracken fern. By mile 0.5, the path comes out into the open, next to a lowland clearing with a cienega. During wet weather, a stream may drain from the cienega and travel down a V-shaped drainage next to the trail. By mile 1, the trail sinks into the wetland and rubs shoulders with a stunning collection of wildflowers that bloom from late July through August.

At mile 1.3, the trail drops into another cienega where it meets the Upper Grant Creek Trail **[2]**. In rainforest fashion, lichen drips from conifers circling the cienega. Turn left onto the Upper Grant Creek Trail to continue on this hike. (This portion of trail to the old cabin is not recommended for people on horseback due to its steep canyon walls.)

The trail squishes through the cienega—the start of Grant Creek—into a fir-aspen forest where it follows the creek as it tumbles down the canyon. The trail constantly crosses the creek, which gets raucous at times, making stream crossings a project if you want to keep your feet dry. Look for a weeping rockwall on the south side of the creek at about mile 2.5 where water drips down a shaggy travertine **[3]** of moss and minerals forming on the wall.

By about mile 3.7, the trail takes to climbing above the creek between crossings as it continues to drop into lower elevations. Watch for poison ivy at creek crossings.

At mile 4.8, the trail arrives at a moonshiner's cabin and corral **[4]**. The well-developed holding, where copper moonshine equipment was found, has a log cabin and wood corral. The trail junctions with the Grant Cabin Trail at mile 4.9, and then the Long Cienega Trail **[5]** at mile 5.1. To continue on this hike, turn right onto the Long Cienega Trail.

The trail begins a steep ascent out of the Grant Creek drainage up a conglomerate bench of bedrock. After topping out at about mile 5.4, enjoy a distinctive overlook of the drainage before the trail heads down into another drainage that leads to Long Cienega. The path climbs and descends with the dips and swells of the slope, landing briefly next to a stream at about mile 6.1. From there it starts a consistent climb up a narrow, rocky canyon cluttered with old conifers, downfall, and moss-covered boulders.

By about mile 6.8, the trail may get masked from downfall and overgrowth. If you start to lose the path, look for blazes on the trees along the trail. You can start to see the meadow where Long Cienega lies by about mile 8.1. The path walks right into the soggy wetland to get to the Steeple Trail **[6]**, mile 8.4, where you turn right to continue on this hike.

The trail climbs out of the cienega over a ridge, then drops into a dense and dark fir-aspen forest, without full sunshine until about mile 9, when the path walks around a meadow in which Willow Spring **[7]** is located. The landscape vacillates between forest and meadow until about mile 10.2, when the path cozies next to a drainage that runs with overflow from a cienega. When the trail reaches the cienega (back at the start of the Upper Grant Creek Trail), continue on the Steeple Trail back to the trailhead.

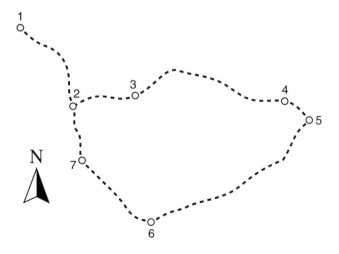

1. Trailhead
2. Cenega/Upper Grant Creek Trail
3. Travertine wall
4. Moonshiner's cabin
5. Long Cienega Trail
6. Steeple Trail
7. Willow Spring

Bibliography

Chronic, Halka. *Roadside Geology of Arizona.* Missoula, MT: Mountain Press Publishing Company, 1983.

Epple, Anne Orth. *A Field Guide to the Plants of Arizona.* Helena, MT: Falcon Press, 1995.

Granger, Byrd Howell. *Arizona Names X Marks the Place.* Tucson, AZ: The Falconer Publishing Company, 1983.

Haak, W.A. *Copper Bottom Tales.* Globe, AZ: Gila County Historical Society, 1991.

Leavengood, Betty. *Tucson Hiking Guide.* Boulder, CO: Pruett Publishing Company, 1991.

Molvar, Erik. *Hiking Arizona's Cactus Country.* Helena, MT: Falcon Press, 1995.

Trimble, Marshall. *Arizona—A Cavalcade of History.* Tucson, AZ: Treasure Chest Publications, 1989.

Tweit, Susan J. *The Great Southwest Nature Fact Book.* Seattle: Alaska Northwest Books, 1992.

Tweit, Susan J. *Meet the Wild Southwest.* Seattle: Alaska Northwest Books, 1995.